DATE DUE

Newspapers and Empire in Ireland and Britain

Newspapers and Empire in Ireland and Britain

Reporting the British Empire, *c.*1857–1921

Simon J. Potter

EDITOR

FOUR COURTS PRESS

Set in 10.5 on 12.5 Ehrhardt for
FOUR COURTS PRESS LTD
7 Malpas Street, Dublin 8, Ireland
e-mail: info@four-courts-press.ie
http://www.four-courts-press.ie
and in North America for
FOUR COURTS PRESS
c/o ISBS, 920 N.E. 58th Avenue, Suite 300, Portland, OR 97213.

ISBN 1-85182-832-x

Printed in England
by Antony Rowe Ltd, Chippenham, Wilts.

Contents

Illustrations and tables

This publication was grant-aided by the
Publications Fund of National University of
Ireland, Galway

Notes on contributors

JACQUELINE BEAUMONT is a freelance scholar and Visiting Research Fellow at Oxford Brookes University. She has published a number of articles on the British press during the South African War and is currently writing a book on the reporting of the South African War sieges.

JILL C. BENDER received her BA in history from the College of William and Mary in 1999 and her MA from the National University of Ireland, Galway in 2002. She is currently working on a PhD in history at Boston College.

RICHARD J. FINLAY is Director of the Research Centre in Scottish History at the University of Strathclyde. His latest book is *Modern Scotland, 1914–2000*.

ALED JONES is Sir John Williams Professor of Welsh History at University of Wales, Aberystwyth, and is the author of *Press, politics and society: a history of journalism in Wales* (1993) and *Powers of the press: newspapers, power and the public in nineteenth-century England* (1996).

BILL JONES is Senior Lecturer in Modern Welsh History at Cardiff University, and is the author of *Wales in America: Scranton and the Welsh, 1860–1920* (1993).

Bill Jones and Aled Jones have co-authored *Welsh reflections: Y Drych and America, 1851–2001* (2001) and 'The Welsh world and the British empire, c.1851–1939: an exploration', *Journal of Imperial and Commonwealth History*, 2:31 (May, 2003) also published as Carl Bridge and Kent Fedorowich (eds), *The British world: diaspora, culture & identity* (London, 2003).

FELIX M. LARKIN studied history at University College Dublin and has been a public servant in Dublin for the past thirty years, most recently with the National Treasury Management Agency. He has a continuing research interest in the history of the press in the late nineteenth and early twentieth centuries in Ireland, especially the *Freeman's Journal*. He is an external contributor to the Royal Irish Academy's forthcoming *Dictionary of Irish biography* and is hon. treasurer of the National Library of Ireland Society.

DONAL LOWRY is Senior Lecturer in History at Oxford Brookes University, and Tutorial Fellow in Modern History, Greyfriars Hall, University of Oxford. He has published articles and essays on various aspects of southern

African, British and Irish history, and had edited, and contributed to, *The South African War reappraised* (Manchester, 2000). He is currently working on a study of Ireland's relationship with the British empire.

JOHN M. MACKENZIE is Emeritus Professor of Imperial History at Lancaster University and an Honorary Professor at the University of St Andrews. He has been the general editor of the Manchester University Press 'Studies in imperialism' series for almost twenty years.

PATRICK MAUME is the author of biographies of Daniel Corkery and D.P. Moran and of *The long gestation*, a study of nationalist political culture, 1891–1918. He has spent three years working on the history of the *Irish Independent*, and is currently a researcher on the *Dictionary of Irish biography*.

ANGUS MITCHELL was the post-doctoral Millennium scholar at Mary Immaculate College, University of Limerick (2001–4) and Visiting Assistant Professor in the Global Studies Department at the University of St Lawrence, Canton, New York (2004–5). His published works on Roger Casement include *The Amazon journal of Roger Casement* (London, 1997), *Sir Roger Casement's heart of darkness* (Dublin, 2003) and *Casement* (London, 2003).

ÚNA NÍ BHROIMÉIL is a lecturer in the Department of History, Mary Immaculate College, University of Limerick. She is the author of *Building Irish identity in America, 1870–1915: the Gaelic revival* (Dublin, 2003).

SIMON J. POTTER lectures in Imperial History at the National University of Ireland, Galway and is currently working on a study of the media and the British empire in the twentieth century. Recent publications include *News and the British world: the emergence of an imperial press system, 1876–1922* (Oxford, 2003) and 'The imperial significance of the Canadian-American reciprocity proposals of 1911', *Historical Journal*, 1:47 (March 2004).

IAN SHEEHY has recently completed a DPhil thesis at the University of Oxford entitled 'Irish journalists and litterateurs in late Victorian London, *c.*1870–1910'.

Introduction: empire, propaganda and public opinion[1]

SIMON J. POTTER

The essays collected in this volume explore the varied attitudes towards empire once sustained by different groups in Ireland, England, Wales and Scotland, and by their diasporic descendants. They also examine the images of the British empire that were projected by newspapers and periodicals in Ireland and Britain. By dealing with each of the 'four nations' that predominated in Britain and Ireland in the late nineteenth and early twentieth centuries, the collection reveals the complex role played by empire, mediated through the press, in the construction of identity among each of the different groups. It also emphasizes the need to view the press from a range of local, national and trans-national perspectives.

Many historians and theorists have emphasized the role played by the press in the forging of national identities. Marshall McLuhan, the influential Canadian communications theorist, argued that the emergence of modern print culture, and particularly newspapers, allowed people to 'see' their vernacular tongue for the first time, and to identify it with national unity and power.[2] This argument was picked up and popularized by Benedict Anderson, who stressed the role of newspapers in encouraging individuals to 'imagine' themselves as part of a national community, linked to people whom they never meet and yet consider to be members of the same group.[3] Ernest Gellner similarly argues that the significance of the press as a promoter of nationalism lies in its provision of 'abstract, centralized, standardized, one to many communication'. By its very nature, such communication supposedly helps define membership of the nation by incorporating those who can understand the language and style of transmission.[4]

1 The idea for this collection emerged at a colloquium on the subject of 'The imperial press and Ireland', held at the National University of Ireland, Galway in March 2002. I would like to thank Dr Deirdre McMahon for her advice in putting together the programme of speakers for this event, some of whom have contributed papers to this volume. I would also like to thank NUI, Galway for making the colloquium possible, and for providing the generous financial support that has allowed the publication of this volume. 2 M. McLuhan, *The Gutenberg galaxy: the making of typographic man* (London, 1962) 1–9, 138, 199, 217; see also M.L. DeFleur and S.J. Ball-Rokeach, *Theories of mass communication* (New York, 1989, 5th edn) 4. 3 B. Anderson, *Imagined communities: reflections on the origin and spread of nationalism* (London, 1991, 2nd edn) 35–6, 92–4, 119–20. 4 E. Gellner, *Nations and nationalism* (Oxford, 1983) 127.

While it would be wrong to exaggerate the impact of this theoretical work on historical accounts, it is striking to note how many historians of the press have adopted an avowedly national perspective. British histories of the press – often flimsily disguised English histories – frequently portray newspapers as contributing to a national media tradition, combining freedom from government regulation (unlike the Continental European experience) with a Liberal mission to educate the public (in contrast with market-oriented American practices).[5] Irish histories of the press have meanwhile generally focussed on the role played by newspapers in the nationalist movement.[6]

Historians have also (perhaps somewhat paradoxically) followed national agendas when examining how empire interacted with the development of the press. British historians have focussed on gauging how far the working classes supported an empire from which they derived no obvious benefits. While some doubt whether empire had a direct or even a particularly significant impact on working-class thinking,[7] others have argued that the media and other forms of popular culture played a significant role in creating a 'false consciousness'.[8] Although historians have not devoted serious attention to examining the role of the press in this regard (as John MacKenzie points out in his chapter below), there remains a pervasive assumption that newspapers proved crucial in whipping up popular support for empire. The British Liberal journalist and political theorist John A. Hobson, whose shadow looms large in most studies of popular attitudes to empire, gave an early lead here, claiming that the press had degraded public opinion and created an atmosphere favourable to the waging of an unjust war in South Africa.[9]

It is not just English historians who have sought to measure and explain popular support for empire,[10] and as Ireland was part of the United Kingdom until 1922 it might be valid to ask similar questions about Irish attitudes. In

---

5 On the 'free press' tradition see J. Curran, 'Press history' in J. Curran and J. Seaton, *Power without responsibility: the press and broadcasting in Britain* (London, 1985) and work on wartime censorship such as P.M. Taylor, *The projection of Britain: British overseas publicity and propaganda, 1919–1939* (Cambridge, 1981); M.L. Sandars and P.M. Taylor, *British propaganda during the First World War, 1914–18* (London and Basingstoke, 1982); and G.S. Messinger, *British propaganda and the state in the First World War* (Manchester and New York, 1992). On Liberal ideas see Aled Jones, *Powers of the press: newspapers, power and the public in nineteenth-century England* (Aldershot, 1996) 155. 6 See for example Hugh Oram, *The newspaper book: a history of newspapers in Ireland, 1649–1983* (Dublin, 1983) and Marie-Louise Legg, *Newspapers and nationalism: the Irish provincial press, 1850–1892* (Dublin, 1999). 7 Jonathan Rose, *The intellectual life of the British working classes* (New Haven and London, 2001) 321–64. 8 See in particular the Manchester University Press 'Studies in imperialism' series, which includes pioneering works by John MacKenzie such as *Propaganda and empire: the manipulation of British public opinion, 1880–1960* (Manchester, 1984). 9 John A. Hobson, *The psychology of jingoism* (London, 1901). 10 Henry Pelling, 'Wales and the Boer War' and Kenneth O. Morgan, 'Wales and the Boer War: a reply', *Welsh History Review*, 4:4 (Dec. 1969) 363–6 and 367–80, respectively.

his chapter below, MacKenzie does just this, but finds few answers, for Irish historians have generally had a different agenda. In recent years, this has involved debating Ireland's exact relationship with the British empire. For while Ireland was to some extent part of the imperial core during the nineteenth and early twentieth centuries, with direct representation at Westminster, in other respects her position seemed distinctly colonial. The Union of the kingdoms of Great Britain and Ireland, lasting from 1801 until 1922, was always incomplete, and manifestations of Ireland's former colonial status remained, in terms of fiscal and commercial legislation, administrative structures, policing models, military garrisoning policies and racial attitudes. Officials and others sometimes drew implicit and explicit parallels between the administration of Ireland and of colonies such as India.[11] Regulations imposed on the press in Ireland could also seem distinctly colonial.

At the same time however, Ireland did form part of the imperial core in at least some respects, and Irish men and women played a crucial role in the maintenance and extension of British colonial rule overseas. In part, the pattern of participation reflected the divided and unequal nature of Irish society. Protestant engagement with empire was especially marked, with the Anglo-Irish disproportionately represented in the ranks of imperial administrators and military commanders, and businesses such as the shipbuilders Harland and Wolff deriving particular benefits.[12] Catholics also served the empire however, largely but not exclusively in the lower ranks of the administrative and military machine, and through migration helped shape the development of the settler colonies in Canada, Australia, New Zealand and South Africa.[13] While Indian nationalists would later draw on Irish examples in their own attempts to shorten the road to independence, the practical impact of such 'subversive' connections can be exaggerated.[14] Indeed, through its unionist tradition, Ireland may have provided a more significant model for die-hard empire loyalist settler groups in Rhodesia, Kenya and Natal.[15]

Like imperial subjects in the settler and crown colonies, and indeed in Britain itself, Irish men and women developed an ambiguous, sometimes volatile, but often viable mixture of identities as members of a global empire, as the essays in this collection demonstrate. As well as associating themselves with the local and national bases of identity that proved paramount for many, a section of the Irish population also saw themselves as British, and as mem-

11 David Fitzpatrick, 'Ireland and the empire' in Andrew Porter (ed.), *The Oxford history of the British empire*, iii: *the nineteenth century* (Oxford, 1999) 494–501. 12 Philip Ollerenshaw, 'Businessmen in Northern Ireland and the imperial connection, 1886–1939' in Keith Jeffery (ed.), *'An Irish empire'? Aspects of Ireland and the British empire* (Manchester, 1996). 13 Fitzpatrick, 'Ireland and the empire', 509–15. 14 T.G. Fraser, 'Ireland and India' in Jeffery (ed.), *'An Irish empire'?*, 77–92. 15 Donal Lowry, 'Ulster resistance and loyalist rebellion in the empire' in Jeffery (ed.), *'An Irish empire'?*

bers of a broader, imperial 'British world'[16] that other Irishmen explicitly rejected.[17] Both unionists and nationalists were often only interested in empire insofar as it could be used to serve domestic Irish agendas: Alvin Jackson rightly doubts the extent to which Irish engagement with empire was driven by any 'widespread philosophical commitment'.[18] However, a similar point could be made about the imperial enthusiasms of many in England, Scotland and Wales, as Richard Finlay's essay below indicates. Empire proved a variable component in a complex cocktail of identities. Steven Howe has recently highlighted the need to 'configure simultaneously the *multiple* interrelationships of national, racial, regional and other imaginings ... We need to think [about] Irishness and Englishness also in their relation to Welshness and Scottishness, Yorkshireness and Kerryness, as well as all the multiple, non-territorial other social identifications in which individuals engage.'[19] An imperial dimension also needs to be factored into this equation.

In relation to the British empire, Ireland's status during the nineteenth and early twentieth centuries remained ambiguous – as Keith Jeffery concludes, Ireland was both 'imperial' and 'colonial'.[20] This ambiguity was crucial, as it in turn allowed contemporaries to present Ireland as 'an integral part of the United Kingdom, a peripheral, backward sub-region, or a colony in all but name' in order to suit their wider purposes.[21] This reflects a wider issue. As Howe has pointed out, processes of economic, political, social and cultural integration can either be seen as 'state-building' or 'colonialism'.[22] The labels applied by contemporaries and historians essentially reflect differing, present-minded perspectives – in the context of this collection of essays for example, contributors have been aware that terms such as 'imperialism' and 'colonialism' are often unhelpful, loaded as they are with a variety of implicit and explicit meanings. In the essays below, contributors have either avoided the use of such terms, or have attempted to define them for the purposes of their own analysis.

16 On the idea of a 'British world' see Carl Bridge and Kent Fedorowich, 'Mapping the British world', *Journal of Imperial and Commonwealth History*, 2:31 (May 2003) 1–15; also available in Carl Bridge and Kent Fedorowich (eds), *The British world: diaspora, culture, identity* (London, 2003). 17 The nuanced attitudes of Irish at home and overseas are brought out nicely in Donal Lowry, 'The crown, empire loyalism and the assimilation of non-British white subjects in the British world: an argument against "ethnic determinism"', *Journal of Imperial and Commonwealth History*, 2:31 (May 2003) 96–120; also available in Bridge and Fedorowich (eds), *The British world*. On Ulster attitudes see Thomas Hennessey, 'Ulster unionist territorial and national identities, 1886–1893: province, island, kingdom and empire' in *Irish Political Studies*, 8 (1993) 21–36. See also Stephen Howe, *Ireland and empire: colonial legacies in Irish history and culture* (Oxford, 2002 edn) 201–2 and Jeffery, 'The Irish military tradition and the British empire' in Jeffery (ed.), *'An Irish empire'?*, 105–18. 18 Alvin Jackson, 'Irish unionists and the empire, 1880–1920: classes and masses' in Jeffery (ed.), *'An Irish empire?'*, 124–30. 19 Howe, *Ireland and empire*, 240. 20 Jeffery (ed.), *'An Irish empire'?*, 1. 21 Fitzpatrick, 'Ireland and the empire', 494. 22 Howe, *Ireland and empire*, 19.

Given these ambiguities it could be argued that, for the historian, analysis of the actual 'colonial' and 'metropolitan' attributes of Ireland's past development is less important than developing an understanding of how different groups at different times perceived the relationship between Ireland and the British empire. Here, it is apparent that elements of Ireland's diverse population adopted varied viewpoints. These perspectives also changed over time, partly as a result of conscious attempts to influence them. Newspapers offer a means to examine the variety of Irish views of empire, and the strategies adopted by contemporaries to alter them.

As Jill Bender's essay in this volume points out, in 1857 there was a wide variety of contrasting and conflicting views as to the affinities between Ireland and India. For some Irish nationalists, the Indian Mutiny did offer an opportunity to demonstrate, through comparison, Ireland's colonial status. Conversely, many unionists emphasized Ireland's status as an integral part of the imperial power challenged by the Indian uprising, and demanded a loyal response from their countrymen. For many others, the comparison between Ireland and India was unclear, and Ireland's status remained ambiguous.

Attempts to discuss Ireland's status through comparison with other parts of the empire probably rarely reached the level of sophistication that they achieved during the Mutiny, for several reasons. For members of the Irish Parliamentary Party, Home Rule was a modest measure that would not take Ireland out of its position in the imperial centre.[23] Many advanced nationalists meanwhile desired a constitutional settlement that would allow Ireland to leave the empire entirely. It thus made little sense for Irish nationalists of either persuasion to tie their fate to that of the colonies. The idea of granting Ireland 'Dominion status' – the same powers of 'responsible' self-government in internal affairs enjoyed by the settler colonies or 'Dominions' of Canada, Australia and New Zealand – did introduce a colonial comparison to the debate over the Irish issue, a theme to which we return below. In general however, the status of Britain's colonies overseas seldom provided a natural yardstick against which to measure Ireland's own position.[24]

Moreover, during the Mutiny readers of Irish papers could have become particularly well informed, if they so desired, about events in India. At other times, as many of the chapters in this collection make clear, Irish readers, like British readers, could have gained only an incomplete, vague and generalized picture of empire. They lacked detailed knowledge.[25] As a result, during the South African War for example, while contemporaries certainly took sides in an imperial conflict, few attempted to draw more than rudimentary compar-

23 See chapter 6 below. 24 Howe, *Ireland and empire*, ch. 4. 25 See John M. MacKenzie (ed.), *Imperialism and popular culture* (Manchester, 1986) 8–9. See also MacKenzie, *Propaganda and empire*, 253–4.

isons between Ireland's position and that of the Boer republics.[26] As Donal Lowry's chapter below shows, the conflict was primarily significant in terms of the opportunities that if offered to advance different domestic Irish political agendas. As in 1857, Irish responses to the war were thus predictably varied.

As Ben Novick has argued, in order for propaganda to be successful, it must resonate with the existing beliefs and prejudices of the intended audience. For most of the nineteenth century, and during the early twentieth century, anti-colonial rhetoric did not resonate with Irish audiences, largely because knowledge of empire was limited. During the First World War, it thus made little sense for nationalist propaganda to stress Ireland's colonial status or affinities with other colonies and, as during the South African War, few attempted to present a picture of Irish fellow suffering with the subjects of Britain's African and Asian colonies. Indeed, advanced nationalists indulged in racist attacks on the colonial troops fighting for Britain and France on the Western Front, arguing that the presence of such people in the ranks of the army of a supposedly civilized power was but another example of British barbarism. Advanced nationalist propaganda sought to associate Ireland with a European, Catholic world, rather than a colonial one.[27] Ireland's semi-colonial status did not prevent Irish men and women from sharing the racial prejudices and stereotypes held by many in Britain at the time, as several chapters in this collection make clear.[28]

It was perhaps only with the creation of the Irish Free State (when, ironically, Ireland formally became a colony for the first time since the Act of Union) that the colonial comparison really began to resonate with a nationalist audience. Seeking to challenge the compromise solution of Dominion status that had been introduced by the Treaty, Eamon de Valera attempted to associate Ireland with an array of burgeoning anti-colonial nationalist movements elsewhere in the world. One of the preconditions for success in this campaign was to inform the Irish public about such movements. Here, de Valera's close links with the *Irish Press* proved extremely useful, and the paper's editors explicitly encouraged the publication of news of anti-colonial agitation around the world.[29]

This raises a more general methodological issue seldom dealt with satisfactorily in histories of the press. When historians examine newspapers, how representative are the opinions that they encounter? Do they reflect popular views or merely those of the paper's editorial staff? By the early twentieth century, following the improvement of printing and distribution techniques,

26 See chapters by Larkin, Maume and Lowry below. See also Howe, *Ireland and empire*, 56–7. 27 Ben Novick, *Conceiving revolution: Irish nationalist propaganda during the First World War* (Dublin, 2001) 103–20, 208.   28 See also Bryan Fanning, *Racism and social change in the Republic of Ireland* (Manchester, 2002).   29 Mark O'Brien, *De Valera, Fianna Fáil and the Irish Press* (Dublin, 2001) 31.

and the emergence of the penny press, millions of people were buying newspapers. Can we then take the views and opinions expressed by these papers
as representative of the views and opinions of their readers, people who would
otherwise remain silent in the historical record?

There are obvious attractions in seeing press comment as a missing link
in the traces that have survived from the past, as representative of 'public
opinion'. In his analysis of British attitudes to Irish policy in the period
1918–1922, for example, D.G. Boyce drew much of his evidence from press
sources, supplementing this with an examination of the views of individual
politicians and pressure groups. Boyce was aware of some of the pitfalls
involved in using the press as a means to gauge public opinion, and stressed
the need to work with a representative cross-section of newspaper opinion.[30]
He did not however grapple with a broader conceptual issue – even if we can
discern a wide spectrum of views, as expressed in the pages of the newspapers,
how can we know how those opinions in turn relate to the ideas of those
reading the papers?

One alternative approach is to stress the role of the press in leading rather
than reflecting public opinion. In a recent survey of British attitudes towards
Irish self-government that similarly relies on newspapers and periodicals for
much of its source material, G.K. Peatling presents the press as a 'substantial
influence on the British population' that set the agenda and shaped the outlines of political debate. Peatling relates the views expressed in the pages of
selected journals to the broader aims of a small number of groups of identifiable press commentators, each with their own ideological convictions about
Irish Home Rule.[31]

In debating the relationship between the press and public opinion, many
Victorian and Edwardian commentators would have agreed with Peatling's
argument that the press helped shape the views of readers.[32] For Liberals like
James Bryce, this influence was seen as positive and healthy, ensuring that a
responsible and enlightened elite could guide public opinion.[33] By the end of
the nineteenth century, others were not so sure. As mentioned above, Hobson
expressed the growing contemporary concern that an increasingly commer-
cialized press, linked to powerful economic interests outside the newspaper
industry, would corrupt rather than enlighten the public. This concern would
later shade into the debate over government propaganda sparked off by state
intervention in press affairs during the First World War. As a result, many
contemporaries and historians have argued that the press frequently distrib-

---

30 D.G. Boyce, *Englishmen and Irish troubles: British public opinion and the making of Irish policy,
1918–22* (Cambridge, Mass., 1972). **31** G.K. Peatling, *British opinion and Irish self-government,
1865–1925: from unionism to liberal Commonwealth* (Dublin, 2001). **32** On Victorian debate
about this issue see for example Jones, *Powers of the press*, 87–94. **33** J. Bryce, *The American
commonwealth*, 3 vols (London, 1888) iii, 3, 6–13, 99–106.

utes propaganda, issued by private commercial interests as well as by governments.[34] This tendency has been particularly marked in writing about connections between the press and empire. British historians interested in the link between press comment and popular attitudes towards empire have often claimed that newspapers led public opinion and whipped up enthusiasm for overseas expansion. Here, Hobson's lead has been followed by historians such as MacKenzie, who argues that propaganda issued through the press, together with other forms of popular culture, provided the means by which state and commercial interests could popularize a core or dominant ideology, of which empire formed an important part.[35]

If press coverage of imperial events constituted propaganda, what does this tell us about popular attitudes to empire? NATO has defined propaganda as 'Any information, ideas, doctrines or special appeals disseminated to influence the opinion, emotions, attitudes or behaviour of any specified group in order to benefit the sponsor, either directly or indirectly.'[36] On one level, we might argue that if propaganda reflected the pre-existing views of the target audience, then there would be no need for it. Propaganda is by its very nature unrepresentative of genuine popular attitudes, and only becomes representative when it succeeds in persuading its target audience to think in a way that does not necessarily represent their own interests. MacKenzie has thus argued that, while the British working classes did not necessarily benefit from empire, the saturation of popular culture with images of empire eventually generated working-class consent and even enthusiasm. The working classes were won over to supporting empire against their best interests. In the same way, we might assume that the press in Ireland helped shape public attitudes towards empire in an unnatural way, building strong opinions about empire where none had previously existed, or perhaps even altering existing beliefs.

As already noted, others stress that, in order to succeed, propaganda must 'resonate' with the pre-existing attitudes of the target audience, and tap into shared ideologies and stereotypes. If we accept this, then we must assume that, if pro-imperial propaganda stimulated enthusiasm for empire among the British working classes, then there must have been at least some degree of pre-existing support. Similarly, this argument would tend to indicate that in Ireland the anti-imperial rhetoric of advanced nationalist propaganda, and unionist propaganda in favour of empire, must both have harmonized with the existing sentiments of at least sections of the public. It is difficult, if not impossible, to know how to choose between these different formulations, when we can never have pure, unmediated expressions of 'public opinion' to com-

---

34 Edward S. Herman and Noam Chomsky, *Manufacturing consent: the political economy of the mass media* (New York, 1988). 35 MacKenzie restates this argument in chapter 1 below. For a similar argument see also chapter 4 below. 36 Quoted in Novick, *Conceiving revolution*, 38.

pare against the propaganda – even letters to the editor are generally written only by a small, self-selecting cadre of readers, and go through a process of editorial selection that makes it difficult to see how representative they are.

Many of the chapters in this collection accept that news and comment about empire in British and Irish papers can often be seen as attempts to influence the opinions of readers, forwarding a variety of, often conflicting, agendas. To some extent, such initiatives were determined by party political interests, reflecting the strong links between press and parliament that endured well into the twentieth century.[37] As the essays by Felix Larkin and Patrick Maume below show, reactions to imperial events, and discussion of issues such as Dominion status for Ireland, were bound up with internal divisions within the Irish nationalist movement. In Scotland, as Richard Finlay demonstrates, press debates over empire and the Irish issue were closely connected with Liberal and Unionist party agendas, while in England, as Simon Potter's essay reveals, coverage of empire was influenced during the early twentieth century by the attempts of 'constructive imperialists' to develop greater popular knowledge of and enthusiasm for the empire.

However, as the collection also shows, it was not just political affiliations that shaped press coverage of empire. As Potter demonstrates, white settlers in Canada, Australia, New Zealand and South Africa sought to influence opinion in Britain and Ireland by influencing the views communicated back 'Home' by the press. Individuals also sought to use the press to popularize their own ideas about empire, as Bill and Aled Jones show in their analysis of the varied agendas promoted by different Welsh journalists and political thinkers. Working at the intersection of British and Irish affairs, individuals with very different perspectives on empire such as W.F. Monypenny and Sir Roger Casement similarly used the press to wage their own propaganda campaigns, as chapters by Jacqueline Beaumont and Angus Mitchell below suggest. Casement was in turn the target of a range of press campaigns, waged with the intention of influencing debate about his activities.

The essays that follow also help to reveal how the press in England, Scotland and Wales, as well as Ireland, was bound up into a range of different regional, national and trans-national contexts – or, to use Howe's phrase already quoted above, '*multiple* interrelationships of national, racial, regional and other imaginings'. Local perspectives were obviously extremely important, as essays by Finlay and Lowry below demonstrate. At the same time, however, it is clear that newspapers in Ireland and Britain were tied to their counterparts around the English-speaking world by a range of connections that linked and transcended local groupings.

---

37 On Britain see S. Koss, *The rise and fall of the political press*, 2 vols (London, 1981 and 1984). On the provincial press in Ireland see Legg, *Newspapers and nationalism*.

While this collection emphasizes the diverse approaches to empire adopted by newspapers in Ireland, Scotland, Wales and England, it is important to remain conscious of the connections and similarities between newspapers within what was then the United Kingdom. Despite the political antipathies and upheavals that wracked the relationship between Ireland and Britain, there remained for example intimate connections that linked the press across the Irish Sea. Printed editions of newspapers travelled back and forth between Britain and Ireland. British papers were read by the Anglo-Irish and by Britons living in Ireland, but also by the Irish.[38] In the early 1920s, up to 165,000 copies of English papers were being sold daily in Ireland, and almost 430,000 copies of English Sunday papers. Fleet Street journalistic models were also imported, along with journalists who had previously worked for British papers and news agencies.[39] Irish journalists meanwhile travelled to Britain to work on Fleet Street, where they could express their own views on Irish issues, as Ian Sheehy's chapter below suggests.

Irish journalists also travelled farther a field, and played an important part in journalism in the British colonies, as Beaumont's analysis of Monypenny's career demonstrates. The Irish Australian journalist Daniel Joseph Quinn was similarly able to move freely between journalism in Britain and Australia, working for the London *Evening News*, the *Daily Mail*, the *Daily Express* and the Brisbane *Courier*.[40] During the First World War he acted as London correspondent for the *Sydney Daily Telegraph*.[41] Irish journalistic models were also adopted in the settler colonies – the *Freeman's Journal*, founded in Sydney, Australia in 1850, explicitly drew on the model provided by its Dublin-based namesake. The first editorial stressed that the conductors of the journal would 'do their best to render the paper worthy of the *name* it bears; and will endeavour to make it imitate the spirit and character of its namesake and model in Dublin, as nearly as circumstances will permit'.[42] The paper reprinted significant amounts of news about Ireland from the Irish and British press. The *New Zealand Tablet* similarly drew heavily on Irish journalistic models, and reprinted copy directly from the Irish and Irish American press.[43]

Irish newspapers were also read by Irish emigrants and their descendents, not just in the British settler colonies, but also of course in the United States, helping to keep a diasporic consciousness alive.[44] De Valera's *Irish Press* was partly funded by bonds sold in Australia by Archbishop Mannix, and further

38 Legg, *Newspapers and nationalism*, 43, 152–3.   39 O'Brien, *De Valera*, 14.   40 Mitchell Library, Sydney, MS 48 D.J. Quinn papers, 48/4 S.S. Saile to D.J. Quinn, 6 March 1900. 41 Ibid., 48/1 'Jogging along the inky way: recollections of a peripatetic journalist', printed and typescript MSS [1938].   42 Sydney *Freeman's Journal*, 27 June 1850.   43 Kevin Molloy, 'Victorians, historians and Irish history: a reading of the *New Zealand Tablet*, 1873–1903' in Brad Patterson (ed.), *The Irish in New Zealand: historical contexts & perspectives* (Wellington, 2002).   44 Legg, *Newspapers and nationalism*, 174

support came from the Irish community in the USA.[45] Irish diasporic groups also maintained their own newspapers, offshoots of Irish journalism, which reinforced local perspectives on Irish and British affairs. As the Irish Canadian journalist Grattan O'Leary recalled of his youth in Gaspé County, Quebec, 'We had lots of Irish newspapers, from Dublin the *Freeman's Journal*, from New York the *Irish World*, from Minneapolis the *Irish Standard*. We knew more about British politics than about Canadian.'[46] These diasporic perspectives could differ markedly from the attitudes expressed by papers back in Ireland. As Úna Ní Bhroiméil shows below, Irish American journalism expressed a particularly bitter anti-Englishness, but also opposed the South African War in the context of a broader anti-imperialism that, in contrast with newspapers back in Ireland, was less preoccupied with Irish domestic issues. Irish migrant communities elsewhere meanwhile maintained their own perspectives[47] – as Mark McGowan has shown, in Ontario the Irish community responded to the South African War very differently.[48] We are only now beginning to appreciate how groups such as the Welsh also used the press to shape a sense of diasporic identity, and of how this related to broader ideas about Britishness.[49]

A number of essays in this collection focus on the South African War (Boer War) of 1899–1902. This is unsurprising. The war has always been seen as playing a significant role in the development of Irish nationalism. The recent centenary has meanwhile provoked new studies of virtually every stage and aspect of the conflict, including several re-evaluations of the role of the press.[50] Looking at the South African War also reinforces the sense of connection between the press in Ireland, Britain and the settler colonies. Chapters in this collection reveal that while an Irish nationalist interpretation of the conflict certainly emerged, it was not all that different from that deployed by radical Liberal critics in Britain. Such links reflected other institutional as well as political links between the two groups – for example, radical Liberal papers often employed Irish correspondents associated with the nationalist movement and the literary revival.[51]

45 O'Brien, *De Valera*, 14–27. 46 Quoted in I.N. Smith, *The Journal men: P.D. Ross, E. Norman Smith and Grattan O'Leary of the Ottawa Journal* (Toronto, 1974) 132. 47 Lowry, 'The crown'. 48 Mark G. McGowan, *The waning of the green: Catholics, the Irish and identity in Toronto, 1887–1922* (Montreal, 1999). 49 See Aled Jones and Bill Jones, 'The Welsh world and the British empire', *c*.1851–1939: an exploration', *Journal of Imperial and Commonwealth History*, 2:31 (May 2003) 57–81; also available in Bridge and Fedorowich (eds), *The British world*. 50 See for example Donal Lowry (ed.), *The South African War reappraised* (Manchester, 2000) and David Omissi and Andrew S. Thompson (eds), *The impact of the South African War* (Basingstoke, 2002). On the press see for example J. Beaumont, '*The Times* at war' in Lowry (ed.), *The South African War reappraised*; Simon J. Potter, *News and the British world: the emergence of an imperial press system, 1876–1922* (Oxford, 2003), ch. 2; and John Gooch (ed.), *The Boer War: direction, experience, and image* (London and Portland, Oregon, 2000), chs. 11–14. 51 Peatling, *British opinion*, 64.

The South African War and the subsequent creation of the Union of South Africa reinforced these connections, as British Liberals, strengthened in their commitment to Irish home rule, drew analogies between the South African settlement and the future of Ireland. The perceived success of self-government in South Africa in the wake of the war bolstered Liberal enthusiasm for a similar devolution of power in the case of Ireland. As the essays below by Finlay, Maume, Larkin, Beaumont and Sheehy show, the applicability of Dominion status to Ireland was widely debated in both nationalist and unionist circles, demonstrating how the press facilitated the flow of ideas and debates between Britain, Ireland and the settler colonies.[52]

The decision to include in this collection single, survey essays on England, Wales and Scotland, together with a number of more detailed studies of the Irish press, reflects the relative state of historical writing about the press in these places. While the history of the press in Britain has been well explored, the history of Irish newspapers is still a field awaiting detailed and comprehensive scrutiny. In order to examine responses to empire, many of the chapters included in the latter part of this collection present for the first time essential background material on the history of Irish newspapers and journalism. Nevertheless, there remain gaps in our knowledge that this collection has been unable to fill. We still lack a basic understanding of the subtle and changing attitudes express by the Dublin *Irish Times* for example, and little work has been done on the press in Northern Ireland – a topic touched on in essays by Jill Bender and Donal Lowry below. It is hoped that this collection will help to stimulate further work on the Irish press, building up a more comprehensive picture of a particularly important institution in Irish and British life.

52 See also ibid. 61–2, 90, 131–2.

1. The press and the dominant ideology of empire[1]

JOHN M. MACKENZIE

Few institutions stimulate more anxieties and fears in modern society than the press. Newspapers represent a concentration of power that, allegedly, can make or break governments, not to mention individual reputations. Yet this is nothing new. Everyone remembers Stanley Baldwin's celebrated remark about power without responsibility, but he was merely encapsulating in a memorable epigram a deep resentment, a recurrent nervousness about press power that had been prevalent from the late eighteenth century onwards. These apprehensions, perhaps inevitably, spread to the British empire. Major controversies about the freedom of the press and about the alleged power of journals to foment dissidence or revolt broke out in the Cape, Canada, India and elsewhere in the first half of the nineteenth century. By the second half, press freedoms had been established in some territories, stifled in others, and politicians had already come to recognize the convenience of buying into the press as a major propaganda tool.

Yet the surprising fact is that, until recently, study of the press in the anglophone world has been limited. This is particularly true of the British empire, where one would think that press studies ought to be legion.[2] This is the case both in terms of the treatment of imperial issues in the British press and in respect of the colonial press in the many territories of empire. Although the work of Potter, Kaul and a number of others is now rectifying this[3], there has still not been a study of press content to compare with William Schneider's *An empire for the masses*, which was something of a revelation when it came out in 1982.[4] Schneider examined the French popular image

---

1 A version of this paper was originally given as a keynote address at the colloquium on 'The imperial press and Ireland' held at NUI, Galway. 2 One of the few exceptions is J.D. Startt, *Journalists for empire: the imperial debate in the Edwardian stately press, 1903–13* (Westport, Conn., 1991) – this focussed however on one fairly restricted sector of the press over a relatively brief period. 3 Simon J. Potter, *News and the British world: the emergence of an imperial press system, 1876–1922* (Oxford, 2003); Chandrika Kaul, *Reporting the raj: the British press and India, c.1880–1922* (Manchester, 2003). For another example of a new approach to the history of the press see Rodanthi Tzanelli, 'The "Greece" of Britain and the "Britain" of Greece: performance, stereotypes, expectations and intermediaries in Victorian and Neohellenic narratives, 1864–81' unpublished PhD thesis, Lancaster University, 2002. 4 William H. Schneider, *An empire for the masses: the French popular image of Africa, 1870–1900* (Westport, Conn., 1982).

of Africa in the late nineteenth century as revealed in illustrated and other papers. Strikingly, Schneider undertook statistical work on the quantity of articles, the number of front-page stories and even the extent of column inches occupied by material on Africa.

There may be several explanations for the underdeveloped nature of similar studies of the British press. One is that researchers have invariably found it a major problem to access the British Library's newspaper collections in the wastes of North London, at Colindale, particularly as microfilm readers were not always available when they got there. And those microfilm readers are of course also part of the problem. The fragility of newspapers is such that we can very seldom get at the originals. So, even if you do get a microfilm reader, excessive use can lead to early forms of scholarly blindness, while even the most equable temperament can be driven to fits of monumental rage at one's efforts to maintain focus on that tiny, dancing and – given the technology of the period – highly variable print. Practical limitations have also distorted the scope of what research has been undertaken. Microfilms of *The Times* are available in almost every university library in the English-speaking world. There has therefore been a tendency to concentrate on the 'Thunderer' to the exclusion of all other newspapers, whose milder meteorology might nonetheless conceal real national and local significance (see chapters 2 and 3 below). Moreover, it is possible to question how representative the views expressed by *The Times* really were – its circulation was in steep decline by the end of the nineteenth century.[5]

There have of course been a large number of histories of the press as a business, as a site of developing technologies, as a field for the progressive removal of fiscal and other restraints and as a characteristic of societies with incomplete or growing literacy.[6] There have been very few detailed studies of the press as a means of mediation and communication among the classes, or indeed among ethnicities, as a major conduit between elite and masses, rulers and ruled. Nor have there been significant studies of the press as a key disseminator of popular culture, as a means for the transmission and reinforcement of ideologies of consensus and controversy, compliance and conflict, interacting with other popular cultural forms such as sport, theatre, exhi-

5 Jacqueline Beaumont, 'The Times at war, 1899–1902' in Donal Lowry (ed.), *The Boer War reappraised* (Manchester, 2000) 67.   6 S. Koss, *The rise and fall of the political press*, 2 vols (London, 1981 and 1984); Alan J. Lee, *The origins of the popular press, 1855–1914* (London, 1976); L. Brown, *Victorian news and newspapers* (Oxford, 1985); J. Shattock and M. Wolff (eds), *The Victorian periodical press: samplings and soundings* (Leicester, 1982); B. Harrison, 'Press and pressure group politics' in Shattock and Wolff (eds), *Victorian periodical press*; D.L. LeMahieu, *A culture for democracy: mass communications and the cultivated mind in Britain between the wars* (Oxford, 1988); A. Jones, 'The image makers: journalists in Victorian popular politics' in C.C. Eldridge (ed.), *Empire, politics and popular culture: essays in eighteenth and nineteenth century British history* (London, 1990).

bitions, advertising and, later, cinema, broadcasting, fashion and the like. As if that were not enough, we have not yet seen sufficient attention paid to newspaper design and the deployment and potential deconstruction of illustrations and cartoons.[7] Above all, we have not yet aspired to the sophistication of examining the manner in which representations of various phenomena differed from newspaper to newspaper, and from location to location, as between, for example, England, Scotland, Wales and Ireland, and between the towns and cities of empire in North America, southern Africa, India and Australasia.

Most significantly, in terms of this volume at least, little work has been done on the impact of empire and imperialism on the emergence of a modern press in the later nineteenth century.[8] It is one of those extraordinary conjunctions of modern history that the 'imperialising of the British press', as Andrew Thompson has called it, took place at exactly the time that obvious restraints on the press were being removed and newspaper technologies were undergoing a period of rapid development.[9] In this, the repeal of stamp and paper duties in 1855 and 1861 were key to the emergence of a more popular press. In exactly the same years, the development of the rotary press and web feed transformed newspaper production, as did the progression from rag to esparto grass and then crucially to wood pulp as the source of paper by the 1880s. Linotype also developed in the 1880s.[10] At the same time, special newspaper trains created a revolution in distribution from the 1870s; the Press Association secured cheaper telegraph rates and the domestic telegraph was taken over by the Post Office. It is true that international cable costs were exorbitant until at least the end of the century, but the Press Association and Reuters greatly facilitated the transmission of international and imperial news.[11]

From the point of view of the transmission of imperial ideas, this transformation of the press as a business was clearly very significant. Start-up costs for newspapers increased by a factor of 20 between 1850 and 1900, resulting in the concentration of ownership of the press in fewer hands. Vast numbers of papers in the London suburbs and the British provinces, in the latter case running to nearly a thousand, survived until the 1880s, but thereafter a more national press began to take over. The status of journalists rose and the phe-

---

7 Ramamurthy's research on advertisements, though not restricted to the press, is important here. Anandi Ramamurthy, *Imperial persuaders: images of Africa and Asia in British advertising* (Manchester, 2003). Roy Douglas, *Great nations still enchained, 1848–1914: the cartoonists' vision of empire* (London, 1993) offers some preliminary ideas on cartoons, though nothing on Ireland. 8 For the purposes of this paper, I would define empire as the existing territories of white settlement together with India, while imperialism would be the tendency towards expansionism, in this instance mainly formal, in the later nineteenth century. 9 Andrew S. Thompson, *Imperial Britain: the empire in British politics, c.1880–1932* (London, 2000) 61. 10 See Lee, *Origins of the popular press* for an account of these technical developments. 11 Donald Read, *The power of news: the history of Reuters* (Oxford, 1999, 2nd edn).

nomenon of the press baron became more apparent. However, historians who
have charted these changes have often played down the continuing power of
some provincial, urban papers. In the Scottish case, the *Glasgow Herald*, the
Scotsman in Edinburgh, the *Dundee Courier* and the *Aberdeen Press and Journal*
continued to be very important in communicating with at least the professional and business middle classes of those places long after a national press
had become more widely distributed. The situation was probably similar elsewhere in Britain and Ireland.

To some extent, the factor of locality coincided with class distinctions. By
the late nineteenth century, a popular press had begun to capture a mass
readership on something approaching a national basis. *The Times* meanwhile
continued to communicate with an elite that was spread across the various
ethnicities of the United Kingdom, but it was an elite readership that was
apparently shrinking in the era of popular imperialism. On the other hand,
more local, quality papers spoke to a bourgeoisie who seem to have retained
a sense of regional chauvinism or, in more practical terms, required to be
informed about local business and commercial conditions. Of course, in such
an analysis we have to recognize the possibility of multiple purchase and we
also have to remember that throughout most of the Victorian era, readership
was much greater than circulation. Over the queen's reign, newspapers were
available in pubs, news rooms, coffee houses, mechanics' institutes, working-
men's clubs (as well as clubs for the elite) and the increasingly ubiquitous
town and district libraries. Additionally, more expensive illustrated and
humorous papers like the *Illustrated London News*, the *Graphic*, *Punch* and
Fun, though too costly for a mass readership, would probably have been available not only through some of the locations of public reading, but also to
those 'below stairs' who may have laid hands on copies no longer required
by those 'above stairs'.

The conjunction of the technical and organizational transformations that
overtook the newspaper industry, and the simultaneous 'imperialising' of the
press, was not planned, but neither was it coincidental. For the industrialization of the press, and late nineteenth-century imperialism, were facilitated
by similar technological developments. Overseas expansion (and its attendant
commercial, strategic, social and political processes) was propelled by some
of the same technical changes as were transforming the press. Hence, the
press was truly facilitator, instrument and reflector, all at the same time. To
combine the ideas of Marshall McLuhan and Daniel Headrick in a modern
version, the press thus offered the medium and the text messaging by which
both the motives and the means of imperialism could be transmitted.
Moreover, the conditions under which the press operated ensured that information readily shaded into propaganda, news into forms of instrumental
knowledge, and culture into aspects of control. This was not just the case for

newspapers that took an imperialist stance. Politics tended everywhere to be polemicized by imperialism. Radical papers and the Irish nationalist press tended to have their positions conditioned by what I have long described as the dominant ideology, the ideological cluster that embraced militarism, monarchism and Social Darwinism. In the case of Ireland some might add Protestantism to that heady brew, although there were of course plenty of Catholics who were seduced by this potent concoction. And many others, often in want, were prepared to take its shilling to survive.

While we have strong indications of the pervasive nature of the imperial ideology in the press, the fact is that this has never been properly analysed or quantified. As noted above, few historians look beyond the pages of *The Times* for evidence of attitudes towards empire, and some shun even this limited source. For example, neither A.P. Thornton's *The imperial idea and its enemies* nor Bernard Porter's *Critics of empire* made much use of the press, even though the reader would expect that it would be central to their themes. Perhaps the same charge could be levelled against my own *Propaganda and empire* of 1984, although there are some key references.[12]

We do have some insights into press coverage of particular events or themes. Andrew Thompson has examined major controversies that took place in the early twentieth century press over issues such as the tariff reform campaign and naval defence. His work on the Imperial Press Conference of 1909 constitutes one of the very few attempts to look at situations in which journalists and press owners and executives from around the British empire came together formally to discuss common concerns.[13] Chandrika Kaul's new book meanwhile examines the press and the British *raj* in India in the late nineteenth and early twentieth centuries, focussing on key moments and issues. Kaul analyses the manner in which the press was manipulated and its content massaged by the official capacity to release information and control the news that actually reached the public.[14] Others have examined the role of particular individuals in exploiting the press for their own purposes.[15]

Susan Carruthers has done something similar for the press in relation to the colonial conflicts of the 1950s, particularly those in Kenya, Cyprus and

---

12 A.P. Thornton, *The imperial idea and its enemies* (London, 1959); Bernard Porter, *Critics of empire* (London, 1968); John M. MacKenzie, *Propaganda and empire: the manipulation of British public opinion* (Manchester, 1984). Robert H. MacDonald's *The language of empire: myths and metaphors of popular imperialism, 1880–1918* (Manchester, 1994) contains some, but not extensive, references to the significance of the press. Neither Edward Said's *Culture and imperialism* (London, 1993) nor Frederick Cooper and Ann Laura Stoller (eds), *Tensions of empire: colonial cultures in a bourgeois world* (Berkeley, 1997) contain references to the press.   13 Thompson, *Imperial Britain*, chapter 3.   14 Kaul, *Reporting the raj*.   15 Heather Streets, *Born warriors? The military, martial races and masculinity in British imperial culture, 1857–1914* (Manchester, forthcoming, 2004) particularly chapter 4, where Streets examines the manipulation of the press by the leading British imperial general, Frederick Roberts.

Malaya.[16] From her work it is apparent that information was still being carefully controlled at that time, while the larger part of the British press, the section that had the greatest circulations, also continued to exercise the consensual restraint that generally characterized its approach to imperial events. Some would say that this was still very apparent at the time of the Falklands campaign in 1982.

Another approach has been to examine the press in respect of a single incident or set of events. Perhaps the most interesting of these in the Irish context have been the publications of De Nie and Gray, examining press responses to the Irish Famine.[17] In a wider imperial context, the role of the press in the outbreak of the South African War has received a great deal of attention, although most of this work still shies away from wide-ranging representational or statistical analysis. The agenda was set by J.A. Hobson's contemporaneous surveys, which sparked off a continuing debate about whether the press stimulated or merely reflected popular 'jingo' support for the war.[18] It cannot be denied that press coverage of the public fervour that welcomed the Relief of Mafeking on 17 May 1900, for example, was truly striking. The quite extraordinary descriptions to be found in almost every newspaper in England, Scotland and Wales at this time indicate a degree of popular and universal rejoicing that seems unprecedented in the nineteenth century, surpassing the response to earlier events such as Trafalgar and Waterloo. Richard Price's contention that such activity was restricted to the bourgeoisie in the West End of London is holed below the waterline by an examination of almost any paper you care to pick up.[19] The wild celebrations in Lancaster, as recounted in the local press, were quite remarkable.[20] Perusal of the Scottish press reveals that 'mafficking' seems to have taken place to an inordinate degree from Kirkwall to Kirkcudbright, from Lewis to Langholm, and particularly in Glasgow, where shipyard and other workers were benefiting financially from the war.[21]

16 Susan L. Carruthers, *Winning hearts and minds: British governments, the media and colonial counter-insurgency, 1944–1960* (London, 1995). 17 Michael De Nie, 'The Famine, Irish identity and the British press', *Irish Studies Review*, 1:6 (1998); Peter Gray, '*Punch* and the Great Famine', *History Ireland*, 2:1 (1993). 18 J.A. Hobson, *The war in South Africa* (London, 1900) and *The psychology of jingoism* (London, 1901). 19 Richard Price, *An imperial war and the British working class* (London, 1972). 20 C. Good, '"Perfect saturnalia" – Mafeking night in Huddersfield and Lancaster', unpublished MA dissertation, University of Lancaster, 1998. 21 The *Glasgow Herald* (21 May 1900) contained extraordinary descriptions of celebrations in Glasgow over the weekend, when 'business and household arrangements were forgotten in the universal joy' in which 'everyone [was] anxious to have a share'. A 'general strike' was resolved upon and processions of workers headed for the centre of the city, while all ships were dressed overall and the wharves and principal docks were decorated. Bonfires were lit in every corner of the city; firecrackers set off; bands played and there was general rejoicing everywhere, carrying over into the church services of the Sunday morning. The *Herald* itself suggested that there was more money about as a result of the full employment engendered by the war. The

The press is of necessity our prime source for examining this phenomenon, but newspaper reports, often ecstatic, need to be analysed with that necessary shrewdness born of scepticism. How far were newspapers reporting genuine events? To what extent were they seeking out or fabricating evidence for what was considered to have become, or ought to have become a national, if brief, passion? Were the populace displaying genuine imperial fervour or were they merely exploiting an excuse to take a day off work that employers could not argue with, not to mention a perfect reason to get drunk? To what extent were the bonfires, the processions, the bands, the effigies of Kruger and other Boer leaders, the photographs of Baden-Powell just part of a Bakhtinian carnivalesque, a glorious opportunity to turn the world upside down in the otherwise drab existence of industrial workers? We need to distinguish between enthusiasm for general celebration, whatever the occasion, and buying into the dominant ideology of empire.

From the reports that appeared in the press, it seems that few of those who thronged the streets seem to have minded the loss of pay that celebration involved. Indeed, most seem to have been prepared to spend good money on flags, bunting and other forms of extravagant display. Moreover, again if reports are to be believed, almost all of the population, both urban and rural, seem to have been involved, including clerics and church-goers, many of whom may have thoroughly disapproved of excess of any sort, particularly drunkenness. All the pent-up pressures of late nineteenth-century life seem to have been released in this one orgiastic moment, perhaps facilitated by the fact that the news arrived on a Friday night, permitting all the celebrations to take place on a Saturday. The extent of mafficking in Ireland is less clear, although, as might be expected, the shipyard workers of Belfast were as active as their cousins in Glasgow in losing both their heads and their sobriety. I have found nothing about mafficking in Dublin, although the queen's visit in April 1900 stimulated celebrations that were reminiscent of those that had attended the Relief of Ladysmith just a short time before, or so at least *The Times* alleged.[22]

Mafeking was, perhaps, the high point of a process that had been developing over the previous few decades, as press coverage of imperial events gained increased prominence. The 1870s were crucial. It is true that single climactic events had caused major perturbations in the newspapers before this

---

Herald also produced a round-up of celebratory activities in no fewer than 107 Scottish towns from Alyth to Wick (following with several more on the following day). It then surveyed the celebrations in English cities and towns, as well as offering a description of 'extraordinary displays of loyalty' across the empire, including the celebrations of black inhabitants of Jamaica. Some recent research, conducted by myself, into the Nova Scotian press of Halifax and other towns indicates that the Relief of Ladysmith (perhaps more so than Mafeking) was also received with wild celebrations in that Canadian province. **22** *Times*, 2 Apr. 1900.

decade, moments like the Indian revolt of 1857 (see chapter 5 below) or the Morant Bay rebellion in Jamaica in 1865. But the 1870s opened with those celebrated markers of a new enthusiasm for imperial expansion and consolidation, Ruskin's inaugural lecture as Slade Professor at Oxford and Disraeli's Crystal Palace speech, which were not notably sensational press events, and then continued with many that were. These started out with David Livingstone's disappearance and his discovery by Henry Morton Stanley on the shores of Lake Tanganyika in 1871, followed by his death in 1873 in Central Africa, surprisingly as resonant to Catholics as to Protestants, and his extraordinary funeral in Westminster Abbey. They continued with Disraeli's flamboyant purchase of the Suez Canal shares, the visit of the Prince of Wales to India in the winter of 1875/76, the passing of the Royal Styles and Titles bill and Lord Lytton's extraordinary durbar in India, the Russo-Turkish war with the imperial implications of the Berlin Conference of 1878, and the striking as well as chastening events in Zululand and Afghanistan in 1879. By then empire was firmly established as a source of spectacular events worthy of prominent press treatment.

The illustrated press neatly bears this out. The *Illustrated London News* issued a special supplement for the visit of the Prince of Wales to India and Ceylon in the mid-70s.[23] In 1879, the *ILN* devoted a very high proportion of its pages to the Zulu and Afghan wars and many of the engravings it used are lodged in our consciousness as images of those campaigns. An examination of *Punch* also reveals the extent to which cartoons and joke doggerel shifted to include imperial events or European events associated with empire.[24] This seems to be equally true of other sections of the illustrated and humorous press.

It is hard to see Gladstone's 1880 victory as heralding a reversal of this imperial thrust. The apparent resolution of the Afghan conflict and the withdrawal from the Transvaal after Majuba Hill in 1881 might indicate this. But of course Gladstone was soon embroiled in Egypt, while the affairs of the Sudan, and in particular the death of General Gordon, indicated the extent to which Little Englander politics seemed to be an impossibility in the climate of the time. In any case, a series of other conjunctions during the 1880s reinforced the trend towards growing press engagement with empire. These included improved steam and cable communications, the developing professions of war correspondents and artists,[25] the emergence of geographical education and the founding of geographical societies across the country,[26] as well

23 'India and the Prince of Wales' by George Augustus Sala, *Illustrated London News* supplement (1875). This was written ahead of the Prince's visit and described a 'programme which may or may not be followed'.   24 I have surveyed *Punch* from vol. 13 (1847) to vol. 88 (1883). 25 Roger T. Stearn, 'War correspondents and colonial war, *c.*1870–1900' in John M. MacKenzie (ed.), *Popular imperialism and the military, 1850–1950* (Manchester, 1992).   26 John M.

as the increased influence and visibility of the missionary societies, Protestant and Catholic, with their ready access to the agency and propaganda opportunities of churches conveniently dispersed around the country.

Hence, in the 1880s, empire as a source of spectacular theatrical events became even more prominent. An examination of selected issues of *The Times* helps in charting the growth of what was from the 1870s to the Edwardian era described as 'colonial intelligence'. In the 1870s, coverage seems to have been driven by specific events, but from the 1880s and, particularly, the 1890s, more bread and butter happenings in the territories of white settlement also came to have greater prominence (see chapter 2 below). Columns headed Canada, Australia, as well as occasionally the West Indies, the Cape or South Africa, came to join India and, above all, Egypt in the press coverage of the day. Such material included trade figures, the comings and goings of vessels, political developments, the award of mail contracts, and sometimes matters from the law courts, but of course revolt and war, together with royal visits, tended to secure the greatest prominence. By Edwardian times, larger newspapers had bulked up on colonial and imperial matter.[27]

How did British papers cover Irish affairs? Preliminary research, mainly using *The Times*, the *Glasgow Herald* and *Punch*, provides some clues. Just as the daily papers offered formalized columns devoted to imperial matters, so did *The Times* and the *Glasgow Herald* invariably contain a column headed 'Ireland'. This is interesting in itself. I have yet to find, although they may exist, columns headed either 'Scotland' or 'Wales'. Thus, the press accorded Ireland a liminal status, a separation within the Union that was not accorded to Scotland, even after the creation of the Scottish Office in the 1880s. This marginal status was confirmed by the content of these columns, mainly taken up with crime, 'outrages', news from the law courts, electoral and local government matters, the comings and goings of the lord lieutenant and chief secretary, distress, land reform and increasingly from the 1880s, of course, Home Rule. In a sense much of this could be seen as constituting issues of imperial concern, as Stephen Howe has shown.[28]

We can moreover attempt a distinction between news stories that were about the implicit 'imperialising' of Ireland as well as others that sought to set Ireland in a wider and explicitly imperial context. Curiously, this latter category seems to have encompassed a relatively small proportion of press coverage of Ireland. The sense that Irish affairs could be related to problems

MacKenzie, 'The provincial geographical societies in Britain, 1884–1914' in Morag Bell, Robin Butlin and Michael Heffernan (eds), *Geography and imperialism, 1820–1940* (Manchester, 1995). **27** These conclusions are derived from a survey of selected issues from each decade. **28** Stephen Howe, *Ireland and empire: colonial legacies in Irish history and culture* (Oxford, 2000); see also David Fitzpatrick, 'Ireland and the empire' in Andrew Porter (ed.), *The Oxford history of the British empire*, iii: *the nineteenth century* (Oxford, 1999).

in other parts of the British empire may seldom have been noticed, but was probably pregnant with meaning when it was.

In order to examine these themes further, preliminary research was undertaken using the CD-ROM of the Palmer's index to *The Times*, to establish how many hits were registered in searches combining references to Ireland and various imperial possessions between 1790 and 1914. Clearly we need a health warning here. Indexes are notoriously fallible. The indexer has to be able to recognize whether a particular piece really relates to the topic that it is ostensibly about. Significant allusions to other topics might not be picked up. Yet following up index entries shows that indexers did not operate solely on the basis of headings – they also noted individual paragraphs in articles that the heading would not necessarily have signalled. So indexing could be quite sophisticated.

Taking Ireland and India as key words produced only nineteen hits for the long nineteenth century, and only eight of them from 1880. Several of these related to comparisons between peasant proprietors in Ireland and India; some to troops from Ireland leaving for India, occasioning civil disturbance as they did so; and at least one compared evictions in India and Ireland. In the earlier period, there was an extraordinary account in 1847 of relief collections made in India for distress in Ireland, in which it was said that 'sepoys' (Indian Bengali soldiers) had contributed as generously as European regiments.[29]

To continue with this statistical survey, Ireland and Canada produced 49 hits, Ireland and South Africa 19, plus another five for the Cape. Ireland and Australia produced eleven, Ireland and New Zealand only two, Ireland and empire four, five each for Egypt and Newfoundland and a few for the West Indies and Hong Kong. Some may doubt whether these statistics are of much interest, but the character of these multilateral imperial connections, as reflected in *The Times*, does offer insights into significant aspects of press coverage of events in Ireland. This is confirmed by analysis of specific items turned up by the searches, providing an outline of the main obsessions of papers such as *The Times* and the *Glasgow Herald*.

Despite the possibility of skewed results arising from such a limited sample, a definite pattern seems to emerge. Inevitably, the activities of the Fenian Brotherhood featured prominently. There was a succession of news stories relating to the Fenian raids upon Canada in 1870, revealing an intriguing difference between the views expressed by *The Times* and the *Glasgow Herald*. *The Times* tended to be complimentary to American efforts in controlling the raids, while the *Glasgow Herald* quoted a speech by General Lindsay to the effect that the Americans had been hopeless and had stood to one side.[30] Interestingly, *Punch*, dealing with an earlier incident, changed its

29 *Times*, 7 June 1847. **30** *Times*, 30 May and 16 and 23 Oct. 1870; *Glasgow Daily Herald*, 31

tune. One cartoon showed an American fireman sitting back and refusing to extinguish the flames, while a later one showed the same functionary fully involved.[31] Other prominent stories related to visits to the Dominions by Irish nationalists (notably John Redmond, William O'Brien and T.P. O'Connor) seeking to raise money, and to resultant resistance and support in Australian, Canadian and other communities.[32] Another category indicated the backing of Dominions politicians, such as Richard John Seddon in New Zealand and Wilfrid Laurier in Canada, for Irish Home Rule in the context of wider imperial reorganization.[33]

There were periodic round-ups of the treatment of imperial events by the Irish nationalist press in both *The Times* and the *Glasgow Herald*. These were not always the same and contained different emphases. They included the Fenian raids in Canada and General Sir Garnet Wolseley's invasion of Egypt and his defeat of Colonel Urubi (then Arabi) Pasha.[34] Their main thrust seems to have been to indicate the presence in Ireland of dangerously seditious views, such as the widespread support for Urubi as a fellow anti-royal nationalist.

The *Glasgow Herald* carried annual statistics of Irish emigration, carefully charting lows and highs right through to the First World War.[35] Inevitably, the *Herald* also carried news of Irish organizations in Glasgow, covering the escalating passions of Orange and unionist communities in the city in response to Home Rule.[36] The *Herald* was, as might be expected, a staunchly unionist paper and its reports and leaders were probably fiercer than those of *The Times*. It tended to ridicule such notions as 'Home Rule all round', and organizations like the Young Scots Society that promoted them.[37] In terms of sectarian interests, it is also noticeable that the *Herald* carried annual reports of the general assemblies of the Irish Presbyterians, no doubt of interest to its clerical and missionary readership. English papers like *The Times* showed no interest in such arcane discussions. The *Herald*, and no doubt other Scottish newspapers, also tended to pursue a historical interest in the Scottish settlements in Ulster, with correspondence and much discussion about the role of migrants from specific Scottish counties.[38]

The other major area of reporting on Ireland was in relation to royal visits. Those of Queen Victoria, culminating in 1900, of Edward and Alexandra in 1907 (associated with the opening of the Irish National Exhibition in Dublin), and of George and Mary in 1911 were reported as

May and 1 and 4 June 1870.　**31** *Punch*, 7 Apr. and 30 June 1866.　**32** For example, *Times*, 9 and 16 Aug. 1883 and 25, 29 and 30 Apr. and 2 May 1887; *Glasgow Herald*, 6 Oct. 1910 and 14 Sept. 1912.　**33** *Glasgow Herald*, 17 Feb. 1904, 15 Oct. 1906 and 22 Mar. 1907.　**34** *Glasgow Daily Herald*, 6 June 1870; *Times*, 25 Aug. 1882.　**35** For example, *Glasgow Herald*, 3 Apr. 1907; 28 Mar. 1908; 5 May 1911.　**36** *Glasgow Herald*, 14 Apr. 1908; 18, 20 and 30 Dec. 1909; 9 Nov. 1914.　**37** *Glasgow Herald*, 5 Feb. 1909.　**38** *Glasgow Herald*, 5 Oct. 1910; 12 Oct. 1912.

extensively in the *Herald* as in *The Times*.[39] Such visits acted of course as litmus tests for supposed loyalty and disloyalty. They seem to have been used to reassure specific constituencies in England and Scotland that Irish nationalism could be separated from the genuinely loyal sentiments of the populace. Each royal visit was described as eliciting loyal demonstrations in the working-class districts of Dublin, though this contrasted rather strikingly with the allegedly churlish resistance of, for example, the striking carters and dockers in 1907 or the Dublin Corporation's refusal to be involved in 1911.[40] Victoria's visits in 1849 and 1900 produced extraordinary material in the elite press, coverage that seems strangely out of its time in its chatty style and extensive and lurid descriptions. Do we have the Mafeking effect here? Did the phenomena so avidly portrayed really happen or did the press engage in a degree of wish-fulfilment?

Some may say that this kind of selective analysis does not get us very far. So what can we make of it? The first point is that, in dealing with the press, we have to be as aware of silences as we are of noise. Silence is difficult to identify, but there can be little doubt that it exists and that it exists for a reason. Any analysis of the press and its influence on public opinion, elite, bourgeois and mass, has to deal with silence. To take but one example, the press, like other forms of imperial literature, gave greater prominence to Irish Catholics and Scottish Protestants in the empire, even though there were of course many prominent Protestants from across Ireland and a large Scottish Catholic population from the Highlands and Islands, involved in the running of empire.

The second point is that in order fully to understand press coverage of Ireland, we also need to examine press comment on events in England, Scotland and Wales. For example, the treatment of Ireland by British papers was clearly an implicit, and sometimes explicit, means of dealing with Scotland, and vice versa. To apply Steven Ellis' phrase to a later period, pluralistic Celtic worlds overlapped with an English one, throughout the empire.[41] Scots in the empire tended to be talked up by such disparate figures as Edward Long, the eighteenth-century historian of Jamaica, and imperial travellers like Sir Charles Dilke and J.A. Froude in the nineteenth, as a means of critiquing the Irish.[42] Highlighting the perceived disloyalties of some was conversely a technique for defining and spotlighting the reassuring loyalties of others. The press was surely in the same game (see chapter 3 below).

39 See, for example, *Times*, 2, 4, 5, 6, 12 and 27 Apr. 1900; *Glasgow Herald*, 11 and 12 July 1907 and 10 and 11 July 1911. **40** *Glasgow Herald*, 12 July 1907 and 11 July 1911. **41** Quoted in Howe, *Ireland and empire*, 15. **42** John M. MacKenzie, 'Essay and reflection: on Scotland and the empire', *International History Review*, 4:15 (1993) 714–39 at 725–6; see also John M. MacKenzie, 'Empire and national identities: the case of Scotland', *Transactions of the Royal Historical Society*, sixth series, 8 (1998) 215–31.

Scots were also assimilated into the controversy over Irish Home Rule. The debate was described by opponents of devolution such as Joseph Chamberlain as constituting the 'most dangerous time in the history of the British race'. In this context, we can note that English and British were always used in a fascinatingly specific way in writings about empire: 'English' for national characteristics, perceived qualities and the dissemination of notable institutions; 'British' when there was a threat or when there was a need for incorporation of Welsh and Scots into a particular imperial laager. The English expanded and the British defended.

All of this helps reveal highly pluralistic forms of 'othering'. Writers such as Said or Colley have tended to present ideas about 'the other' in the context of essentially binary and oppositional sets of constructs.[43] I have always felt uneasy about this. Writers and artists also create ideal and exemplary others, as happened with certain representations of the Middle East in the second half of the nineteenth century, and above all in relation to Japan.[44] Within the archipelagic world of Britain and Ireland and its wider imperial connections, very complex processes of overlapping, positive and negative othering were at work. English and Scots, Scots and Irish, some Scots and some Irish – particularly in military contexts perhaps – were consciously contrasted in these ways. The peregrinations of politicians and fundraisers, the celebration of royal visits, the fighting of colonial wars, all seem to have acted as arenas in which these implicit debates on identities and supposedly common or contrasting characteristics could take place.

A third and related, some may think contradictory, point arising from our analysis is connected with iconography, where stereotyping might often be more prominent than in prose. Illustrations and cartoons relating to the ethnicities of the British and Irish islands, particularly in relation to empire, are another grossly under-worked field. Of course, there has been some important work done here, particularly in relation to race, but much more is needed. One interesting example of the contrast between the iconography deployed to represent the Irish and the Scots is a gendered one. Ireland was invariably depicted as Hibernia, or sometimes Erin, a much put-upon iconic female figure frequently seeking the sisterly consolation of Britannia.[45] Cartoon after cartoon used this conjunction. Of course Britannia was supposed to stand for all of Britain, but it is interesting that there has never been a specific female signifier for Scotland. Neither Scotia nor Caledonia has ever been strongly featured within this sisterhood. It may be possible to theorize here about the feminization of Ireland, and to draw a contrast with the portrayal of Scots as

43 Linda Colley, *Britons: forging the nation, 1707–1837* (London, 1992); Edward Said, *Orientalism* (London, 1978) and *Culture and imperialism*. 44 John M. MacKenzie, *Orientalism: history, theory and the arts* (Manchester, 1995). 45 See, for example, the *Punch* cartoons, 30 Sept. 1865, 127; 3 Mar. 1866, 89; 8 Dec. 1866, 233.

a manly martial race. Queen Victoria on her first visit to Ireland wrote about both the supposed degradation of the Irish and the beauty of Irish women. In Scotland she was always more interested in the manly, kilted, male figure (witness John Brown). Similarly, it is worth noting the extent to which the Scottish soldier, through the exotic character of his dress, became a major imperial icon in the nineteenth century, belying the statistical realities of his more limited position in the British army.[46]

An analysis of volumes of *Punch* from this period reveals that there were more small cartoons relating to the Scots than to the Irish. The Irish tended to figure more in the large engraved cartoons, although there were never particularly many of these. The Scots were always inevitably kilted and much fun was poked both at their alleged national characteristics, as well as at their landscape as a huntin', shootin' and fishin' playground for the English. Those English who became surrogate Scots (for example by finding parliamentary seats there) and supposedly adopted the kilt, were also satirized.[47] The Irish on the other hand were almost always characterized as Fenians.[48] And I need not dilate on the notorious depiction of the Fenian that appeared in cartoon after cartoon throughout the final decades of the century. These illustrations were underpinned by prose and doggerel items. A striking one was a discovery *Punch* made from *The Times* in 1866 that the army's medical college at Netley was having difficulty in recruiting Scots and English doctors and was turning to the Irish – as indeed the Indian Medical Service was doing at the same time. *Punch* promptly turned such recruits into Fenian doctors who were going to inflict more injuries on the British soldiery than they would receive on the battlefield.[49] Thus, in the iconography, while Scots were collapsed into engagingly funny kilted figures, the Irish were stereotyped as dangerous Fenians. Such stereotyping can also be found in prose. In 1866, *The Times* reprinted an article from *Blackwood's* which, in the aftermath of the Jamaican revolt, likening 'Sambo' to 'Paddy' – both stereotypes of disloyalty, violence and danger.[50] It is surely the case that the effects of this visual and verbal imagery retained their potency throughout the late nineteenth and early twentieth centuries. As I have long argued, popular cultural forms, their conventions and their predilections, tend to have a long shelf life, often outliving political and intellectual developments which may seem to have rendered them redundant. Intriguingly and paradoxically, longevity in the press of such stereotypes may have disrupted efforts to identify a more positive 'other' that seem to lie behind so much press coverage.

46 MacKenzie, 'On Scotland and the empire', 726–7.   **47** Both Gladstone (regularly) and Goschen were depicted in kilts. See, for example, *Punch*, 16 Aug. 1884, 78–9; 30 Aug. 1884, 103; 25 Oct. 1884, 203–4; and 18 Apr. 1885, 183.   **48** *Punch* in 1866 was full of Fenian cartoons; many more are to be found in subsequent volumes. See also for example the Land League cartoon in *Punch*, 22 Dec. 1883, 295.   **49** *Punch*, 17 Nov. 1866, 207.   **50** *Times*, 1 Feb. 1866.

Such stereotyping may also explain the dilemmas and contradictions that seem to underlie so many press reports of Irish events within the empire. On the one hand, emigration helped to people the empire and provide labour for its development. Yet Irish emigration could also seem tantamount to exporting disloyalty. Fenians in North America, however inept, but more particularly nationalist travelling fund-raisers seemed to demonstrate that Irish migrants, together with their priests, constituted an endemic imperial problem, however much processes of integration as well as ample evidence of political and cultural pluralism seemed to indicate the contrary. Even aristocratic governors general were not immune to exported controversy as Lord Lansdowne discovered when William O'Brien turned up in the United States and Canada in May 1887 to agitate on behalf of the tenants of Lansdowne's Luggacurren estate.[51] Dominions' premiers, whose loyalty seemed unimpeachable, meanwhile took up the cause of Irish Home Rule in pursuit of an empire based on consultation. Such contradictions seem to become more pronounced as the years wore on towards the First World War.

It may well be that this chapter asks many more questions than it answers. But when considering newspapers and empire in Ireland and Britain, we need pluralistic rather than dualistic modes of analysis. Far too much imperial history has been written from the viewpoint of the amorphous Briton juxtaposed against the supposedly rebellious Irish. The role of the Irish within the British empire, and the manifold press depictions of that complex connection from both the imperialist and the nationalist perspective, can only be understood in terms of the broader ethnic breakdown of Irish, Scots, Welsh and English. Beyond that, Irish attitudes towards empire also need to be related to the emerging identities of Canadian, Australian, New Zealander and, later, white South African.

This is neatly illustrated by a classic parliamentary gaffe in the Commons in 1911. After the presentation of the Irish emigration statistics, Captain Craig quipped that all the migrants were desperate to escape from the dangers of Home Rule. John Redmond rose to suggest, to the contrary, that they were all eager to get to the joys of Home Rule. This exchange was gleefully reported by the *Herald*, which in turn perhaps scored an own goal as sure-footedly as Craig had done.[52] This example raises broader questions. Lots of Scots had also left the UK to find Home Rule, while working-class Britons, sometimes seen as alarming and disruptive at home, came to be represented as loyal and civilized in the armed forces and in the empire. Could versions of such an imperial transformation also be found for the Irish? Or does the imperial press suggest, in the obsessive aspects of its coverage, that the multiple forms of redemption born of mobility and of colonial opportunity,

51 *Times*, 2 May 1887. 52 *Glasgow Herald*, 19 May 1911.

achievement and defence were more possible for the English, Scots and Welsh than for the Irish? Can we therefore see the relationship between Ireland and empire, as portrayed by the press, as being about the optimistic search for common identities, repeatedly disappointed by stereotypical differences that could never be gainsaid? Press coverage of Ireland and empire seems to reveal a desperate effort to find the wished-for 'other' in the face of less promising stereotypes. The realisation seemed gradually to dawn that this was tantamount to searching for the unattainable.

2. Empire and the English press, *c*.1857–1914[1]

SIMON J. POTTER

How did English newspapers provide their readers with coverage of events taking place in the British empire? To what uses did editors put this news? Was English press coverage of empire distinctive in relation to that provided in other parts of what was then the United Kingdom? Can coverage and comment be taken as representative of an 'English' national response to empire? In attempting to answer these questions, this chapter examines the tensions that existed between forces acting to encourage diversity and homogeneity of press coverage of empire in Britain and Ireland. It also emphasizes the importance of placing the UK press in a broader imperial context, examining links with newspapers and journalists in the far-flung territories of the British empire.

Throughout the period studied in this chapter, the English press was characterized by marked divisions. In part, these were regional in nature. The political centralization of the UK certainly meant that many leading dailies, weeklies and periodicals were London-based. There existed something that at least resembled a national press, with such papers circulating throughout Britain and Ireland and even further a field. But, particularly in the earlier part of our period, many of these papers were still perceived essentially as London papers, rather than national papers, with little appeal to provincial readers. As one contemporary argued in 1851, 'There are many persons in the country who are utterly unable to understand a London paper.'[2] Space existed for a flourishing provincial press, particularly in the years after the abolition of the Newspaper Stamp Tax in 1855.

Provincial papers catered to (and perhaps stimulated) perceived differences in regional priorities and perspectives.[3] They were keen to stand up for local interests, not least in order to develop their own circulation. In the 1850s the *Manchester Guardian*, perhaps England's most influential provincial paper,

1 The research for this chapter was conducted with the generous financial assistance of a Royal Irish Academy – British Academy Exchange Scholarship. I would like to thank Professor Andrew Porter for his support, and seminar audiences at the Imperial History Seminar, Institute of Historical Research, London, and the University of Sussex for their questions and comments. I would also like to thank Jacqueline Beaumont for several helpful suggestions. 2 Quoted in A.J. Lee, *The origins of the popular press in England, 1855–1914* (London, 1976) 73. 3 Francis Williams, *Dangerous estate: the anatomy of newspapers* (London, 1959 edn) 96–7.

thus emphasized its devotion to 'the interests of the locality in which it cir-
culates', while the Manchester *Courier* proudly proclaimed its penchant for
'provincial aggrandisement'. Even a national paper like *The Times* admitted
that its sympathies lay more with mercantile communities such as London
and Bristol, than with the industrial midlands and north.[4] When examining
coverage of empire, it is important to consider how far the amount of attention devoted to imperial affairs differed between the London and provincial
press and between papers in the different provinces, and whether distinct
regional perspectives can be detected.

Like the press in the rest of the UK, the English press was also divided
in terms of political affiliation. Over the course of the nineteenth century the
press came to mirror the partisan divide between Conservatives and Liberals.
Even if commercialization had by the eve of the First World War begun to
dilute partisan vitriol, the fierce political debates of the Edwardian period,
and Liberal attempts to regain the dominance of the press that they had previously enjoyed, helped ensure that newspapers retained their connections
with the major parties and with particular factions within those parties.[5] Irish
Home Rule played a significant part in reinvigorating partisan press debate,
and the resultant controversy acquired an imperial flavour as comparisons
were drawn between Ireland and the Dominions.[6] A more explicitly imperial controversy was sparked off by Colonial Secretary Joseph Chamberlain's
tariff reform campaign, launched in 1903 and designed to promote the economic and political integration of the UK and the Dominions through a
system of protectionism combined with tariff preferences. The debate that
ensued revealed clear, albeit complex, divisions between the political parties
in terms of their approach to imperial issues.[7] It might thus be expected that
coverage of empire might differ, both in scope and content, between Liberal
and Conservative papers, and also between papers affiliated with particular
factions belonging to each party.

While diversity was thus an inescapable feature of English press coverage
of empire, there were at the same time certain factors acting to encourage a
greater degree of homogeneity. Newspapers across England felt the impact
of similar commercial and organizational changes, fundamentally altering the
backdrop against which coverage of imperial events was presented. Such
changes also altered editors' beliefs about the extent to and ways in which
their papers could reflect or lead 'public opinion', and even modified beliefs
about what 'public opinion' actually was.[8] Challenges emerged to the con-

4 *Newspaper press directory*, 1857/8.   5 Lee, *Origins of the popular press*, 133. On the political
press generally see S. Koss, *The rise and fall of the political press*, 2 vols (London, 1981 and
1984).   6 See Introduction above.   7 Simon J. Potter, *News and the British world: the emergence of an imperial press system, 1876–1922* (Oxford, 2003), ch. 7.   8 Aled Jones, *Powers of the
press: newspapers, power and the public in nineteenth-century England* (Aldershot, 1996) 87–94.

viction that the press could help shape and form public opinion.[9] By 1920, Kennedy Jones, editor of the London *Evening News* and co-founder of the *Daily Mail*, could argue that the business of the press was

> to collect news and present it to the public in an intelligible and agreeable form ... This service enables it to form an intimacy with the customer which offers an opportunity to speak advice ... often it is smiled at and answered in the same spirit as a customer smiles at and answers the chatter of the barber who cuts his hair.[10]

This shift reflected the fact that, by the end of the nineteenth century, the traditional organs of the political elite were sharing the market with new mass circulation papers, catering to larger and more socially inclusive audiences than ever before. Commercialization was in part a result of technological change, which allowed newspapers to be printed and distributed on a scale previously unimagined.[11] The spread of telegraph and undersea cable communication meanwhile worked drastically to alter how domestic and overseas news reached the public and, with the emergence of syndicated news services, encouraged a certain homogeneity of coverage. In an age in which the press supplied readers with an essentially uniform budget of news, the extent to which newspapers could sustain diverse public opinions was increasingly constrained.

Historians must thus question not only the connection between the press and public opinion, but also the extent to which homogeneity can be interpreted as proof of distinctively English attitudes. On one level, English papers were bound into a broader UK press industry, in which Scottish, Welsh and Irish papers were subject to similar forces and changes. The ability of English newspapers to develop entirely autonomous coverage of empire, for example, was thus limited. Moreover, as this chapter seeks to demonstrate, English papers were also integrated into a broader imperial network of communication, creating links with the overseas press, and particularly with newspapers in the settler colonies, or Dominions, of Canada, Australia, New Zealand and South Africa. Any attempt to examine the English press in isolation, from an essentially national perspective, misses these important connections.

THE MID-NINETEENTH CENTURY

For much of the nineteenth century, newspapers relied for their coverage of overseas events on news arriving by ship, brought through the mails in the

9 On this conviction see Introduction above. 10 Kennedy Jones, *Fleet Street and Downing Street* (London, 1920) 308–9. 11 See here especially Lucy Brown, *Victorian news and newspapers* (Oxford, 1985).

form of letters from correspondents or printed newspapers from abroad. In the age of sail, news did not travel fast. In the 1850s it could take three months for news to reach the UK from Australia. Even with the introduction of steamships, in the late 1860s it still took 45 days for ships to complete the journey. However, from the late 1840s onwards, telegraph networks began to snake across the landscape, allowing the more rapid overland distribution of news. Information could now travel faster than people could, and over long distances. By 1851 the first submarine cable between Britain and France was also operational, opening up possibilities for the rapid transmission of news around the world.

English papers were quick to adopt the new technology, and to use the promise of generous supplies of cable news as a means to attract readers. In the *Newspaper press directory* for 1857–8, the London *Morning Post* stressed its efforts to expand the amount of overseas intelligence supplied, claiming that 'no journal [goes] to greater expense for telegraphs and Continental information'. The London *Times*, which claimed to represent 'the voice of the English nation', also emphasized its global reach.

> This, the leading journal of Europe, has for the field of its circulation, emphatically, the WORLD, and its influence is coextensive with civilisation ... within two or three hours after sunrise, the wonderful machinery of this great journal throws off its fifty or sixty thousand impressions, instinct with the intelligence which, from every quarter of the globe, at an incalculable outlay, is night by night acquired.[12]

A desire to advertise their commitment to providing telegraphic news also obviously motivated the founders of the *Daily Telegraph*, established in 1855.

In reality however, the ability of mid-nineteenth-century English newspapers to supply their readers with plentiful services of cable news was limited, not just by the expense of such reports, but also by the inadequacies of the cable infrastructure. Even the relatively short cables laid under the Mediterranean during the 1850s proved unreliable, while cables over the longer distances to British colonies in North America, Africa, Asia and the Pacific had yet to prove practicable. Papers thus continued to rely on letters mailed by correspondents, and on copies of overseas newspapers carried to the UK by ship. This clearly had an effect on coverage of events around the empire. Even when news of imperial events of unusual interest to English audiences occurred, papers could provide little in the way of regular, up-to-date coverage – and the emergence of telegraph technology was leading readers to expect such a service.

12 *Newspaper press directory*, 1857–8.

With the outbreak of the Indian Mutiny in 1857, a flood of reports from the subcontinent inundated English newspapers. Papers such as the *Daily News* devoted special sections of each edition to 'The Indian Mutinies'. However, this news took a considerable amount of time to reach the English press, as it had to come overland by mail until it reached points where it could be fed into the European telegraph and cable network. This resulted in serious delays, and reports of the relief of the siege of Lucknow, for example, took over a month to reach the UK.[13] Readers became increasingly frustrated as a result. One correspondent, noting the 'intense anxiety for early news by [*sic*] the English public', bemoaned the unnecessary delays in forwarding reports caused by 'the utter carelessness or absolute incompetency [*sic*] of certain officials' at Alexandria and elsewhere.[14] The irregular and disjointed nature of reports also made it impossible for papers to present continuous, coherent accounts of events. Editors thus had to put considerable effort into interpreting and explaining the fragmentary cable reports to their readers, joining the dots with conjecture.[15]

Delays in supply probably acted to reduce the appeal to English readers of everyday news from the colonies, and few papers published much news from the empire. For news from Britain's main commercial and military outpost in southern Africa, the Cape Colony, the UK press was entirely reliant on mailed reports, which in 1857 could take two months or more to arrive. This must be borne in mind when examining how the English press reported the disturbing events occurring on the boundaries of the Cape Colony during 1856–7. The expansion of white settlement and British military influence into the lands of the Xhosa (referred to as Kaffirs, Caffirs or Caffres in the English newspaper reports of the 1850s) during the previous decades, and the sudden impact of a major epidemic of lungsickness among the Xhosa's herds of cattle, had culminated in the emergence of a millenarian movement. Prophets urged people to kill their cattle and cease cultivating their crops, in order to speed up the arrival of spirit warriors who would sweep the British into the sea. The resultant famine not only led to the death of an estimated 40,000 Xhosa, but also provided the Cape government with an opportunity to move the Xhosa off their land and into the waged colonial economy, opening up more opportunities for white settlement and providing a much needed source of labour. By the end of June 1857, over 13,000 Xhosa had been sent into the Cape Colony to work on settler farms.[16]

---

13 The *Morning Post* and the *Daily News* both reported on 24 December that Lucknow had been relieved over a month earlier, on 21 November. News came from India by ship to Suez, from whence it took a further five days to travel between Alexandria and London by telegraph, cable and ship. 14 Letter to the editor from Francis M. Jennings of Cork, *Daily News*, 22 Dec. 1857. 15 See for example the editorial in the *Daily News*, 24 Dec. 1857 attempting to interpret reports from India. 16 See J.B. Peires, *The dead will arise: Nongqawuse and the great*

In general, the London papers did not start to alert their readers to these events until late in 1857. On 10 December *The Times* published extracts from a letter from an anonymous female settler at King William's Town, describing the effects of the famine. This was forwarded to *The Times* by Edward Fry of Bristol, probably the lawyer great-grandson of Joseph Fry, the Quaker cocoa manufacturer. The next day the *Daily News* published a short extract from the *Grahamstown Journal*, which referred to the large numbers of Xhosa migrating into the Cape Colony, and a question was asked in the British House of Commons about the famine.[17] A week later, the *Daily News* reported 'great distress' among the Xhosa, estimating that up to 25,000 had migrated into the Colony over the previous months.[18]

Papers such as the *Daily Telegraph* and the *Morning Post* did not provide readers with any news of this until 8 January 1858 however, when the provincial press also began to include coverage. The amount of space devoted by provincial papers to these events, while universally small, varied considerably, with readers outside of the larger manufacturing centres being the least well informed. Papers such as the *Manchester Guardian* and *Aris's Birmingham Gazette* provided roughly as much news about the fate of the Xhosa as did their London contemporaries.[19] Other provincial papers contained markedly less, generally only one or two short paragraphs.[20] Weekly papers such as the *Durham Chronicle* contained no news at all about events at the Cape during this period.

While the level of coverage varied considerably, the tone of comment on events at the Cape was strikingly uniform. Both in London and the provinces, papers seemed to have relied in general on the same reports, often reprinting news using exactly the same wording as each other, with or without acknowledgment of the original source.[21] There seemed few divisions among editors either, and apart from the letter forwarded to *The Times* by Edward Fry, little evidence of humanitarian sympathy. The *Daily Telegraph* argued that the famine had prevented the outbreak of another war between the British

Xhosa cattle-killing movement of 1856–7 (Johannesburg, 1989).   **17** *Morning Post*, 12 Dec. 1857. **18** *Daily News*, 18 Dec. 1857.   **19** The *Manchester Guardian* provided reports on 8 and 12 January, 9 February and 4 and 11 March 1858.   **20** The *Manchester Courier* carried two short reports on 9 January and 6 March 1858. Similarly, while the Exeter *Western Times* contained lengthy reports about events in India, it only carried a short paragraph concerning the Cape on 13 February 1858, and a reprinted article from the *Grahamstown Journal* (6 March). The *Durham County Advertiser* contained only an un-attributed copy of a report from *The Times* of 11 January, reprinted on 15 January, and a short report on 12 February. On 16 January the *York Herald* reprinted a short paragraph from the London *Standard* of 8 January. The only news published by *Woolmer's Exeter and Plymouth Gazette* on the subject came on 13 February 1858.   **21** The *Manchester Guardian* reprinted news in the same form as published in the London *Times* on 8 and 12 January, 9 February and 11 March 1858. *Aris's Birmingham Gazette* meanwhile published short reports from the Cape on 11 January, 15 February and 8 March 1858, mostly reprinted verbatim from London papers.

and the Xhosa, thus guaranteeing the increased prosperity of the Cape. 'Out of the evil, therefore, which has occurred, a redeeming good may arise.'[22] Even Liberal editors shed few tears. On 24 October 1857, the *Manchester Guardian* reprinted an editorial from the London *Globe*, on 'The state of Kaffraria'. Both were avowedly Liberal papers and, to some degree, we can see here the operation of a network of politically like-minded papers sharing their news and views – on 31 October the Liberal *Lancaster Guardian* reprinted the same extract. The tone of the editorial was hardly favourable to the Xhosa however. The author concluded that the cattle killing was probably part of a plot among the Xhosa's leaders to drive them into attacking the Cape Colony – 'the foolish Kaffirs are the victims of their silly trust in supremely silly advice'. The editorial went on to detail the results of the famine, in terms of mortality and migration, and to endorse the Cape government's attempts to ensure that only those willing to work received public relief. On 11 March the *Daily Telegraph* recorded that 'Those received as servants promise to become a valuable portion of the public.'[23]

The *Globe* editorial also suggested raising a 'brigade of Kaffirs for the Indian war', treating the displaced Xhosa as a potential source of manpower now at the empire's call. The *Morning Post* similarly noted that

> Among the warlike native tribes of Southern and South-Western Africa, the Kaffirs and the Zulus, it is quite within the bounds of possibility that we might find a large body of men who would be peculiarly fitted, by constitution and previous habits of life, for military service in India, ready to enter the armies of the Crown, especially as at this moment these unfortunate people are suffering the most severe distress and privation from want of food. To convert these borderers from troublesome enemies into well-paid soldiers would not be an unprofitable way of securing peace upon our Cape frontier.[24]

This is a remarkably early reference to the possibility of recruiting African troops for imperial service.

Where did the uniformity of English press coverage of events in Xhosaland originate? The dependence of provincial papers on their London contemporaries for news meant that they tended to echo the editorial comments of metropolitan papers.[25] More significantly, English papers generally, in London and the provinces, were in turn dependent on the settler press at the Cape for much of their news, and generally summarized or reprinted reports from

22 12 Jan. 1858.   23 See also *Daily News*, 8 Jan. 1858.   24 *Morning Post*, 6 Feb. 1858.   25 A rare example of a provincial paper with access to its own source of news was the *Lancaster Guardian*, which on 26 December 1857 printed a letter from 'a correspondent, writing from King William's Town', referring to the plight of the Xhosa.

the three main Cape papers, the *Cape Town Mail*, the *Grahamstown Journal* and the *South African Advertiser*. These sources were in turn the origin of the English emphasis on the Xhosa as a valuable new source of manpower. On 1 January 1858 the *Daily News* for example reprinted a remark from the *Cape Town Mail*, to the effect that the influx of Xhosa would help relieve the colony's want of servants and labourers.

The idea that the famine was the result of a plot by the Xhosa's leaders to foment an attack on the Cape was also picked up from the settler papers. The *Morning Post* thus reprinted an article from the *Cape Town Mail*, which argued that

> It has long been suspected that the infatuation of the Kaffirs, which has ended in the destruction of their tribes, originated with their chiefs ... and that the orders to kill all the cattle and to abstain from cultivating the ground were simply preparations for a desperate effort to recover their independence and avenge themselves on the colony. The proof of this has at last been obtained, and we have now one of the most instructive narratives for those Governments that have to deal with barbarians.[26]

The same report was reprinted on the same day, without attribution, by the London *Standard*. On 4 March the *Post* meanwhile reprinted an article on 'The late Kaffir plot' from the *Grahamstown Journal* of 5 January, an article also carried by the *Daily News* and the *Daily Telegraph* (4 March), *The Times* (5 March), the Exeter *Western Times* (6 March) and probably by other papers as well.[27] This article clearly served settler interests, not only endorsing Governor Grey's actions during the famine, but also again presenting the catastrophe as the result of a plot by the Xhosa chiefs rather than of pressure placed on the Xhosa by the expansion of settler influence. The article also concluded that the supposed plot demonstrated the need to extend the Colony's borders into Xhosaland, in order to prevent such a threat re-emerging.

> While there is a large savage population upon and within our border, with little or no possible check upon their habits and training, it is impossible that the frontier districts of the colony can ever be safe. Only in taking advantage of the providential turn things have taken, as far as possible; only by the extension of British rule over the whole of Kaffraria, and planting it with British settlers, can we hope to see any real help for the colony or any effective measure of civilisation applied to the Kaffir.

26 *Morning Post*, 8 Feb. 1858. 27 On 4 March the *Standard* reprinted a different article from the same paper, dated 29 Dec. 1857.

Reliance on the settler press (combined with changing attitudes following the Indian Mutiny) also helps explain the lack of humanitarian sympathy displayed by English papers towards the plight of the Xhosa. Settler humanitarian sentiment had already collapsed at the time of the 1846–7 frontier war.

As Alan Lester has recently demonstrated, in the mid-nineteenth century contact between newspapers around the empire helped create complex networks of communication between Britain and its settler colonies, and between the settler colonies themselves. Settler papers were adept at using these connections to urge their views on British readers, in order to stand up for the perceived collective interests of settler communities.[28] Their editors were well aware that British papers were reprinting their news, and indeed actively encouraged this by providing regular summaries of local events, published to coincide with the departure of the overseas mails. These summaries could be used as a soapbox for targeting British audiences on particular issues. For example, on 11 March 1858 *The Times* republished verbatim a summary from the *Cape Town Mail*, which stressed that disturbances in Xhosaland were no reason for Britons not to migrate to the Cape. Even when not directly reliant on summaries, British papers tended to adopt the settler perspective, as settlers were often employed as local correspondents. In a letter published by *The Times* on 11 January 1858, an 'Occasional Correspondent' at the Cape presented a strikingly similar interpretation of events to that provided by papers such as the *Grahamstown Journal*.

The limited supply of news available from the Cape meant that those reports that were available to English readers could only really have appealed to or informed a small, elite audience with prior knowledge of affairs at the Cape, able to supplement the newspapers with additional sources of information.[29] How representative this group was of anything other than an elite level of 'public opinion' is debatable. Taking the striking level of uniformity displayed by newspapers around England as evidence for some form of common English 'national' perspective on events at the Cape is rendered even more problematic by the fact that uniformity was in many cases the result of reliance on the settler press. This is particularly apparent when one takes into account the fact that papers elsewhere in Britain, and in Ireland, were dependent on the same sources of news. Neither the Edinburgh *Daily Scotsman* nor the Dublin *Freeman's Journal* contained much news from the Cape, bar a paragraph on 8 January 1858, repeating verbatim a report appearing in the English press culled from the settler papers. During the mid-nineteenth cen-

28 Alan Lester, 'British settler discourse and the circuits of empire', *History Workshop Journal*, 54 (2002) 24–48.   29 One of the sources available to nineteenth-century readers to help interpret newspaper reports from overseas is discussed in Michael Hancher, 'An imagined world: *The Imperial Gazetteer*' in Julie F. Codell (ed.), *Imperial co-histories: national identities and the British and colonial press* (Cranbury, NJ, 2003).

tury British and Irish press coverage of imperial events was influenced by the fact that newspapers were bound into a broader imperial network of communication, encompassing settler colonies at the Cape and elsewhere.

THE LATE NINETEENTH CENTURY

This network remained in place throughout the decades that followed, although its nature was modified by organizational and technological change. In particular, improvements in telegraph and cable communication came to offer newspapers opportunities for providing greater amounts of up-to-date news from around the empire. During the 1860s and 1870s, undersea telegraph cables were constructed linking Britain with each of its major colonies. Along with the expansion of the cable infrastructure, syndicated news services began to emerge. This reflected the fact that cable news remained extremely expensive. Across the UK, newspapers could generally only afford to provide overseas news by cooperating with others, to share the cost of a common service among many subscribers.

One of the first organizations to recognize the opportunities that this niche offered was Reuters Telegram Company, founded in 1851 by a German Jewish émigré, initially in order to transmit commercial information between London and the European capitals of finance. Reuters subsequently took advantage of cable and telegraph technology to become one of the world's first truly global corporations.[30] As a result of cartel agreements with the world's other major news agencies, dating back to 1856 and formalized in 1870, it acquired the sole right to collect and sell news in most parts of the British empire.[31] London papers subscribed directly to Reuters' services while, after 1868, provincial papers in Britain and Ireland were served with Reuters' syndicated news through the medium of the Press Association, a co-operative organization that also provided subscribers with domestic news.[32] By the end of the nineteenth century, the Press Association could supply members with a range of overseas services, depending on their requirements, costing between £40 and £300 per annum.[33] In 1897 the Press Association was paying

30 O. Boyd-Barrett and T. Rantanen (eds), *The globalization of news* (London, Thousand Oaks and New Delhi, 1998) 1–5.   31 Donald Read, *The power of news: the history of Reuters* (Oxford, 1999, 2nd edn) 49, 55–65; Read, 'Reuters: news agency of the British empire', *Contemporary Record*, 2:8 (autumn 1994) 195–212.   32 Alexander Turnbull Library, Wellington, New Zealand Press Association (NZPA) Archive, box 68, 'Press Association Limited prospectus', [*c.*1906]; box 71, E. Robbins to W.H. Atack, 21 Apr. 1899 and memorandum by Atack for the Directors of the UPA, 14 Aug. 1899. See also 'The Press Association', *Monthly Circular of the Empire Press Union*, Jan. 1913.   33 NZPA Archive, box 71, 'Press Association Limited tariff for newspapers', 1899.

Reuters £8,000 for news, and spending an additional £48,245 on telegraphing and cabling reports to subscribers.[34]

As a result of the increased reach of the cable network, and the availability of syndicated news, readers of English papers could expect to be provided with a much greater amount of up-to-date coverage of imperial events than had been possible in the past. As will be discussed later, existing connections within the network of imperial communication grew stronger. In addition, new and more isolated areas could be bound into the network, at least temporarily, as English public interest was aroused. Here, the 'small wars' of the late Victorian period were crucial, as English papers sought to provide their readers with reports from colonial conflict zones such as Zululand, Ashanti and the Sudan. Here, there were no existing settler papers to provide news. Instead, a new breed of professional war correspondent accompanied the troops to the front.

War correspondents were particularly active during the Sudanese campaign of 1896–8, when Herbert Horatio Kitchener, a major-general in the British army seconded as Sirdar to the Egyptian army, employed a joint Anglo-Egyptian force to re-conquer the region from the Mahdist forces that had taken Khartoum and killed General Gordon in 1885.[35] Kitchener provided the press with a suitably dramatic climax to his lengthy campaign when, at the battle of Omdurman, his force wiped out an enormous Mahdist army, killing an estimated 10,000 Dervish fighters, while sustaining casualties amounting to only 48 dead and 434 wounded.

From the start, contemporaries expected the provision of plentiful supplies of up-to-date news from the front detailing Kitchener's exploits, especially as the British force had erected its own telegraph line as it advanced into the Sudan. As one member of the force noted, 'It is impossible not to experience a glow of confidence in the power of Science which can thus link the most desolate regions of the earth with its greatest city and keep the modern pioneer ever within hail of home.'[36] However, in reality the press did not act to keep the public as well informed about events in the Sudan as had been expected. In part this reflected the eccentricities and alcoholism of the war correspondents. One officer with the force criticized the correspondents for their 'extravagant mess arrangements' and continual drinking, and Kitchener generally seems to have viewed the pressmen as a nuisance.[37] Other commanders saw that cultivating the press could enhance their own reputations however. Lionel James, the Reuters correspondent, enjoyed particularly

34 Ibid. 'The Press Association Limited: report of the thirtieth annual meeting' (London, 1898).
35 See Edward M. Spiers, *Sudan: the reconquest reappraised* (London, 1998).   36 'Letter received by a correspondent from a friend in the Nile Expeditionary Force, Wady Halfa, August 10', *Morning Post*, 2 Sept. 1898.   37 West Sussex Record Office, Chichester, Leopold Maxse papers, vol. 446, W756–8 Ivor Maxse to Leo Maxse, 23 Nov. 1897.

good relations with General Gatacre and other officers, facilitated by connections fostered while living in India.[38] Indeed, perhaps inevitably, the correspondents all worked and associated closely with the military. This provided some protection from the perils of covering a military campaign, but
the profession remained a dangerous one. Henry Cross, special correspondent of the *Manchester Guardian*, died of enteric fever during the campaign,
while *The Times* correspondent Colonel Frank Rhodes was wounded during
the battle of Omdurman. His colleague Hubert Howard was killed.

Further restraints were placed on the flow of news by the practical limitations of the cable system, which became apparent in the build up to
Omdurman. On 1 September, as Kitchener neared Khartoum, telegraphic
communication was suddenly cut off, prompting contemporaries to wonder
if a storm had severed the line, if Kitchener had imposed censorship, or if
the force had engaged with the enemy.[39] Most papers had still received no
news on 3 September, when the *Daily Telegraph* scooped its competitors, and
beat the War Office itself, in announcing the fall of Omdurman. It printed
11 lines of undated, unattributed cable news bulked up with huge headlines
and plenty of background material written by the London staff and presumably kept on file. For most papers it was not until 5 September that news of
Kitchener's victory four days earlier could be printed. Moreover, initial reports
were short and fragmentary. It took several days for more detailed news to
dribble in, much of it seriously delayed by the communication breakdown
and subsequent congestion of the cables. In the cases of the *Morning Post*,
Daily News, *Daily Mail*, *Daily Telegraph* and the *Standard* it was not until
10 September that the detailed telegraphic reports of the battle, sent at great
expense by their war correspondents, could be published. *The Times*, with
both its correspondents becoming casualties, was meanwhile forced to rely
on summarized accounts taken from other papers.

Despite the increasing use of telegraphic news reports, late nineteenth-
century newspapers also continued to print dispatches that arrived by mail.
In the case of the Sudan campaign, most war correspondents sent descrip-
tive letters in addition to their terse, summarized cable reports. There was
however a considerable lag between when letters were mailed and when they
arrived and were printed. This meant that the basic news they contained had
often been rendered outdated by earlier cable summaries. Obsolescence became
a real problem for editors. In the case of the *Morning Post*, on 7 September,
the same day that it published telegraphic news of the memorial service for
General Gordon held by the British forces at Khartoum, it also published a
letter from its war correspondent, Winston Churchill, dated 21 August and

38 See Bodleian Library of Commonwealth and African Studies at Rhodes House, Oxford,
Lionel James papers.   39 *Morning Post*, 2 Sept. 1898; *Daily News*, 1 Sept. 1898; *Birmingham
Daily Mail*, 1 Sept. 1898.

entitled 'On the way to the Front'. Such letters continued to arrive for weeks after the victory at Omdurman, and it was not until 23 and 24 September that the *Post* was able to print Churchill's letters containing details of the actual fighting. Reports continued to drift in over the weeks that followed. *The Times* even found itself printing letters from Hubert Howard after having published telegraphic news announcing his death.

The problem was particularly marked in the case of the illustrated press. The *Illustrated London News* for example continued to publish sketches by its artist in the field, Frederick Villiers, showing the slow advance of the Anglo-Egyptian force, until 17 September. While telegraphic reports published by other papers advised readers of the victory at Omdurman, the *Illustrated London News* was able only to publish general stock photographs, such as a file photo of the 21st Lancers, who had got cut up at Omdurman. The paper also reprinted pictures taken from books such as Slatin Pasha's *Fire and Sword in the Sudan*, with photographs of Kitchener and of Gordon's statue in Trafalgar Square superimposed.[40] It was not until 24 September that the paper was able to publish artistic impressions of scenes from Omdurman, based on sketches sent by Villiers and British officers in the field.

Newspapers had various strategies for dealing with the time lag between the arrival of news by cable and mail. The *Daily News* only printed a few of the letters mailed by its correspondent, while the *Daily Mail* attempted to make the lag less obvious by omitting dates when it printed its correspondent's letters! When the *Daily Telegraph* published letters from the celebrated Bennett Burleigh, it claimed that, although a month old, 'the universal enthusiasm excited by the Sirdar's successful campaign in the Sudan gives them a peculiar interest of their own'.[41] Perhaps this was true, and audience interest was maintained. Later pressmen were not so sure, arguing that mailed reports had been rendered useless by the cable. As Richard Jebb of the London *Morning Post* commented, 'It is an incident of modern civilization that people will not read the letters in their newspapers, however excellent those letters may be, with the same avidity as the cabled intelligence – they must have everything red-hot!'[42] H.A. Gwynne of the *Standard* similarly noted that 'In my newspaper experience I find that the only matter that is read with avidity and almost without question is telegraphic despatches.'[43]

Most provincial papers were reliant on supplies of syndicated news provided by Reuters, the Press Association and other news agencies (such as the

40 *Illustrated London News*, 10 Sept. 1898. **41** 15 Sept. 1898. **42** National Archives of Canada, Ottawa, Sandford Fleming papers, 24/173 R. Jebb to Fleming, 7 June 1905. **43** Durham University Archives, Durham, Grey Family papers, 176/5/1 copy of extract from H.A. Gwynne to 3rd Earl Grey, 27 Apr. 1906. See also Lord Crewe's comments at the 1909 Imperial Press Conference, reprinted in T.H. Hardman (ed.), *A parliament of the press: the first Imperial Press Conference* (London, 1909) 135–6.

Central News). Some provincial papers had access to their own additional sources of news, primarily in the form of mailed reports. The Birmingham *Daily Mail* printed a letter from an anonymous Birmingham man fighting at the front.[44] The Birmingham *Daily Gazette* meanwhile printed letters sent from its special correspondent, Frederic Villiers, who it shared with the *Manchester Courier* (as noted above, Villiers was also the special artist for the *Illustrated London News* – according to Lionel James, he belonged to 'the one shirt school, which means that he does not consider it incumbent on a war correspondent to keep clean').[45] As in the 1850s, different types of provincial paper provided readers with varying amounts of coverage of imperial events. In 1898, this was most apparent in the case of weekly papers published on Fridays such as the *Durham County Advertiser*, the *Lancaster Standard and County Advertiser* and the *Lancaster Guardian*. Such papers printed very little news about the battle, perhaps unsurprising given that the news had broken at the beginning of the week and had already been well-covered by the dailies.

Provincial papers also continued to derive news from the London press, supplementing the Reuters service by reprinting the reports provided by the correspondents of the big London papers. Sources chosen, as in 1857, had little to do with political allegiance. The *Manchester Guardian* reprinted the special correspondent reports of the Liberal *Daily News*, but also republished accounts provided by the Conservative *Daily Telegraph* and *The Times*. The Liberal *Exeter Western Times* similarly reprinted reports taken from Conservative papers such as *The Times* and the *Standard*, as well as the Liberal *Daily News*, and obtained much of its coverage by reprinting reports from Bennett Burleigh, the war correspondent of the Conservative *Daily Telegraph*. Many other papers of varying political hues also reprinted Burleigh's reports, unsurprising given his reputation.

Papers of different shades of political opinion thus continued to take the same raw news, even if their criteria for selection varied somewhat. Where partisan divisions really came in was in terms of how cable news was used for editorial purposes. Papers drew very different conclusions from identical reports.

Most papers agreed that the victory at Omdurman had ended the rule of a cruel and tyrannous regime, and represented a triumph for Kitchener's skills as a military planner.[46] There was some disagreement as to whether it was

44 21 Sept. 1898.   45 James papers, James to Maggie, 9 Aug. 1898. I would like to thank Ms. P.L. Buckler for permission to quote from the James papers.   46 'The fall of Omdurman', *Daily News*, 5 Sept. 1898; *Daily Telegraph*, 5 Sept. 1898; *Manchester Guardian*, 6 Sept. 1898 (although the *Manchester Guardian* noted that too much should not be made of the 'humanitarian' side of the victory, and by 10 Sept. was noting 'how tasteless and disproportioned some of the more fulsome self-congratulations of the past week have been').

proper to celebrate the victory as vengeance for the death of Gordon – it was pointed out that Gordon's Christian principles were incompatible with the concept of a war of revenge.[47] Most papers also presented the slaughter on the field as a necessary evil, and noted the bravery of the Dervish fighters.[48] The *Manchester Guardian* however saw an estimated 8,000 Dervish casualties as 'too grim an offering on the altar of humanity.'[49] Its special correspondent, Henry Cross, sent a letter shortly before his death hinting that the British force's African camp followers had killed wounded Dervish troops after the battle in order to loot their bodies. The *M.G.* would eventually use this evidence to challenge a proposed government grant of £30,000 to Kitchener for his services.[50] The editor, C.P. Scott, continued to push the matter until the summer of 1899, following up further reports that British soldiers had bayoneted Dervish wounded, some of whom were believed to be shamming death in order to launch surprise attacks. Scott believed that genuine wounded had also been killed in the process. One journalist at the *M.G.*, L.T. Hobhouse, noted that a crusade on this issue was likely to encounter a 'hostile audience', arguing that the paper would be trying to lead opinion and convince a reluctant public that a British force had committed atrocities.[51] Scott agreed that the paper faced 'an ugly job', but believed that parliament and people could ultimately be convinced that Kitchener's force was in the wrong.[52]

However, in the short term the main debate relating to Omdurman occurred over the issue of what Kitchener's next objective should be. Conservative papers tended to advocate a continued advance that would eventually unite and secure Britain's east African territories. The *Daily Mail* argued that once Mahdism had been comprehensively crushed, Kitchener should consolidate Britain's hold in the region against any French threat. 'The Equatorial Provinces southward – even to Uganda – need the wholesome breath of this pioneering force of civilisation ... the path from Cape to Cairo must be made straight.'[53] Liberal papers were less enthusiastic. The

47 The *Daily Mail* claimed that 'Gordon is avenged', 5 Sept. 1898, sentiments echoed by the Birmingham *Daily Mail*. The London *Star* dismissed the idea that the war was one of revenge however. See also *Standard*, 5 Sept. 1898 and *Times*, 5 Sept. 1898. 48 *Star*, 5 Sept. 1898; Birmingham *Daily Gazette*, 5 Sept. 1898. 49 *Manchester Guardian*, 6 Sept. 1898. 50 Henry Cross, 'The battle of Omdurman', *Manchester Guardian*, 24 Sept. 1898. 51 University of Manchester John Ryland's Library, Manchester, *Manchester Guardian* Archive, 132/48 L.T. Hobhouse to C.P. Scott, 7 Apr. 1899. 52 Ibid. 132/49 Scott to Hobhouse, 11 Apr. 1899. The *Manchester Guardian* also related how, after Omdurman, Kitchener had ordered the Mahdi's tomb to be opened and the body thrown into the river. Soldiers had cut off the head and sent it back to base en-route for England in a packing case, although ultimately the British authorities in Egypt had intercepted the case and prevented it returning to Britain. See D. Ayerst, *Guardian: biography of a newspaper* (London, 1971) 266–72. 53 *Daily Mail*, 5 Sept. 1898. Again, the *Birmingham Daily Mail* echoed this editorial line. See also *Daily Telegraph*, 5 Sept. 1898 and *Manchester Courier*, 6 Sept. 1898.

Manchester Guardian argued that 'in the future only such steps should be taken in continuation of the campaign as are necessary for the protection of the frontiers of Egypt ... we believe with Gordon that such a frontier may be found at Khartoum ... at Khartoum the tide of territorial conquest should stop.'[54] The Liberal *Exeter Western Times* similarly argued that the Anglo-Egyptian advance up the Nile 'ought not to be continued simply to fulfil the Rhodesian plan for a British continuity of territory from Cairo to the Cape'.[55]

Papers in the rest of the UK also drew on the same essentially homogenous cable reports. The Edinburgh *Scotsman* reprinted reports from Reuters, the *Daily Telegraph*, the *Times*, the *Standard* and the *Daily News*. The Dublin *Irish Daily Independent* drew its news from Reuters and London papers such as the *Daily Mail*, *Daily News*, *Standard* and the *Daily Telegraph*. Again, identical cable reports did not preclude very different editorial opinions. The *Independent* took an extremely hostile line regarding the British victory at Omdurman, presenting it as the result of an unfair military advantage, and claiming that British troops had committed atrocities – 'killing the wounded and even the women caught on the field of battle has been amongst the habitual horrors practised by the British in every campaign in the Soudan in the past'.[56] There would have been little in the news reprinted from papers like the *Daily Mail* to support such claims.

THE EARLY TWENTIETH CENTURY

For historians and other commentators discussing press coverage of empire, attention has often focussed on bloody outbursts of expansionism such as the Sudanese campaign. This is partly due to methodological convenience. When sampling the press, examining a dramatic event that would have elicited considerable coverage allows the historian to derive the maximum amount of useful material from a notoriously diffuse and unmanageable primary source. The tendency to examine episodes of imperial violence also reflects suppositions shared by many contemporaries and historians, in particular the idea that empire was synonymous with violent expansionism and that the media helped propagate public enthusiasm for such excesses. Contemporaries of a Liberal persuasion blamed 'jingoism' on the press, while historians seeking to explain 'popular imperialism' have often targeted the mass media as the source of propaganda.

However, while empire certainly did involve aggressive expansion and repression, this did not mark the totality of the imperial experience, and was certainly not the only way that contemporary readers were made aware of the

54 *Manchester Guardian*, 5 and 6 Sept. 1898.   55 6 Sept. 1898. See also editorial on 7 Sept. 1898. 'Rhodesian' is meant here in the sense of being advocated by Cecil Rhodes.   56 Dublin *Irish Daily Independent*, 5 Sept. 1898.

existence of Britain's empire. As discussed above, newspapers devoted significant resources to providing full coverage of Omdurman. However, some
of the variations in that coverage were surprising. Traditionally, a great deal
of criticism has been heaped on the mass-circulation press in particular for
stimulating popular support for imperial expansion, with papers such as the
Daily Mail attracting contemporary and historical opprobrium. It is perhaps
surprising then to note that some sections of the popular press showed considerably less enthusiasm for expansion. When reporting Omdurman, the
London *Star*, one of the pioneers of the new form of popular journalism,
paid a lot less attention to events in the Sudan than did many other, more
traditional papers. After the initial news of the victory at Omdurman had
been published, the *Star* took little interest in events in east Africa. This
partly reflected its Liberal editorial line, but was also a result of its greater
interest in pursuing journalistic crusades about domestic and local issues, such
as the water shortage in London's East End and the sale of potentially incen-
diary low-flash lighting oil. The *Star*'s radical leanings later led to it being
burnt on the London Stock Exchange during the South African War.[57] It is
not known whether it was first immersed in low-flash lighting oil.

Moreover, while papers such as the *Daily Mail* were keen to provide full
details of the military drama of Omdurman, they also attempted to put across
to their readers an idea of everyday life in the empire – political, but also
economic, social and cultural. According to Northcliffe's lieutenant at the
Daily Mail, Kennedy Jones, this pandered to a perceived increase in public
interest in the empire.

> We discovered [during the Jameson Raid] an abounding desire for
> knowledge of all matters affecting the Empire ... It had been over-
> looked in Fleet Street how largely the British Empire is a family
> affair; that there is hardly a household or a family circle of any size
> which does not have one or more of its members earning a livelihood
> somewhere in the outer wards.[58]

The founders of the *Daily Mail* ensured that it would have an unrivalled network of correspondents to provide such news.[59] As a result, at the same time
as it covered Omdurman, the *Daily Mail* also related to its readers news about
the elections then taking place in the Cape Colony, providing daily cable reports
from its own correspondent at the Cape, including voting figures for each local
election as they became available. The paper also published articles contextu-
alizing the election and its outcome.[60] Other papers proved similarly keen to

57 Lee, *Origins of the popular press*, 165.   58 Jones, *Fleet Street and Downing Street*, 146.   59
R. Pound and G. Harmsworth, *Northcliffe* (London, 1959) 248.   60 See for example editorials
and articles published on 3 and 8 Sept. 1898.

cover the Cape elections. The *Manchester Guardian* published a substantial number of reports from Reuters and *The Times* covering the elections, alongside letters from individuals such as H.R. Fox Bourne explaining why the progress of the Afrikaner Bond party was a positive thing for British interests. Indeed, the *Guardian* had no compunction about reprinting cables from the *Daily Mail*, despite the papers' opposing views about South African politics, showing again the separation between raw news and editorial response.[61]

The attention devoted by English papers to events in Southern Africa reflected the growing crisis in the region in the wake of the Jameson Raid, as agents of the British empire began to square up to the Boer republics of the Transvaal and Orange Free State. As the conflict escalated towards war, connections between the press in England and settler newspapers in South Africa again became apparent, and this time became a focus for Liberal criticism. Here, the radical journalist and political theorist John A. Hobson played a prominent role. Hobson visited South Africa in the months before the outbreak of the war, on behalf of the *Manchester Guardian*. While in South Africa, discussions with leading Cape Liberals convinced Hobson that the crisis was the result of the machinations of the region's mining magnates. These men he believed were seeking to destroy President Kruger's Boer republic in the Transvaal and create a political environment more suited to their economic interests. Hobson also picked up the Cape Liberal argument that the mining magnates were using the South African press to secure popular support for their schemes.[62] Hobson claimed that control of newspapers in South Africa allowed diamond and gold mining capitalists to feed the British press with misinformation, as British papers had been tricked into reliance upon South African journalists and newspapers for information about events in the region.[63]

61 *Manchester Guardian*, 26 Aug. 1898.   62 For early statements of the Cape Liberal conspiracy theory see for example J.X. Merriman to F.J. Centlivres, 4 Apr. 1898; Merriman to J. Bryce, 29 Mar. 1896; and Merriman to Bryce, 5 Dec. 1899 printed in P. Lewsen (ed.), *Selections from the correspondence of J.X. Merriman* ii: *1890–1898*, 4 vols (Cape Town, 1963) 303–6, 214–16 and 110–14 respectively. See also J.W. Sauer to P.A. Molteno, 8 Sept. 1897 and Molteno to A. Cartwright, 28 Apr. 1899 printed in V. Solomon (ed.), *Selections from the correspondence of Percy Alport Molteno, 1892–1914* (Cape Town, 1981) 59 and 83–4 respectively.   63 Hobson wrote a number of articles for the *Manchester Guardian* and the *Speaker*, providing an argument that was repeated and expanded in *The war in South Africa: its causes and effects* (London, 1900) 206–28 and *The psychology of jingoism* (London, 1901) 108–21. Other contemporaries also used this argument. See for example British Library, London, J.A. Spender papers, Add. MSS. 46391 ff. 50–1 Bryce to Spender, 9 Nov. 1899; G.P. Gooch, 'Imperialism' in C.F.G. Masterman (ed.), *The heart of empire: discussions of problems of modern city life in England* (London, 1901, new edn Brighton 1973) 309–63; 'ILP resolution at Blackburn' and 'Transvaal Committee – report of six month's work', both printed in S. Koss (ed.), *The pro-Boers: the anatomy of an antiwar movement* (Chicago, 1973). For the broader intellectual context of Hobson's ideas see P.J. Cain, *Hobson and imperialism: radicalism, New Liberalism, and finance, 1887–1938* (Oxford, 2002).

However, when seen in the broader context of information exchange within the empire, the fact that English papers were drawing their news from the South African press was hardly surprising. They had done the same in 1857, without the need for any capitalist intervention. Telegraphic communication did not destroy English newspapers' reliance on the settler press for news, but merely changed the way that news flowed between the two. In the early stages of the South African crisis, cooperation was to some extent inevitable, as English papers were forced to rely on local journalists who were already on the spot, at least until their own special correspondents could get to the scene.[64] However, the links went deeper than this. During the war, *The Times* exploited its existing connections with the Cape *Argus*, and the London *Daily Mail* worked closely with the *Cape Times*. Even the radical *Manchester Guardian* was able to find suitable journalistic collaborators, in the form of the staff of the *South African News*, to supply reports.[65] This provided the cheapest and most effective means for English papers to gather news from the Cape, and most contemporaries found nothing exceptionable about it. By the end of the war, British papers were dependent on Cape journals, and South African papers were in many cases staffed by British and Irish migrants – the British and Cape press had begun to merge.[66]

In the wake of the South African War, it also became apparent that while the cable could act to temporarily tie new areas into the imperial network of communication, links with the settler colonies and with the settler press would continue to dominate. Here the activities of a new generation of young men, who returned to British politics after having gained their formative experiences in South Africa while working as correspondents or administrators during and after the war, proved crucial. Devoted 'constructive imperialists', these men sought to use the press as a tool of imperial integration. They believed that through active intervention, and in particular with the support of the state, the press could become a key means to bind Britain and the colonies of settlement more closely together. The new generation of constructive imperialist journalists worked to overcome the limits imposed on press coverage of empire. Newspapers like *The Times* and the *Standard* sought subsidies from Dominion governments and private companies, in the form of lucrative advertising contracts, in order to pay for increased supplies of cable news from the colonies and the publication of special empire supplements. Journalists and proprietors also lobbied for government intervention to secure the reduction of press cable charges. The hope was that an ignorant and apathetic British public could be taught to 'think imperially'.[67]

64 The National Archive: Public Record Office, London, WO32/7141 'Report on the issues of licences to correspondents accompanying troops in the field' (1901). **65** Potter, *News and the British world*, 42–3. On the *Manchester Guardian* and the South African War in general see Ayerst, *Guardian*, 273–86. **66** See chapter 10 below. **67** See Potter, *News and the British world*, chs. 3 and 5.

What effect did these schemes have on English press coverage of empire? Content analysis of three English newspapers, the *Daily News*, the *Daily Telegraph* and the *Manchester Guardian*, for three week-long sample periods, 9–14 March 1903, 20–25 July 1908 and 17–22 November 1913, suggests some preliminary answers to this question (see Table 1).

Table 1: Columns of cable news printed in three English papers, 1903–13

a) *Daily News*			
	9–14 March 1903	20–25 July 1908	17–22 November 1913
White Dominions (Canada, Australia, New Zealand, South Africa, Newfoundland)	2.65	3.2	6.3
Asia (incl. India)	0.8	1.2	1
Africa	4.3	0	0.1
Europe	11.5	11	8
USA	3.25	0.5	3.9
Other	0.16	0	0.7

b) *Daily Telegraph*			
	9–14 March 1903	20–25 July 1908	17–22 November 1913
White Dominions (Canada, Australia, New Zealand, South Africa, Newfoundland)	0.7	12.4	7.4
Asia (incl. India)	0.2	2.7	3.2
Africa	3.2	1.3	0.8
Europe	14.1	17.8	22.3
USA	6.3	4.7	14.6
Other	0	0.1	2.4

c) *Manchester Guardian*			
	9–14 March 1903	20–25 July 1908	17–22 November 1913
White Dominions (Canada, Australia, New Zealand, South Africa, Newfoundland)	1.4	7.8	3.7
Asia (incl. India)	0.2	3.9	1
Africa	2.4	0	0
Europe	3.6	7.8	1.3
USA	1.4	1.7	3
Other	0.1	0	1.6

Despite the activities of constructive imperialist journalists, European and, to a lesser extent, United States news clearly continued to dominate the cable columns of these English newspapers throughout the early twentieth century. Paris in particular proved an important and regular source of reports. Conflict in the Balkans in the 1903 sample period, the Turkish revolt in 1908 and tensions between Mexico and the United States in 1913 all received substantial cable coverage. On an everyday basis, news from the Dominions occupied but a small part of the cable budgets published in the English press. Australia and New Zealand in particular received short shrift, with Canada and South Africa benefiting from only marginally greater coverage.

However, while large quantities of news did not flow to Britain on a daily basis from the Dominions, by the end of the period in question significant events in the Dominions were being covered in much greater detail than before, and certainly in more depth than were events in the crown colonies. The Quebec Tercentenary celebrations of 1908 received massive attention, accounting for the bulk of coverage in the relevant sections of the content analysis table. Similarly, Indian protests in Natal in 1913 led English papers to publish substantial amounts of cable news from South Africa. Indeed, by the early twentieth century, sufficient amounts of news were flowing between Britain and the settler colonies to make it possible to sustain inter-linked debates over matters of common concern. As for example debate over the 1911 Canadian-American reciprocity proposals demonstrated, newspapers in Britain had no difficulty in finding Canadian journalists to provide ample supplies of news to support their own positions on matters of imperial interest. Canadian papers were similarly able to find British allies.[68]

Constructive imperialist activities thus clearly did have an impact upon English press coverage of empire, bringing increasingly detailed accounts of events in the Dominions. This widened the gap between coverage of the settler colonies on the one hand, and of the crown colonies on the other. While new areas in the tropical empire were being integrated into the imperial network of communication, this was often a temporary phenomenon, and English press coverage subsided after events of interest had ended. The avid attention devoted to Omdurman did not result in a sustained increase in coverage of Sudanese affairs. Military campaigns in Somaliland and Nigeria in 1903 similarly received limited coverage. It was the settler colonies, with their long history of connection to the imperial communications network, which benefited disproportionately from improvements in communications technology and the efflorescence of constructive imperialism.

68 See Simon J. Potter, 'The imperial significance of the Canadian-American reciprocity proposals of 1911', *Historical Journal*, 1:47 (March 2004) 81–100.

CONCLUSIONS

In some ways, an exploration of English press coverage of empire confirms
a picture of diversity. Papers in London and the provinces provided readers
with different amounts of news about imperial events, and there was a clear
gap between the amount of news available in the larger cities of the midlands
and industrial north, and that published in other provincial areas. Moreover,
while much of the raw news published by papers around England was similar or even identical in content, there remained room for differing editorial
interpretations, allowing marked partisan divisions between and among Liberal
and Conservative papers.

At the same time, coverage of empire was characterized by a striking
degree of homogeneity. The raw news that reached the press was often the
same all around England, and in some cases, such as the Xhosa cattle killing,
editorial comment did toe a remarkably similar line. This partly reflected the
mechanics of news supply in England. Provincial papers relied on London
papers for much of their news, a dependency that was reinforced by the
advent of syndicated news reports provided by agencies such as Reuters. As
this essay has sought to demonstrate, homogeneity also reflected the fact that
the English press was bound into a broader imperial communications network, that linked papers to their counterparts not just in the rest of the UK,
but also in the colonies. News and views flowed easily across the internal
boundaries of empire, and particularly between the UK and the colonies of
settlement. Settler interests thus gained a privileged place in English discussions of imperial issues, a fact that became more, not less marked over time.
On issues where there was a diversity of settler opinion, English responses
were often similarly varied, as during the Canadian-American reciprocity
debate of 1911. But at other times, when settler opinion was united, for example in response to the Xhosa cattle killing, then that unity could be transmitted to the English press.

The survey of the English press presented in this chapter highlights the
danger of seeking to associate the views of even a wide cross-section of newspapers with 'public opinion'. Diverse editorial opinions were offset, and sometimes precluded, by reliance on increasingly uniform supplies of news, often
provided by interested parties. Similarly, the above analysis shows how difficult it is to associate press comment with any English 'national' set of perspectives. In the case of the Dominions, news of empire was often supplied
by settlers, and was tinted by their own particular perspectives on local events.
English readers were thus exposed to 'propaganda', intended to influence how
they felt about specific issues in the colonies, with the aim of benefiting settler interests. These attempts may well have been successful, but, as discussed
in the introduction to this volume, this could have been because settler views

already resonated with English audiences. While perspectives on specific issues might have differed, how divergent were the general attitudes, assumptions and beliefs of Britons in the Dominions and back 'Home'?

A more obvious consequence of the strong link between the English and the settler press was the emergence and subsequent widening of a significant gap between coverage of tropical and settler colonies. English readers would have developed a much fuller knowledge of events in the settler colonies than about the affairs of the crown colonies. This reflected both the nature of the imperial communications network and, in the early twentieth century, the priorities of constructive imperialist journalists. It was a divergence that, thanks to other media institutions such as the BBC and the Empire Marketing Board, would continue to characterize media coverage of empire into the interwar years and beyond.

3. The Scottish press and empire, 1850–1914

RICHARD J. FINLAY

We are feared for oor road to India, but hoo has it come aboot
that we hae sic a deep interest in a road to India? Hoo did we
get a haud o' India? Was it no by the sword? Ay, an' aften by
the maist ootrageous proceedin's that were ever see or heard tell
o' in this world! We got India by murder, treachery, an
stouthreif, an' we hae the cheek to blackguard Rooshia for
annexin' her neebors! What did we do the ither day in the Sooth
of Africa? Did we no annex an independent republic ca'd the
Transvaal? O yes, but it was for the guid o' the inhabitants.[1]

Until recently, the Scottish contribution to British overseas expansion was
either down-played or relegated to the sphere of 'British' history by Scottish
historians. There is now however not only growing interest in the role played
by the Scots in the British empire, but also an increasing awareness of the
impact of British imperial expansion on Scotland's economic, social, cultural
and intellectual development in the period after the Union of 1707.[2] An older,
anglocentric view of British imperial history has given way to a much more
nuanced reading of the subject, and a willingness to examine how different
national groups experienced empire.[3]

During the nineteenth century, the Scottish economy was highly dependent on the expansion of imperial trade. Ships were needed to serve the development of the global economy and warships were required to defend sea-
lanes carrying such trade. Locomotives had to be built to move goods from

1 Tammas Bodkin, *People's Journal*, 2 June 1877, quoted in William Donaldson, *The language of the people* (Aberdeen, 1989) 89–90. 2 See J.M. Mackenzie, 'Essay and reflection: Scotland and the British empire', *International History Review*, 4 (1993) 714–39; R.J. Finlay, 'The rise and fall of popular imperialism in Scotland, 1850–1950', *Scottish Geographical Magazine*, 113 (1997) 13–21; J.M. MacKenzie, 'Empire and national identities: the case of Scotland', *Royal Historical Society Transactions*, sixth series, 8 (1998) 215–33 and T.M. Devine, *Scotland's empire, 1660–1830* (London, 2003). 3 See for example Aled Jones and Bill Jones, 'The Welsh world and the British empire, c.1851–1939: an exploration', *Journal of Imperial and Commonwealth History*, 2:31 (May 2003) 57–81; David Fitzpatrick, 'Ireland and the empire' in Andrew Porter (ed.), *The Oxford history of the British empire, iii: the nineteenth century* (Oxford, 1999); P. Payton, *The Cornish overseas* (Fowey, 1999).

the interior to coastal entrepôts in North and South America, and to facili-
tate transport within the Indian sub-continent. Machines and engineering
skills were needed to encourage extraction, production and distribution in the
emerging global economy. All of these demands were of critical importance
to the Scottish economy. The extent to which imperial trade was the engine
of Scottish economic development in the nineteenth century has not been
sufficiently assessed, and no historical consensus exists, but it can be said
with confidence that contemporaries certainly perceived British imperial
expansion as necessary for Scottish economic well-being. Tea merchants, shipping magnates and industrialists benefiting from the expansion of demand
for steel, iron and coal all believed that empire was a good thing.[4]

At the same time, the Scottish universities had too much productive capacity, and engineers, doctors, scientists and clergymen depended on imperial
postings for work. Hundreds of thousands of Scots sought to improve their
standard of living by emigrating to the settler colonies of Australia, New
Zealand, South Africa and Canada.[5] Scottish aristocrats and gentry, challenged by the growth of democracy and falling land values at home, could
similarly avail themselves of the opportunities offered by empire, becoming
soldiers or administrators. In the period from 1850 to 1939, a third of colonial governors general were Scots.[6]

Having exhausted the possibilities of religious zeal within the homeland
the Scottish churches were meanwhile keen to embark on ever more ambitious endeavours of conversion in the imperial territories. John Ritchie, publisher of Christian literature in Kilmarnock, had a fifteen-page catalogue of
'Gospel gift books and Sunday school rewards' to inspire the youth of
Scotland.[7] Despite such incentives, obstinate heathenism in the cities at home
could be contrasted with the success stories of thousands flocking to the
banner of Christ in Africa, India and the South Seas, where paganism was
being pushed back by a Scottish religious onslaught.

Empire thus entered into Scottish national consciousness and became a
fundamental part of Scottish national identity. In political circles, the Union
was more and more associated with empire and the Anglo-Scottish relationship was characterized as an imperial partnership. Empire became an important cement in the manufacture of British identity in Scotland in the sense
that the Scots could be presented as making their own distinctive national
contribution to the British imperial mission. As such there was no contra-
diction or conflict in being both Scottish and British – dual identities dove-
tailed perfectly. Glaswegians exalted themselves as citizens of the 'Second
City of Empire', the economy was portrayed as the 'workshop of Empire' and

4 R.J. Finlay, *A partnership for good? Scottish politics and the Union since 1880* (Edinburgh, 1997)
12–35. 5 Marjory Harper, *Adventurers and exiles: the great Scottish exodus* (London, 2003). 6
MacKenzie, 'Essay and reflection'. 7 *The Christian worker's guide* (Kilmarnock, n.d.).

by the 1880s numerous campaigns were afoot to prohibit the use of 'England' and 'English' in imperial terminology.[8] Empire was even powerful enough to momentarily unite the fractious Scottish churches in 1889, when they petitioned Lord Salisbury to make Nyasaland a British protectorate, lest it fall into the hands of the Catholic Portuguese.[9]

It might be expected that the press played a central role in the promotion of a British imperial identity in Scotland, certainly if the experience of England was anything to go by.[10] The Scots read more newspapers per head of population than any other society in the nineteenth century, and the period from 1850 to 1914 witnessed an explosion in both the number and circulation of Scottish newspapers. The Edinburgh-based *Scotsman* had a weekly circulation of around 2,500 in 1850, while its rival, the *Glasgow Herald* sold about 4,000. The repeal of the Stamp Act in 1855 opened the flood-gates to mass produced, cheap newspapers. Although circulation figures are difficult to gauge, as publishers kept them a closely guarded secret, by the eve of the First World War the *Daily Record* sold more than 150,000 copies and the weekly *People's Journal* had a sales figure in the region of a quarter of a million.[11] Local papers also proliferated. From 1860 to 1914, the number of titles produced and sold in Scotland rose from sixty to almost three hundred.[12] Most of these were weekly papers that served the immediate local community, such as the *Falkirk Herald* or *Stirling Observer*. Others were specialist sports papers and some were weekly editions printed for a more general readership, such as the *Scots Observer*.

In many ways, the Scottish press developed on an autonomous basis, with limited English penetration of the Scottish newspaper market.[13] Nevertheless, English titles such as the *Saturday Review* were read, significant in the context of this chapter given English press coverage of imperial activities. Moreover, for most of the period, Scottish papers cribbed their international coverage from the London press. Indeed, until public clamour dictated otherwise, accounts were reprinted verbatim, and often included the use of the term 'England' when referring to the political nation. When the *Scotsman* and the *Glasgow Herald* employed their own correspondents abroad, it was usually during conflicts such as the American Civil War or the Franco-Prussian War, rather than imperial campaigns. Letters from soldiers were

8 H.J. Hanham, *Scottish nationalism* (London, 1969) 81.   9 A.J. Hanna, *The beginnings of Nyasaland and north-eastern Rhodesia, 1859–95* (Oxford, 1969) 137–8.   10 Simon J. Potter, *News and the British world: the emergence of an imperial press system, 1876–1922* (Oxford, 2003); J. Marriot, *The other empire: metropolis, India and progress in the colonial imagination* (Manchester, 2003) and David Cannadine, *Ornamentalism: how the British saw their empire* (London, 2001). 11 *Newspaper press directory.*   12 Ibid.   13 See R.M.W. Cowan, *The newspaper in Scotland: a study of its first expansion, 1815–1860* (Glasgow, 1946) and Joan P.S. Ferguson, *Directory of Scottish newspapers* (Edinburgh, 1984).

sometimes the only independent sources used in Scottish press coverage of imperial conflicts.

In addition to the daily and weekly press, there were also other specialist forms of literature that helped to convey aspects of the Scots' imperial pursuits. The *Scottish Geographical Magazine* was an effective conduit for the promotion of imperial expansion, printing numerous articles on the opening up of new territories, especially in Africa. The various churches each had their own house journal such as *Life and Work* or *Missionary Monitor* which recounted the activities of the missions established overseas to promote 'Christianity and Civilisation'. When we also factor in children's literature impregnated with an imperial flavour, it is clear that the Scottish reading public was continually kept abreast of Scotland's activities within the British empire. Whether this merely reflected or actively promoted an imperial identity in Scotland is a matter for debate.

Given the dominance of the Liberal Party in Scottish electoral politics throughout this period, it is somewhat difficult to square press enthusiasm for providing accounts of imperial development with the limited support given to the Conservative/Unionist Party. The latter, as the 'natural party of empire', might have been expected to be the prime beneficiary of the promotion of an imperial identity in Scotland. Yet, with the exception of the South African War, this generally seems not to have been the case. Looking in detail at press coverage of empire offers some clues as to the reasons for this disparity.

In Scotland's larger cities, Unionist newspapers prospered despite electoral support for Liberalism. As might be expected, Glasgow, with its strong sense of imperial identity stimulated by the area's commercial and industrial links with the empire, sustained Unionist papers such as the *Glasgow Herald* and its offshoot, the *Evening Times*. The papers appealed to the city's business class. Despite the existence of populist and politically Liberal papers such as the *Daily Record* and the *Evening News*, and the fact that in 1914 five of the seven constituencies were held by Liberals, one contemporary still maintained that 'The four most representative and powerful organs in the western city are frankly Unionist in politics.'[14] Similar, Unionist sentiment expressed by the Edinburgh *Scotsman* and the *Evening Dispatch* went against the city's Liberal electoral politics.

Liberal views were more commonly expressed by papers outside Glasgow and Edinburgh, in areas where Liberal political predominance was most marked during the Victorian and Edwardian period, and where local titles, most of which were locally owned, dominated Scottish society.[15] According

---

14 G.R. Blake, *Scotland of the Scots* (London, 1918) 218.   15 This is an area which requires more research. The work of Catriona M.M. MacDonald on Paisley politics, *The radical thread: political change in Scotland – Paisley politics, 1885–1925* (East Linton, 2000) highlights the role

to Catriona MacDonald, a survey of some two hundred Scottish papers on
the eve of the First World War reveals that more than seventy per cent were
either Liberal or independent.[16] In Dundee, the *Courier* and the *Advertiser*
were staunchly Liberal, while the Aberdeen *Free Press* dominated its Unionist
rival, the *Daily Journal*. This raises a difficultly in assessing the impact of
the press on Scottish ideas about empire – local papers were probably more
influential than the city papers upon which most historical attention has
focused. Historians have tended to present newspapers such as the *Scotsman*
and the *Glasgow Herald* as being representative of national opinion, in the
same sort of way that English historians use *The Times*. This may introduce
a distorting effect. William Donaldson, though more interested in the use of
literary Scots, has highlighted the profusion of Liberal and anti-imperialist
sentiment which dominated the press in the north east of Scotland. Not surprisingly, this was the area most strongly in favour of Irish and Scottish home
rule and against the jingoism of the South African War.[17]

A diverse and varied Scottish press presented readers with a range of views
on imperial issues. In a study of this length, it would be impossible to do
justice to this spectrum of opinion – indeed, there is scope for a larger study
of aspects of newspaper perceptions of empire in Scotland, in the way that
Krisztina Fenyo has recently examined the issue of the Highland clearances.[18]
It is with this in mind that the present chapter will limit itself to certain specific imperial themes in the period between 1850 and 1914. It will examine
the press reaction to the issue of Irish Home Rule, with specific reference to
the idea of restructuring imperial constitutional relations. It will also discuss
coverage of the South African War, particularly its bearing on the issue of
federalism. Finally, it will assess the impact of the campaign for imperial tariff
protectionism. These issues have been chosen because they provided opportunities for questions of empire to interact with Scottish domestic political
agendas.

The Scottish press had little time for Ireland in the second half of the
nineteenth century. As one of the four 'mother nations' of empire, Ireland
was seen to represent the exact opposite of the Scots' own image of themselves, particularly within the imperial context. Even during the Famine, the
Scottish press bemoaned the amount of government subsidies that were being

of the local press in promoting political change. My own graduate student, Ian Cockburn, is
finding the same pattern in his study of Clackmannanshire politics in the same period.   16
Catriona M.M. MacDonald, 'May 1915: race, riot and representations of war' in C.M.M.
MacDonald and E.W. MacFarland (eds), *Scotland and the Great War* (East Linton, 1999) 145–73.
17 Donaldson, *Language of the people*, 1–16; S.J. Brown, 'Echoes of Midlothian: Scottish
Liberalism and the South African War, 1899–1902', *Scottish Historical Review*, 71 (1992) 156–84.
18 Krisztina Fenyo, *Contempt, sympathy and romance: Lowland perceptions of the Highlands during
the famine years, 1845–1855* (East Linton, 2000).

given to the starving of Ireland, and contrasted the situation with that prevailing in the Highlands of Scotland, which had also suffered from potato blight. Both the *Scotsman* and the *Glasgow Herald* used the contrasting experiences of famine in Scotland and Ireland to point out the latter's deficiency as a mother nation of the empire. Bizarrely, most of this denunciation took the form of a condemnation of rising support for Daniel O'Connell and the Repeal movement, at a time when the Scottish press was raising its voice in support of nationalism elsewhere in Europe. The following editorial from the *Glasgow Herald* was typical:

> The state of Ireland is as deplorable as ever, and the measures of the government are said to be inadequate for the relief of the starving millions. It may be of some gratification to the Irish heart to know that the Great liberator is suffering in no perceptible degree from the present dearth. He is domiciled in Darrynane and in the full enjoyment of rural sports ... A Roman catholic priest, who describes his flock as literally starving, has transmitted forty two pounds drawn from them to swell the repeal rent ... the wish to relieve Ireland in her present difficulty is universal here, but is our charity rightly administered when it fills the pockets of O'Connell instead of the starving labourer? We ought certainly not to be prodigal with our supplies to a people who seem habitually disposed to give up their daily bread to feed the luxuries of their pampered and mendacious leader.[19]

Irish examples were used to differentiate between the positive and negative aspects of nationalism. Whereas nationalism of the type associated with Kossuth and the Hungarian revolution was deemed progressive on account of its Liberalism, anti-Catholicism and anti-aristocratic stance, Irish nationalism was portrayed as backward, associated with Catholicism (illiterate and uneducated peasants being roused by Jesuits) and dominated by landlords who used the Famine for their own purposes. Interestingly, the Scottish press initially deployed the same unfavourable Celticist images of the Irish and the Scottish Highlanders during the early period of the Famine. Laziness, squalor and temperament were cited as the chief causes of distress, although in the case of the Highlands blame later shifted as attention focussed on the activities of rapacious landlords.[20] For the Scottish middle class, intent on extending their political power in Scotland, the Famine was a convenient means by which to portray the aristocracy as self-serving, corrupt and incompetent.

Irish immigrants into Scotland also received hostile treatment from the Scottish press, as many scholars have documented. Lurid stories circulated

---

19 9 Oct. 1846. **20** Fenyo, *Contempt, sympathy, romance*, 46–96.

about the Irish Catholic proclivity towards crime and squalor, and this was reinforced by sensationalist accounts of the activities of the Catholic Church which led to one Scottish MP demanding in the House of Commons that nunneries be opened up to public inspection.[21] Furthermore, the press kept up a barrage against what was seen to be overly favourable treatment of the Irish by the British government. Scottish papers presented this as unwarranted and demeaning to Scotland on account of the latter's staunch imperial service.

Such coverage of events in Ireland was important on two accounts. Firstly, Ireland's mixed record as a participant in imperial expansion was used to highlight the success of Scotland within the imperial partnership. Secondly, it was instrumental in conditioning Scottish reactions to the Home Rule crisis of 1886, helping to explain why so much of the discussion surrounding Gladstone's policy took on an imperial flavour.[22]

While much attention has focused on the Scottish domestic political context of the Home Rule crisis, the imperial aspect of the debate has received less coverage. Where the press was influential in this instance was not only in terms of editorial comment, but also through the publication of letters to the editor from key individuals. For example, for many Gladstonian Liberals in Scotland, the widely-circulated letter from the retired radical Liberal, Duncan McLaren, stating his opposition to Irish Home Rule, came as a bolt from the blue. McLaren's technique of sending letters simultaneously to many newspapers was the most effective way to disseminate opinion on key issues and, in this case, was particularly striking. Married to the sister of John Bright and widely described as the 'Member for Scotland' during his parliamentary career, McLaren had an impeccable Liberal pedigree. Throughout his career, he had regularly used parliamentary time to compare and contrast government expenditure on the two nations to show that Ireland had been consistently favoured. As a former journalist, McLaren was able to maximize the publicity that was given to his findings, and present his activities as an attempt to safeguard and promote the interests of Scotland within an imperial context.[23] Such notions of the legitimate Scottish contribution to the empire, and the contrast with Ireland where 'disloyalty was rewarded', were important in defining the Scottish sense of themselves within not only the British domestic context, but also the imperial one.

Scottish newspapers, some of which devoted 50 per cent of their space to advertising, were an important conduit for the promotion of emigration.[24] The steamship companies took out large advertisements promoting the ben-

21 For examples see T. Gallagher, *Glasgow: the uneasy peace – religious tensions in modern Scotland, 1819–1914* (Manchester, 1987) 42–86.   22 R.J. Finlay, 'Radical Liberalism and nationalism in mid-Victorian Scotland' in I. Denes (ed.), *European liberalism and nationalism* (Budapest, forthcoming 2004).   23 J.B. Mackie, *The life and work of Duncan McLaren*, 2 vols (Edinburgh, 1888) ii, 242–64.   24 Harper, *Adventures and exiles*, 71–112.

efits of emigration to North America, and the extensive appearance of letters in the local press written by people who had made good was a further inducement to leave. Such notions were reinforced by the publicity given to the favourable image of Scots as migrants, again in contrast to the Irish.[25] Coverage of Volunteer activity meanwhile helped to promote the idea of Scotland's contribution to British military prowess, which was believed to be essential for the defence of the empire. It was also a way of highlighting the distinctive qualities of Scottish civil society where the citizens would defend the nation and empire, unlike European powers which relied on conscription. Volunteering featured heavily in the local press. Be it the first appearance of the Volunteers in Glasgow for the visit of Queen Victoria to open up the Loch Kartine water works or in Paisley on the eve of the First World War, such coverage highlighted the weekend activities of parading and exercising.[26] In the local press, the influence of notable members of the community within the ranks of the Volunteers was the occasion to provide coverage. Similarly, the activities of the local churches in their missionary endeavours might be discussed – stories associated with a local woman working in southern Africa, Christina Forsythe, appeared regularly in the *Greenock Herald*.[27]

Such examples, which stress the importance of locality, are important because it was through the filter of local identity that much Scottish imperial involvement was experienced. The fact that regiments were recruited locally, that missionaries were sponsored by local churches and that, more often than not, the local economy had some form of connection with imperial trade (such as jute in Dundee, or the locomotive works in Springburn in Glasgow) meant that the focus tended to settle on a limited horizon. That there was a fair amount of imperial coverage in the Scottish press, no one would deny, but its presentation was more often than not wrapped up in and conditioned by local interests, rather than consciousness of a Scottish or British national endeavour.

The exceptions to this occurred in the arena of politics. Here, the Irish issue provided an ongoing source of debate from 1886, and the South African War raised imperial issues to a position of prominence that was sustained throughout the early twentieth century thanks to the campaign for imperial tariff preference. When it came to the discussion of such general imperial issues in the context of Scottish politics, the Scottish press was either limited in its imperial commitment or actively hostile, in marked contrast to its more favourable treatment of local connections with empire.

The issue of Irish Home Rule had a dramatic impact on Scottish politics. It resulted in the secession of a number of Liberal 'Unionist' MPs who ini-

25 Ibid. 154–6.   26 *Glasgow Herald*, 18 Oct. 1859; *Scottish Review*, 30 Jan. 1913.   27 W.P. Livingstone, *Christina Forsythe of Fingoland* (Edinburgh, 1915).

tially formed a distinct political party, but eventually merged with the Scottish Conservatives to form the Scottish Unionist Party in 1912. The cause of imperial unity was most strongly promoted by the Edinburgh *Scotsman* and the *Glasgow Herald*. The former inclined towards the idea of maintaining a distinctive Unionist dimension in the Liberal Party while the latter was more inclined to support a reinvigorated Conservative Party. Although the threat to imperial unity was a mainstay of the Scottish Unionist case against Irish Home Rule, as expressed by the *Herald*, its importance diminished over time. Initial hopes that the threat to imperial unity would be enough to turn the electorate away from the Liberal Party proved forlorn and the paper quickly realized that an extra domestic dimension was needed to beef up the appeal to the voter. The *Herald* summed up its position in 1889:

> It ought now, at all events, to be plain to the two leaders of the two sections of the Unionist Party that, in Scotland, more particularly, they must not confine their exhortations to the negative and defensive work, all important though that is, of opposing the disintegration of the Empire, but must offer the constituencies a programme of moderate yet immediately necessary reforms.[28]

It was the advent of war in South Africa that gave the imperial cause its next significant rallying call. The Liberal Party in Scotland was divided in its response to the conflict. The traditional Gladstonian element stuck firm to its beliefs in 'liberty, retrenchment and peace', while the Liberal Imperialist lobby prepared the way for a reinvigorated Liberalism with Lord Rosebery at its head. The political complexion of the Scottish press meanwhile determined its own response to the South African War. The Unionist *Scotsman* and *Glasgow Herald* threw their weight behind the patriotic cause and even endorsed the break-up of pro-Boer and anti-war meetings.[29] Many Liberal papers meanwhile supported the war in its initial stages but soon began to express reservations. Of greater concern to many, however, was the wave of jingoism across Britain that accompanied the war and contributed to the Unionist Party victory in the 1900 general election. Arguably the role of the press in facilitating this result was most visible in Glasgow, where the *Herald* held sway and the Liberals lost their two remaining seats. This was seen by Liberal publications as a wake-up call. The *Scottish Review* denounced the influence of 'base Anglo Saxon' populism and Hector MacPherson, editor of the *Edinburgh Evening News*, condemned the deterioration of Scottish political culture.[30] MacPherson went on to form the Young Scots Society, a rad-

28 19 Jan. 1889.   29 Brown, 'Echoes of Midlothian', 169.   30 *Scottish Review*, 3 Nov. 1900; *Edinburgh Evening News*, 8 Nov. 1900.

ical ginger group, which was to play an important part in the subsequent development of the Liberal Party in Scotland. Reflecting the attitudes of the city's two pro-Boer MPs, the Liberal *Dundee Advertiser*, which had initially supported the war, similarly expressed reservations at the growth of 'iliberalism' that accompanied the conflict.[31]

Liberal papers also criticized the expected reorientation of the party on imperial issues. The *Young Scot* lambasted the activities of Rosebery, particularly his sniping at the party leadership, while the *Dundee Advertiser* and the *Edinburgh Evening News* criticized the latent imperialism of a speech given by Rosebery at Glasgow University, where he had been elected Rector.[32] Coverage of the concentration camps in South Africa and of Campbell Bannerman's denunciation of the 'methods of barbarism' deployed by the British during the war began to rally traditional Liberal opinion back to the fold and the Young Scots were able to hold an anti-war demonstration in Edinburgh in April 1901 which attracted an estimated 10,000 protesters.

A key component of the Liberal attack on the South African War involved the promotion of a specifically Liberal conception of empire. Thomas Shaw for example called for an empire in which federalism and free association were the watchwords, and also denounced the growing influence of militarism.[33] The Scottish Unionist press meanwhile failed to engage with the issue of imperial federation – the Scottish Tory, Fredrick Scott Oliver, significantly used the letter columns of *The Times* rather than a Scottish paper to make his case.[34] This reflected a broader failure on the part of Scottish Unionists, who as a result left the running to the Liberals, who used the idea of imperial federation as a way to endorse the granting of Home Rule to Ireland as part of a wider package of domestic devolution.

Liberal Scotland was further rejuvenated by Chamberlain's proposals for imperial tariff preference – tariff reform. The threat of protectionism that emerged in 1903 allowed the party to flock to the defence of a classic Gladstonian tenet. The Liberal press did its bit and gave wide publicity to the 'big loaf' versus 'little loaf' argument that formed the mainstay of the Liberal campaign. For the imperially minded Unionists in Scotland, tariff reform was disastrous. The importance of the global free market to the Scottish economy was such that Chamberlain's proposals triggered the defection of two Unionist MPs.[35] The *Glasgow Herald* denounced tariff reform and regularly published (throughout 1903) articles purporting to show the damage it would inflict on the Scottish economy.[36] Championing free trade

31 13 Apr. 1900. 32 Brown, 'Echoes of Midlothian', 170. 33 Thomas Shaw, *Patriotism and empire* (Edinburgh, 1901). 34 John Kendle, 'The Round Table movement and Home Rule all round', *Historical Journal*, 11 (1968) 332–53. 35 I.G.C. Hutchison, *A political history of Scotland, 1832–1924: parties, elections and issues* (Edinburgh, 1986) 219. 36 Re-published as *Fiscal facts and policy* (Glasgow, 1904).

and a social reform agenda helped ensure a successful Scottish outcome for
the Liberals at the 1905 general election.[37]

The inability of the Unionists to recover ground in Scotland during the
general elections of 1910 led to an increasing focus on the issue of Irish Home
Rule. The main complaint of the Unionist press was that Home Rule was
being driven through by the minority Liberal government's dependence on
the support of the Irish nationalists to form a majority. Even before the election the *Glasgow Herald* claimed that a Liberal/Irish nationalist coalition was
a possibility: '80 Irish votes, the price of Home Rule', which would mean the
'bartering of British unity and security for the support of the Irish revolutionary party'. The *Herald* argued that loyal Protestants would not forsake
their countrymen in Ulster and 'would fight as never before for the maintenance of the Union'.[38]

With a Liberal parliamentary majority and reform of the House of Lords
complete, Irish Home Rule seemed unavoidable after 1910, and what is interesting about the Unionist press in Scotland is how the imperial perspective
simultaneously more or less vanished from the Home Rule debate. Opposition
tended to centre on the rights of the Protestant minority in Ulster, the fear
of land confiscation and the threat to property that might come from an Irish
parliament. By the time of the post-1910 'crisis', both the *Scotsman* and the
Herald increasingly focused on the plight of Ulster.

> When the problem of national self-government ripens for solution –
> and this will not be until the Radicals lay aside their Irish policy for
> something entirely different – Ulster will have an indisputable claim
> for her peculiar circumstances being effectively provided for. But at
> present so such claim is made.[39]

Right up to the eve of the war, the position of the *Scotsman* was to endorse
the right of Ulster to veto any proposals for Irish Home Rule. While the
paper has been absolved of some of the most virulent anti-Catholicism associated with the press during this period by Tom Gallagher, such sentiments
did, however, seep in from time to time and were used to question the suit-
ability of Irish nationalists for government: 'The appearance, ill or well timed,
of Papal Decrees, that have revealed how unchanged in spirit is the *ultramontane* power with which the Nationalist party is associated, how it continues to be opposed to freedom of conscience, in the home and in public
affairs.'[40] The *Herald* was even more extreme in its opposition and often made
reference to the historic links between Scotland and Ulster and the shared

---

37 R.J. Finlay, 'Continuity or change? Scottish politics, 1900–1944' in T.M. Devine and R.J.
Finlay (eds), *Scotland in the twentieth century* (Edinburgh, 1996) 66–9.   38 29 Dec. 1909.   39
Scotsman, 5 Jan. 1912.   40 18 Jan. 1912.

religion of Presbyterianism, which was portrayed as being under threat. As far as the editorial line of the paper was concerned, there could be no question of any scheme of Home Rule that did not include Ulster and, equally, there could be no question of the Province being coerced into any such scheme: 'it is improbable that the British people would consent to employ the British army in driving Ulster out of the Union'.[41]

Despite the disappearance of the imperial perspective, the *Scotsman* was not averse to using ideas of imperial federation as a means to slow down or halt Irish Home Rule. In a bizarre twist of argument, an editorial put the case for Scottish Home Rule before that of Ireland:

> It [Irish Home Rule] will present itself next session as the basis of a federal scheme. We do not need to be told what this means. Federal Home Rule will be placed in the preamble, as House of Lords Reform was placed in the Parliament Bill. It will be a pious opinion never intended to be put into practice, and provided for the gratification of those, and none else, who are bent on being deceived. If there is to be Federal Home Rule, let it be on the right and natural lines of Devolution, and if it be ground where the experiment would be attended with least risk and with most chance of success. Let the government prove their sincerity by bringing in a Scottish home rule bill, and then wait and see what happens to them and their party.[42]

In spite of its best efforts, the *Scotsman* failed to mobilize public opinion in favour of Ulster and against Irish Home Rule. The narrowing of the issue out of the imperial context into one that focused more directly on domestic British politics was indicative of the failure of wider imperial concerns to condition public opinion. Indeed, one editorial complained that Irish Home Rule was considered 'an occasion to be regarded as lightly as if it referred to the Fiji Islands'.[43]

In the two most unionist papers in Scotland, the question of imperial unity thus came to play only a minor part in the argument against Irish Home Rule. If we examine the correspondence columns for both papers we find that imperial unity is hardly mentioned. Of the sixty-five letters on the issue of Irish Home Rule addressed to the editor of the *Glasgow Herald* in the period from 1 January to 30 April 1912, none placed imperial unity at the centre of their concerns. Likewise, a similar pattern emerges when examining the editorials of the *Scotsman*. Of the twenty-six editorials dealing with the issue of Irish Home Rule in the first half of 1913, none, other than in an incidental manner, raised the threat to imperial unity, and none related it to wider questions con-

41 10 Apr. 1910.   42 18 Jan. 1912.   43 *Scotsman*, 31 May 1913.

cerning the empire. The main thrust of debate concerned the rights of Ulster, constitutional anomalies, comparisons with Scotland and the threat to civil order. To conclude, the Scottish Unionist press viewed the issue of Irish Home Rule from a perspective firmly rooted within a domestic British political context.

Paradoxically, it was the Liberal press that made greatest play of the imperial dimension, by advocating federalism as a means to solve the Irish question, but also by portraying Home Rule as a means to strengthen imperial unity. Correspondents in the *Daily Record* throughout February 1912 used the example of federalism in Canada as a model which might be applied to Britain and stressed that federalism did not constitute a threat either to Canadian unity or to that of the empire. The stimulus to this line of debate was a speech by Winston Churchill in Dundee where a scheme of 'Home Rule all round' – that is for a federated United Kingdom as well as a federated empire – was proposed as the remedy to the situation in Ireland. The editorial line in the *Daily Record* was that this was the best way forward: 'The Bill will either accord with federal ideas or not. The presumption that in the main it will do so grows upon one, although the structure is, as yet, only partly revealed.'[44] Even in the Unionist press, Home Rulers could argue that failure to make concessions to Ireland actually posed a greater threat to the unity of the empire than did Home Rule.[45]

While the Scottish press did pay a lot of attention to imperial matters in the period 1850–1914, imperial debates never proved decisive in shaping the Scottish political landscape. Jingoism of the type witnessed during the 1900 general election attracted widespread condemnation and was arguably most important in providing a vital wake-up call for the dominant Liberal press in Scotland. Even the case of Ireland failed to galvanize imperial sentiment, and Home Rule was increasingly framed in a domestic rather than an imperial context. The empire was probably more important in terms of its appeal to local interests. While much more research need to be done on this area, it is likely that even here, however, imperial issues seldom displaced domestic concerns from the centre of local attention.

44 9 Feb. 1912.   45 For example see the correspondence columns of the *Scotsman*, 4 Oct. 1913 and the *Glasgow Herald*, 8 Feb. 1912.

4. Empire and the Welsh press

ALED JONES AND BILL JONES

Currents of empire flowed through the Welsh popular press of the nineteenth and early twentieth centuries in vigorous but often complicated ways. Attempts to understand the significance of those currents from the vantage point of a post-colonial and devolved British Isles involve conceptual as well as empirical difficulties. What, we may ask, did the 'press' in this period encompass, and whose ideological positions regarding the nature and global reach of 'Britain' and 'Britishness' did its printed pages embody and represent? For the purposes of this survey, we have chosen to focus our attention primarily on the periodical press, including newspapers, magazines and literary journals, produced within Wales between 1804 and 1914. We have further narrowed the field of vision by including only what we consider to be the dominant, that is to say the most formative and widely resonant, voices in certain of the more powerful sections of Welsh society in the same period. Competing readings of British colonial engagement can, of course, be found in Welsh journalism throughout these years, and the following study of how empire was articulated, understood and argued about in, and in response to, the Welsh press is a necessarily partial one which invites others to contest its own readings. But we have to begin somewhere, especially given a past reluctance to address the power exerted by ideas of colonization and empire in the shaping of a 'modern' Welsh identity and a sense of its place in the world. This essay, then, will try to identify some of the more significant streams of 'imperial thinking' that flowed through the Welsh public prints, and, by appraising their roles in the fashioning of a Welsh public life, to render them accessible to broader comparative scrutiny.

The history of the press in Wales has been related in a number of publications, and need not be repeated at length here.[1] Elements of that history, however, do need to be revisited in order to cast a clearer light upon the imperial contexts of its structural development (in particular the evolving technologies of production and distribution), and its news and other content.[2]

---

1 See, for example, Aled Jones, *Press, politics and society: a history of journalism in Wales* (Cardiff, 1993). 2 For an earlier comparative exploration of this theme, see Aled Jones and Bill Jones, 'The Welsh world and the British empire, c.1851–1939: an exploration', *Journal of Imperial and Commonwealth History*, 2:31 (May 2003) 57–81; also available in Carl Bridge and Kent

From its origins in 1804, the Welsh newspaper press had drawn its readers' attention, if not always in equal measure, to both local and international news events. The accelerated expansion in the number of titles and in circulations during the 1850s was as much the consequence of public interest in the events of the Crimean War as it was of the abolition of newspaper taxes. The circulation of news about war, British endeavour overseas and parliamentary debates increasingly familiarized a Welsh readership with the information order of the British state, and thus may be said to have pulled them more firmly into its ideological sphere of influence. However powerful and divisive linguistic and denominational differences were within the expanding press of nineteenth-century Wales, the same kinds of messages regarding Britain's imperial mission circulated in some measure through most of the weekly and monthly publications, albeit often in idiomatically Welsh forms.

As in other parts of the world, outside as well as within western Europe, the growth of the press in Wales was as strongly associated with industrialization, urbanization and the extension of faster and cheaper forms of transport as it was with the development of popular education and the growth of adult literacy. The powerful push of commercial advertising was as critical a motivating force in its growth as was the pull of new consumer demand for up-to-date financial information, political reports or war news. The dissemination of information by the press also furthered an evangelical mission to change the society in which it circulated. Publishers and editors often revealed ambitions to structure the agendas of public discussion and to shape the identities, characters and forms of conduct of their readers. In the main, this was in order to give voice not so much to 'the people', potentially their readers, as to individual, regional or 'belief' based interests, especially in the realms of Victorian religion and politics. The spectacular growth of a Welsh language Nonconformist journalism in particular was both a response to the perceived worsening of the demographic and institutional imbalance between the English and Welsh languages, and an attempt to mobilize support for Wales' incorporation into the mainstream of British Liberalism after the passing of the 1867 Reform Act. Even in the proletarian circles of the south Wales coalfield, where in the early twentieth century opposition to Liberal Nonconformity in the name of an anti-imperial social democracy was strongest, the legacy of such charismatic Welsh Nonconformist Lib-Lab leaders as William Abraham (Mabon) remained significant.[3]

The press not only provides evidence for important elements of an evolving public sphere in Victorian and Edwardian Wales, conducted in two languages and across often acrimonious denominational divisions, but also, to a

Fedorowich (eds), *The British world: diaspora, culture, identity* (London, 2003). 3 The most compelling analysis of Liberal Nonconformity in modern Welsh political life continues to be Kenneth O. Morgan, *Wales in British politics, 1868–1922* (Cardiff, 1970).

considerable extent, created the networks and communications flows which sustained the emerging political culture. Debate within that public sphere tackled the specificities of party allegiances, labour-capital relations and the future prospects of the Welsh language, and also routinely and continuously addressed the Welsh people's place in the world in the broadest possible sense, including their relationship with British imperial power.

We have shown elsewhere how the press actively encouraged emigration by means of advertisements and vivid descriptions of the life and employment opportunities on offer in the settler empire and the USA.[4] The press also fed emigrant experiences back to a Welsh public by printing letters and items of news from widely-distributed centres of Welsh settlement. These entered political debate in Wales, providing divergent attitudes regarding, *inter alia*, state authority, the law, constitutional and civil rights and social reform. In these and other ways, both the English and the Welsh language press regularly and continually reinforced the presence of empire and a British world in the public life of Wales.[5]

The following vignettes, exploring three 'Welsh readings' of empire in the Welsh press, reveal the extent to which the Welsh public sphere was the site of interlocking empires within and outside the British imperial world. These included Wales as the centre of a Protestant pseudo-empire that linked the Welsh in Wales with Welsh migrants and settlements throughout the world by means of a print-based communications network; its structural position in a global, and especially Atlantic, labour market as an economy based first on wool, then on metals, coal and slate exports; and, finally, Welsh involvement in the formal administrative and military structures of the British empire.

As in other parts of the British Liberal and democratic press at the time, the term 'empire' in Welsh journalism of the 1840s tended primarily to refer to the imperial monarchies of continental Europe re-established in 1815 after the defeat of Napoleonic France. The tone of comment on European affairs was, in this specific sense, often 'anti-imperial'. Thus, William Rees, better known by his bardic pseudonym Gwilym Hiraethog, from 1843 the Liverpool-based editor of the first successful Welsh-language newspaper *Yr Amserau* (the Times), not only reported at considerable length the activities of Hungarian and Italian nationalist opponents of the Austro-Hungarian empire, but made his readers aware that he explicitly approved of their struggle. His defence of Mazzini, for example, against 'a host of those curs of

---

4 Aled Jones and Bill Jones, *Welsh reflections: Y Drych and America, 1851–2001* (Llandysul, 2001) and 'The Welsh world and the British empire'. See also Bill Jones, *Emigration and ethnicity: the Welsh overseas, 1790–1939* (Cardiff, forthcoming). 5 See, for example, the reporting of the campaign to end state-funded religion in Victoria, Australia, and discussion on the impact of the secret ballot there in *Baner Cymru* (the Banner of Wales), 30 Sept. and 16, 23 and 30 Dec. 1857.

Continental despots, the Tory organs of the English press, who bark and
gnash their teeth at him', a criticism specifically aimed at the London *Times*
(which Rees both loathed and parodied) and the *Quarterly Magazine*, was
rooted in a conviction that Rees was actively contributing to their anti-imperial efforts 'to proclaim the *Unity* of the human family; and the inalienable
rights of the whole fraternity of man'.[6] Rees further explained that his newspaper campaign had been waged against all repressive imperial states since,
for him, 'an armed government is a traitor … to the nobility of human
nature' which, instead of 'courting [its subjects'] affections through the commanding influence of wisdom and equity, seeks to subdue them by intimidation'.[7] Such heroic treatment of Continental nationalists spawned a literary tradition that continued well into the late nineteenth century, with, for
example, poems extolling Garibaldi and Cavour still being published by John
Ceiriog Hughes in the 1870s, and studies of Mazzini by W. Matthias
Griffiths in the 1890s.[8]

At the same time, however, Rees and other liberal commentators were
signally less critical of Britain's own growing global power, or of Palmerston's
foreign policy, preferring instead to highlight Britain's 'benign' constitutional
monarchy and press freedom as models to which Continental radicals should
aspire.[9] Furthermore, it is evident that Rees' European anti-imperial nationalism had theological origins in an apocalyptic Calvinism that all too often
descended into a crude and visceral anti-Catholicism in which the papacy in
Rome was regarded as being the world's most dangerous imperial power.[10]
Thus, for Rees, the end of empire could only be assured by the collapse of
the papacy, a process which he also explored in such poetical works as
Cwymp Babilon (the fall of Babylon) and *Ffoedigaeth y Pab, yn 1848* (the
flight of the Pope, in 1848).[11] Such sentiments were shared across much,
though not by any means all, of Protestant Wales, Anglican as well as
Nonconformist. The Reverend Evan Evans (Ieuan Brydydd Hir), a cleric

6 William Rees, *Providence and prophecy: or, God's hand fulfilling His word; more especially in
the revolutions of 1848, and subsequent events* (Liverpool and London, 1851) 186. Rees' combination of European republicanism and British constitutionalism was widely shared by contemporary radical-Liberals and Chartists. See Margot Finn, *After Chartism: class and nation in
English radical politics, 1848–1874* (Cambridge, 1993). 7 Rees, *Providence and prophecy*, 18. 8
'I fyny'r mynydd dringai ef/Wrth ochor Garibaldi,/ i wel'd yr haul yn dringo'r nef -/Haul
Rhyddid Itali!' (with Garibaldi he climbed the mountain to see the sun of Italy's freedom climb-
ing the sky), John Ceiriog Hughes, 'Cavour', *Oriau'r Bore*, Llyfr II (Wrexham, 1872) 67. See also
Y Parch. W. Matthias Griffiths, 'Joseph Mazzini', *Y Traethodydd* (May 1897) 186–98. 9 In
his essay on Lord Palmerston, written as a public lecture in 1866, Rees chose to emphasize his
role in the anti-slavery movement. William Rees, 'Arglwydd Palmerston', *Darlithiau gan y
Diweddar William Rees DD (Gwilym Hiraethog)* (Dinbych, 1907) 100–31. 10 For a fuller discussion, see Aled Jones, 'Politics and prophecy in the journalism of Gwilym Hiraethog',
Transactions of the Hon. Soc. of Cymmrodorion 2002, new ser., 9 (2003) 106–21. 11 Gwilym
Hiraethog, *Caniadau Hiraethog* (Dinbych, 1855) 226–8.

with the Established Church, similarly urged his readers to 'abhor the ways of Anti-Christian Rome'.[12]

If Wales' overwhelming Protestantism shaped its journalism's principal attitudes towards the vicissitudes of imperial power on the European Continent, especially during and after the revolutions of 1848–9, it also laid down the parameters for a generally accepted Welsh response to Britishness, and in particular to the institution of monarchy. For much of this period, the British monarchy, and the global empire which it increasingly came to represent, was embodied in the person of Queen Victoria. While some observers had sought to introduce an ethnic dimension to Welsh loyalty, by representing Victoria as a 'Celtic Queen' or, as the poet John Williams (Ab Ithel) fancifully described her in 1853, as a 'Boadicea rediviva',[13] the ties that bound the Welsh to the Victorian crown were effectively those of religion. Richard Parry (Gwalchmai), employing the trope of protectiveness, described Victoria as 'our shield – under the outstretched wing of Jehovah',[14] defending Wales' Protestantism from Catholic Europe, while in a grotesque echo of the growing imperial reach of the British crown, the Calvinistic Methodist weekly *Y Goleuad* (the Illuminator) described Victoria's relationship to the Welsh as being that of *y Fam Wen Fawr* (the Great White Mother).[15] At this time, such pronouncements made from on high by the leadership of Wales' most powerful Nonconformist denomination could not be challenged lightly by any section of Welsh society. This is not to say that there was no criticism of the imperial monarchy in the Welsh press. The mounting cost of the Civil List was from the 1870s subjected to sustained attack by journalists such as Thomas Gee, editor of the main Welsh language weekly newspaper *Baner ac Amserau Cymru* (the Banner and Times of Wales). News of Victoria's assumption of the title of Empress of India in Delhi on 1 January 1877 merited no more than three short lines in Gee's *Baner*, and was otherwise ignored. A decade later, the *South Wales Daily News*, following extensive reporting of public, and publicly funded, celebrations to honour Victoria's 1887 jubilee throughout south Wales, which included street decorations, processions and the lighting of beacons, closed with an editorial column that reminded readers of the conditional and contingent nature of Welsh popular monarchism. 'Welsh loyalty', it proposed, was dependent on appropriate 'royal reward', which palpably had not been forthcoming in the wake of the jubilee. The editorial ended with an acidly-worded warning that 'the Welsh people will

12 D. Silvan Evans (ed.), *Gwaith y Parchedig Evan Evans (Ieuan Brydydd Hir)* (Caernarfon, 1876) 144. 13 John Davies, 'Victoria and Victorian Wales', in Geraint H. Jenkins and J. Beverley Smith (eds), *Politics and society in Wales, 1840–1922* (Cardiff, 1988) 7–28. See also Hywel Teifi Edwards and E.G. Millward, *Jiwbilî Y Fam Wen Fawr Victoria 1887–1897* (Llandysul, 2002) esp. 18 and 31. 14 *Y Celt*, 17 June 1887. 15 Davies, 'Victoria and Victorian Wales', 17.

be able to remember that to those from whom they receive no honours they owe nothing. There are among us many who have been living in a fool's paradise whose eyes will probably be opened by this unfair and scandalous treatment of a nationality everywhere praised for its loyalty and obedience to law.'[16]

In general, however, such criticisms were muted. Both the jubilees of 1887 and 1897 drew effusively monarchist and pro-imperial poems from some of Wales' leading writers. Rowland Williams (Hwfa Môn) in the monthly *Y Dysgedydd* (the Instructor) of July 1897 could hardly contain his enthusiasm in his poem 'Victoria': 'with her golden sceptre on her shining throne, from hour to hour she will reign over BRITAIN great in prestige and INDIA great in size'.[17] Even the radical weekly newspaper *Y Celt*, closely associated with the nationalist and socialist politics of Dr Evan Pan Jones and Dr Michael D. Jones, was placed in a dilemma in 1887 by the show of public loyalty expected by the state. This the editor awkwardly resolved by printing on the paper's front page on 17 June 1887 (see fig. 1) a portrait of Victoria with loyal verses by Richard Parry (Gwalchmai), with the following apologia: 'doubtless, should we see ourselves as we are seen by others ("That resentful republican rag!") we should offer a humble apology for referring to monarchy and empire. We are not quite what some would describe us as being.'[18] The veil of loyalty, however, slipped later in the same article: 'Victoria's Jubilee is being celebrated (in Ireland) by dragging women and girls, the poor tenants of Bodyke, from their homes as the walls are pulled down around their ears.'[19] The Welsh, it implied, would show more loyalty to the crown if it acted to stop such atrocities and allowed evicted Irish tenants to return to their homes.[20] For some readers, such caveats were far from comforting. J. Pryce Davies of Porth complained that he had been 'shocked to see a *picture* of the woman who occasionally sits on Britain's throne on the front page of *Y Celt*, of all publications. I had strongly believed that the constitution of *Y Celt* was beyond the influence of weak-minded Monarchical Jubileeism ...'[21] But such voices of principled opposition to monarchy and empire were few in number, especially during the manufactured euphoria of the jubilee years, although Dr Pan Jones managed another critical gibe at Britain's imperial policy on

16 *South Wales Daily News*, 22 June 1887.   17 'A'i theyrnwialen aur,/Ar ei gorseddfainc glaer,/O awr i awr,/Teyrnasu byddo hi/Ar BRYDAIN fawr ei bri/A'r INDIA FAWR', *Y Dysgedydd* (July 1897) 279.   18 'Diameu pe gwelem ein hunain fel ein gwelir gan eraill ("Y ddalen genfigenllyd a gwerinol!") dylem wneud ymddiheurawd gostyngedig am i ni gyfeirio at frenhiniaeth neu ymerodraeth. Nid ydym yn hollol fel y ceisia rhai ddangos ein bod', *Y Celt*, 17 June 1887.   19 'Dethlir Jiwbili Victoria drwy lusgo gwragedd a merched tenantiaid tlodion Bodyke o'u tai a thynn y muriau i lawr o gwmpas eu clustiau', *Y Celt*, 17 June 1887.   20 Ibid. 21 'Synais weled *darlun* o'r ddynessydd yn eistedd yn achlysurol ar orsedd Prydain, ar wyneb-ddalen y *Celt*, o unrhyw newyddiadur. Yr oeddwn yn credu yn gryf fod cyfansoddiad y *Celt* uwchlaw cael dylanwad arno gan y pen-wendid Jiwbiliaidd Brenhiniaethol ...', *Y Celt*, 1 July 1887.

Y CELT:

Adolygydd Crefyddol, Gwleidyddol a Chymdeithasol.

Rhif 363. Cyf. VIII.   BANGOR, DYDD GWENER, MEHEFIN 17, 1887.   *Registered for Transmission abroad*   Pris 1c.

JIWBILI Y FRENHINES VICTORIA, 1887.

Ein tarian yw Victoria—dan ad·n
   Daenedig Jehofa,
Drwy bynawaodd deyrnasa
A gair doeth ci chynghor da.

A chododd yn serchiadau—ei deiliaid
   Wolir o hob graddau ;
A mawl ei hoes am amlhau
Ei dedwyddyd a'i dyddiau.

Hoddyw, wedi cyrhaeddyd—o'i heiniocs
   Haner can'mlwydd hywyd,
A choledd heb ddymchwelyd,
De wy barch, brif gadair y byd.

Ca'dd hi ei geni i'w gwaith—a'i magu
   Dan edmygedd gobaith ;
Byw i orphen yn berffaith,
Yn llaw Duw, wedl'll y daith.

O oleuni rhagoniaeth—deallwn
   Y deilliodd llywodraeth ;
Ac i'n teyrn fel cenad daeth
I gyrhaedd pob rhageriaeth

Mor wynion mae'r awenau—yn ei llaw
   Mewn llwydd yn mhob parthau,
O fyw'n hir i gyflawnhau
Oes auraidd ei mesurau.

Oddiar graig egwyddor gref—y gwelir
   Goleu ar ein cartref ;
A'n Buddug fyn bawb addef
Am wir nawdd fel morwyn nef.

Mawrhydri ei hymerodraeth—fanw!
   A'i therfynau helaeth,
Ar alwad ei rheolaeth,
Trwy y byd diarob aeth.

Enw'n Banon)
Sy' ar galon } Trwy eu gilydd.
Y trigolion)

A'u hufudd-dod)
I'w hawdurdod } Gân na dderfydd.
Yn ddiorfod)

           GWALCHMAI.

HANER CAN' MLWYDD YN OL.

Ai tybed ei fod yn angenrheidiol i ni wneud rhyw fath o esgusawd dros neilldu o ychydig o'n gofod i jiwbilydda tipyn bach yr wythnos hon. Diameu pe gwelem ein hunain fel ein gwelir gan eraill (" Y ddalen genfgenllyd a gwerinol ! ") dylem wneud ymddiheurawd gostyngedig am i ni gyfeirio at frenhiniaeth neu ymerodraeth. Nid ydym yn hollol fel y ceisia rhai ddangos ein bod.

Er ein bod yn anrhegu ein darllenwyr a llun brenhines Prydain ac ag englynion penigamp y prif-fardd Gwalchmai, nid yw hyny am fod ein llawenydd yn gyflawn, nac am fod pob peth fel y dymunasem iddo fod. Y mae yn wir ein bod wedi cael cryn lawer o bethau yn ystod yr haner can' mlynedd diweddaf, ond o'u cydmaru a'r hyn sydd arnom eisiau a'r hyn ddylasem fod wedi ei gael, nid ydynt oll ond fel gras cyn bwyd. Nis gallwn osod y bai i gyd ar ein penadur, ac efallai nas gallwn ychwaith ymryddhau ein hunain yn hollol oddiwrtho. Y mae Victoria wedi bod yn lled bobloguidd yn mhlith ei deiliaid ar hyd yr haner can' mlynedd diweddaf, nid yn gymaint o herwydd diun a wnaeth, ond hwyrach o herwydd yr hyn y peidiodd ei wneud. Credwn fod y poblogrwydd negyddol hwn wedi cadw yr elfen genedlaethol yn mhell ar ol yn Nghymru. Tefir pob gwelliant mawr, a phob cyfnewidiad gwreiddiol hyd nes y bydd y frenhines wedi myned, yna symudir y gliccied, a daw y byd i'w le ar unwaith. Pe buasai Victoria ychydig yn waeth penadur nag yw, buasem wedi mynu y gwelliantau sydd arnom eu heisiau, a phe buasai ychydig yn well buasem wedi eu cael. Yn lle hyny daliwn i ddisgwyl heb ryw lawer iawn o arwyddion nad disgwyl a gawn.

Ni bu yn Mhrydain ond tri jiwbili fel hyn o'r blaen, a digwyddasant ill trioedd, fel yr un presenol ar adegau lled derfysglyd ar hanes y wlad. Y cyntaf oedd eiddo Harri y trydydd, yr hwn a deyrnasodd 56 o flynyddoedd, ac a gyrhaeddodd ei jiwbili yn y flwyddyn 1266, sef ar ddiwedd rhyfel gwaedlyd y Barwniaid, yr hwn fu y lladdwyd Simon de Montefort, ac o'r hwn gynhwrf y tarddodd ein cynrychiolaeth seneddol. Y nesaf a welodd haner can' mlwydd prin ar orsedd Prydain oedd Edward III., yr hwn a fu farw yn yr haner canfed flwyddyn o'i deyrnasiad, yn 1377. Claddwyd hefyd ei fab, ac aer y goron y Tywysog Du yr un flwyddyn cyn esgyn o hono i orsedd ei dad. Tymhor gwaedlyd oedd hwn hefyd, sef amser rhyfel Ffrainc, pan yr ym ceisiai Edward am orsedd y wlad hono yn rhinwedd ei berthynas a'i fam. Y nesaf gyrhaeddodd haner canrif oedd Sior y trydydd, yr hwn a deyrnasodd 60 mlynedd, ac a gyrhaeddodd ei jiwbili yn y flwyddyn 1810, sef 77 mlynedd yn ol. Yr oedd y tymhor hwn yn nghanol rhyfel yr Hispaen ; pum' mlynedd ar ol brwydr Trafalgar a marwolaeth Nelson, a phum' mlynedd o flaen brwydr Waterloo. Dyma

the occasion of Victoria's death in 1901: 'she died of a broken heart', he concluded, 'caused by the stubborn refusal of the Boers passively to submit to
be killed by her butchers'.[22]

Religion provided the impetus for another compelling though differently
angled discourse of empire in the Welsh press. Missionaries supplied, and
were themselves the subjects of, an impressively wide range of reading matter
in popular journalism. This body of writing, at least from the 1840s onwards,
brought Welsh religious life and the perceived purposes, if not always the
actual conduct, of the British empire into ever closer association in the public
mind. This area has attracted scholarly attention in recent years, though one
important theme that has remained neglected is the way in which the literature of mission generated a cultural defence of empire by a cultural minority located within the imperial metropole. Welsh literary journals such as *Y
Traethodydd* (the Essayist) published a number of lengthy tributes to the work
of, among others, Dr Livingstone in 1858,[23] Dr Duff in 1878[24] and Mackay
in Uganda in 1891.[25] Shorter pieces describing the lives of such British missionaries, and the social and physical landscapes in which they worked, were
also often found in weekly and even daily newspapers, while some book-length
accounts of travel in Welsh acquired considerable popularity during the second
half of the nineteenth century.[26] From the early nineteenth century, however,
when predominantly Nonconformist missionaries from Wales began to offer
their own accounts to the Welsh press, a new genre of specifically Welsh
'imperial' writing began to appear. This was to be substantially augmented
when, in 1840, the Welsh Calvinistic Methodist connexion decided to launch
their own, autonomous missions in north east India and Brittany. William
Pryse, one of the earliest Welsh Calvinistic Methodist missionaries to settle
in the Sylhet region of eastern Bengal (later transferred to Assam) published
in Wales in 1859 and 1860 a series of studies of Sanscrit and Bengali literature, classical and modern.[27] In these, he proposed a number of arguments
based on his translations of the *Katha Upanishad*, the first being the existence
of cultural correspondences between 'the Hindu' and 'the Celt'. In the ante-
diluvian world, Pryse proposed, Hindus and Celts had been 'brothers suck-
ing at the same breasts', and had thence in ancient times developed different

22 Quoted in Davies, 'Victoria and Victorian Wales', 19. 23 *Y Traethodydd* (1858), 186–202.
24 *Y Traethodydd* (1878) esp. 390, discusses connections between Duff and Thomas Jones, the
first independent Welsh Calvinistic Methodist missionary to India. 25 Francis Jones, 'Mackay
o Uganda', *Y Traethodydd* (Mar. 1891) 126–36. 26 For example, a biography of Denbigh-
born Henry Stanley 'hero of the dark continent', published by Thomas Gee and explicitly aimed
at the 'monoglot Welshman', *Hanes Bywyd Henry M. Stanley: arwr y cyfandir du, yn cynnwys
trem ar ei yrfa anturiaethus, a'i archwiliadau llwyddiannus yn nghyfandir tywyll Affrica, at wasanaeth
ei gydwladwyr* (Dinbych, 1890). 27 William Pryse, 'Llenyddiaeth Henafol yr Hindwaid' and
'Cyfieithiadau o'r Sanscrit', *Y Traethodydd* (1859) 320–43, 424–8.

but analogous social and religious codes in which the Brahminical *Rushies* were broadly comparable to the Celtic Druidic order.[28] The standards of linguistic sophistication practiced in the heroic Sanscrit poetry of the ancient world, however, had according to Pryse not been sustained in the modern, and the decline of Hindu civilization could be precisely traced through the degeneration of its language. In a final essay on modern Hindu literature, Pryse was unrelentingly critical of its damaging moral effects on Indian society and its propensity to turn 'truth into lies, and lies into truth'. 'We protest', he concluded, 'against the praise bestowed on Indian literature by some European intellectuals.'[29] This 'fallen' cultural world might only be saved by the intervention of Western, Christian social order and moral values, of which Wales was regarded by Pryse and others as constituting a model for others to emulate. In this evolving cultural discourse of empire, Welsh national self-consciousness was wholly consistent with British imperial expansion.

By the end of the century, such views had acquired a more secular rationale and were widely held by Welsh Liberal leaders. Writing of his journey through Egypt in 1896, J. Herbert Roberts defended British rule on the grounds that it had brought justice for Egyptian farmers, lightened the national tax burden and developed the country's national resources through 'honest and fair' government after decades of native 'corruption',[30] though a later account of British policy in the Transvaal in the same journal was less complimentary.[31] In general, reflections on Wales' position as part of the British empire at the turn of the century remained favourable to the *idea* of empire, as indeed they were to the growth in the use of English, regarded as the language of imperial modernity, among previously monoglot Welsh-speakers.[32] If T.E. Ellis, founder with David Lloyd George and others of the *Cymru Fydd* (Young Wales) movement in the 1880s, and Liberal MP for Meirionnydd from 1886 until his death in 1899, had been among the most public advocates in Wales of a 'liberal' British empire, the task of arguing the case in the Welsh press fell to another leading figure in the journalism of both languages, O.M. Edwards.

Both contemporaries and subsequent commentators have identified Owen Morgan Edwards (1858–1920) as one of the most influential and revealing voices that sought to shape and promote the idea of a re-emerging sense of Welsh nationhood in the late nineteenth century. In March 1907 he was described by the *Welsh Review* as the 'literary apostle' of 'the great revival of Welsh nationality during the last few years',[33] while Hazel Walford Davies

28 William Pryse, 'Yr Hindŵ a'r Celtiaid', *Y Traethodydd* (1859) 64. 29 William Pryse, 'Llenyddiaeth Ddiweddar yr Hindwaid', *Y Traethodydd* (1860) 173. 30 J. Herbert Roberts, 'Tro yn yr Aifft', *Y Traethodydd* (May 1896) 174. 31 R. Gwyneddon Davies, 'Y Transvaal', *Y Traethodydd* (Nov. 1899) 562–71. 32 T.A. Levi, 'Lle Cymru fel Rhan o Ymerodraeth Prydain', *Y Traethodydd* (Nov. 1901) 460–71. 33 'Welsh personalities: II Owen M. Edwards,

has described him as 'the most powerful single influence on his generation in revitalizing the living culture of Wales. As folk hero he held sovereign sway.'[34] Born in Llanuwchllyn, Meirionnydd, Edwards was Fellow in History at Lincoln College, Oxford from 1889 until 1907, when he became Chief Inspector of Schools for Wales, a post he held until his death. He also succeeded T.E. Ellis as Liberal MP for Meirionnydd for a brief period in 1899–1900.[35] The 'Wales' Edwards articulated embodied numerous elements, including the democratic, religious and cultured characteristics of its ordinary people and their quest for greater education, a cause for which he himself worked indefatigably.[36] To Edwards, the late nineteenth and early twentieth centuries saw the coming of age of the Welsh people, linking an ancient and distinguished past with an ever-greater future, measured in terms of the country's service to the rest of the world. His mission was embodied in the motto of his monthly Welsh-language magazine *Cymru* (Wales), which he edited from 1891 until his death in 1920: 'I Godi'r Hen Wlad yn ei Hôl' (to raise up the old country again). He wished to teach the Welsh about their history, to instil pride in their literary and poetic achievements and to foster unity among different, and often antagonistic, cultural, political and religious groups in the Wales of his time.

Edwards' main vehicle was the printed word, in both Welsh and English, and his output was prodigious. He wrote, edited or published scores of books, among them histories in both languages, and Welsh-language anthologies of poetry, children's books and accounts of his travels in his own country and on the European continent. More relevant in terms of this essay is his mobilization of the periodical press in Wales. He edited several Welsh-language journals, including the monthly *Cymru'r Plant* (the Children's Wales), published between 1892 and 1920, and also the English-language *Wales* between 1894 and 1897. As John Davies has emphasized, in the mid-1890s Edwards was the driving force behind the simultaneous publication of five different journals. As well as editing them, selecting illustrations and organizing their distribution, he also wrote much of their content, and often used his own money to pay for them.[37] Of particular note is the innovative and 'powerful and influential'[38] *Cymru*, or as it was popularly known, 'Y Cymru Coch' (red

MA', *Welsh Review*, 3:2 (Mar. 1907) 49–51. See also W. Llewelyn Williams MP, 'Representative Welshmen: VII Owen Morgan Edwards, MA', *Wales* (Apr. 1912) 199–201.   **34** Hazel Walford Davies, *O.M. Edwards* (Cardiff, 1988) 4.   **35** For studies of Edwards, see Davies, *O.M. Edwards*; Hazel Walford Davies (ed.), *Llythyrau Syr O.M. Edwards ac Elin Edwards, 1887–1920* (Llandysul, 1991); John Davies, 'Owen Morgan Edwards', *Welsh Historian*, 7 (spring 1987) 26–7; W.J. Gruffydd, *Owen Morgan Edwards: Cofiant Cyf. 1, 1858–1883* (Aberystwyth, 1937); Emlyn Sherrington, 'O.M. Edwards, culture and the industrial classes', *Llafur*, 1:6 (1992) 28–41.   **36** Edwards regarded Wales as 'the most democratic part of Britain'. O. M. Edwards, *A short history of Wales* (London, 1906) 111.   **37** Davies, 'Owen Morgan Edwards', 26.   **38** Davies, *O.M. Edwards*, 43 and 39–48 for a discussion of *Cymru*.

Cymru), after the colour of its covers. Edwards has been the subject of a fair amount of scholarly study but the fact that his understanding of Wales' past, contemporary profile and future trajectory were interwoven with an interpretation of Wales' relationship with the British empire and the wider world has largely been overlooked. As the following analysis of some of Edwards' commentaries in *Cymru* and other writings suggest, his attitudes towards the British empire and interpretations of its contemporary nature were inseparable from assumptions regarding Wales' developing role within it, and his visions of his native country's past and future.

Edwards' stance towards the empire was positive, not oppositional in any meaningful sense. He apparently disliked the use of the word 'English' when 'British' was meant, and complained about it in one of his articles.[39] The anonymous writer of a 'Welsh Personalities' sketch on Edwards in the *Welsh Review* in 1907 made a direct link between the subject's efforts 'to rekindle the national spirit' and the work of other young historians of small nations in Europe:

> These modern historical students do not necessarily aim at national independence. As long as their countries preserve practically their local independence they consider it an advantage than otherwise to form part, for the purposes of foreign affairs, with great empires. But they do not renounce their own feeling of nationality, and their pride of race is only increased.[40]

Edwards would have concurred fully with this assessment. According to Hon. Judge Sir Gerald Hurst, one of his students at Lincoln College, 'young men found [Edwards'] belief in Greater Britain inspiring'. Edwards had once signed off a letter to Hurst with 'Ever a true imperialist, O.M.E.'[41]

Edwards' perception of a Wales that was emerging on a world stage was complemented by the part he believed it had played in the developing greatness of Britain. As he wrote in his pioneering English-language 'continuous popular history of Wales' for the 'Story of the Nations' series (1901), 'the development of Wales has been twofold – in national intensity and in the expansion of imperial sympathy'. He argued that the Welsh had consistently played an imperial role 'where the surge of the advancing British wave has beaten fiercest' (referring to Welsh activity at battles 'from Cressy to Agincourt to Albuera to Inkerman'), and had also contributed to British art, literature, capitalism and the cause of labour.[42] As we shall see, Edwards' relationship with empire was not one of unconditional acceptance. There were

39 *Wales*, 23:3 (Feb. 1896) 90.   40 'Welsh Personalities: II Owen M. Edwards MA', 50.   41 Alfred T. Davies (ed.), *O.M.: a memoir* (Glynceiriog, 1946) 49.   42 O.M. Edwards, *Wales* (London, 1901) ix, 403.

aspects of British culture of which he did not approve, while his own horror of war and, apparently, his dislike of Joseph Chamberlain qualified his attitude during times of imperial military conflict.[43] Nevertheless, Edwards regarded the British empire as generally a benevolent and necessary institution, partly because of his interpretation of its attitude to smaller nations.

Some measure of this positive perception can be gauged in his belief that Welsh people should form colonies in the British empire, and not outside it as had occurred in the case of the much-publicized *Y Wladfa Gymreig* (Welsh colony), established in Patagonia in 1865. In *Cymru* in May 1900 he reprinted the text of Michael D. Jones' *Gwladychfa Gymreig* (Welsh colony), a pamphlet that had first been published around 1860. Jones was one of the chief architects of the Patagonia project and, as we have seen, was closely associated with *Y Celt*.[44] *Gwladychfa Gymreig* called for the Welsh to establish a Welsh colony or proto-state beyond the reach of English influence, and thus outside the British polity, and had been instrumental in the creation of the Patagonia colony. In a preamble to the reprinted version, Edwards praised Jones' contribution to Wales but stated that it was under the British flag that he himself would like to see Welsh colonies founded, because 'Britain's spirit has changed since M.D. Jones first wrote. It protects its settlers, but doesn't interfere with their internal affairs; in truth, they are independent and free.'[45] He went on to hope that a 'new Wales' might be established in South Africa once the war was over. Earlier in 1900, in remarks occasioned by Russian aggression against Finland, Edwards had declared that ever since the days of George Canning, Britain's behaviour towards small nations had been more tolerant and liberal. 'Our duty as Welsh people', he continued, 'is to serve the empire through raising our voice against the oppression of small nations. We should achieve unity through developing, not suppressing.'[46] Australia and Canada were loyal to Britain because it had given them every freedom. 'Britain', he predicted, 'will be a number of independent countries, but bound together by affection and mutual benefit, so they can be sufficiently united to challenge any power that threatens their freedom or fetters their trade.'[47]

Clues about Edwards' understandings of the relationship between Wales and empire are scattered throughout his writings, but some of its central lin-

---

43 As reported by Gerald Hurst, Edwards believed: 'If only Britain would cultivate a better system of education, care less for sport and work harder, what a future lay ahead.' Davies, *O.M.*, 49.   44 Michael D. Jones, *Gwladychfa Gymreig* (Lerpwl, *c.*1860).   45 'Y mae ysbryd Prydain wedi newid er pan ysgrifennodd M.D. Jones gyntaf. Amddiffynna ei sefydlwyr, ond nid ymyrra â'u materion mewnol; mewn gwirionedd, y maent yn anibynol a rhydd', *Cymru*, 106:18 (15 May 1900) 106.   46 'Ein dyledswydd ni fel Cymry yw gwasanaethu yr ymherodraeth trwy godi ein llais yn erbyn gorthrymu gwledydd bychain. Uno trwy ddadblygu, nid trwy lethu, ddylid wneyd', *Cymru*, 102:18 (15 Jan. 1900) 98.   47 'Nifer o wledydd anibynnol fydd Prydain, ond wedi eu rhwymo wrth eu gilydd gan serch a budd, fel y medrant fod yn ddigon unol i herio unrhyw allu fygthio eu rhyddid neu a lyffetheiria eu masnach', ibid.

eaments are set out directly and revealingly in a series of editorial observations – or what he called a 'conversation' with his readers – entitled 'Yr Ymylwe Geltaidd' (the Celtic Fringe) in *Cymru* in April 1900.[48] His commentary also betrays the influence of the immediate context of the South African War, which, apparently, he regarded with horror but appears not to have opposed,[49] and his perception of the Welsh response to that conflict.[50] The war was extensively covered by the Welsh press in Wales, in both languages, and editorials and letters columns projected diverse, complex views. The columns of the two main Welsh newspapers overseas, the North American *Y Drych* (the Mirror) and *Y Drafod* (Discussion) in Patagonia, also carried discussion and divergent opinions about the war.[51] *Y Drych's* editorials and many of the letters and articles on the subject it published were favourable to Britain's cause.[52] Some newspapers in Wales, such as *Y Celt*, were against the war.[53] Some, like *Tarian y Gweithiwr* (the Worker's Shield) in January 1900, expressed a preference for peace and condemned Britain's statesmen for going to war, but still maintained that hostilities ought to continue until total victory was achieved.[54] Kenneth Morgan has argued that 'the great majority of Welsh-language journals were strongly opposed to the war at the outset', in contrast to the English-language press.[55] The Liberal *South Wales Daily News* and the Tory *Western Mail* were unmistakeably jingoistic, the former's stance being a source of surprise and chagrin to opponents of the war and sceptics.[56] Even voices that interpreted the war as being caused by unwarranted British belligerence were often careful to differentiate between their disapproval in this particular instance and their usual support for the empire. A letter writer in *Tarian Y Gweithiwr* in February 1900 presented readers with a Welsh translation of an extract from an anti-war sermon by Dr Robert F. Horton that argued that the cheap and popular press in Britain had 'impeded the goodness that I believe is still in Britain's spirit – the spirit of justice, mercy and courage that would not knowingly transgress the rights

---

48 'Yr Ymylwe Geltaidd', *Cymru*, 105:18 (15 Apr. 1900) 197–202. 'Conversations' like this one opened each monthly issue between February and June 1900, instead of the usual article on a Welsh historical theme. *Cymru*, 104:18 (15 Mar. 1900) 149. **49** *Cymru*, 103:18 (15 Feb. 1900) 103; 105:18 (15 Apr. 1900) 198; A. Davies, *O.M.*, 49. **50** Historians have disagreed over the extent of pro-Boer sympathy and opposition to the war in Wales. See Henry Pelling, 'Wales and the Boer War' and Kenneth O. Morgan, 'Wales and the Boer War: a reply', *Welsh History Review*, 4:4 (Dec. 1969) 363–6 and 367–80, respectively. Morgan argues that the extent of pro-Boer sympathy in Wales has been exaggerated. **51** For a study of *Y Drych*, see Jones and Jones, *Welsh reflections*. For *Y Drafod*, see Gareth Alban Davies, 'The Welsh press in Patagonia', in Philip Henry Jones and Eiluned Rees (eds), *A nation and its books: a history of the book in Wales* (Aberystwyth, 1998) 265–76. **52** See, for example, articles and editorial in *Y Drych*, 18 Jan. 1900. **53** See, for example, editorial article by 'Ap Y Frenni' in *Y Celt*, 2 Feb. 1900. **54** *Tarian y Gweithiwr*, 18 Jan. 1900. See also 4 Jan. and 7 June 1900. **55** Morgan, 'Wales and the Boer War', 375–6. **56** See, for example, article by John Jones in *Tarian y Gweithiwr*, 10 May 1900.

of any country weaker than itself'.[57] Anti-war Welsh Patagonian correspondents to *Y Drafod* made similar points, one in January 1900 stating that 'no-one needs to fear that the Welsh Colony is less British in spirit' because the sympathies of some of its Welsh inhabitants were with the Boers.[58]

In his 'Yr Ymylwe Geltaidd' article Edwards began by asserting the popularity of Queen Victoria.[59] He maintained also that 'the Welsh are very loyal to the empire of which their country is a part' and had fought bravely and behaved honourably in the war. He claimed that 'it is true that Welsh newspapers have condemned the war that has brought so much grief to our families, because they assume that we could have got everything we wanted by walking the path of peace'.[60] He asserted that Welsh newspapers overseas, though, were even more loyal than the Welsh in Wales. He also observed that Britain was currently friendless among the European nations because of the opprobrium it had attracted by going to war in South Africa. In defence of the empire, Edwards insisted that if the British army was winning victories in south east Africa, then 'more silent but more blessed work' was being done by the British in the north east of that continent.[61] He reported that 23,000 people were at work on the Aswan dam, of whom 20,000 were Egyptians. Edwards believed the huge lake created by the project would be 'a fountain of life and comfort for a country that would have been wasted and parched'.[62] In a complex passage, Edwards compared the liberal British empire favourably with the despotic Pharaohs, and at the same time praised the benefits the British empire had brought through peace rather than military might.

> It is so much better to make the wilderness blossom like a garden than erect massive pyramids to commemorate oppressors. Yes, so much better is the work of the twenty three thousand who are constructing the dam than the work of the two hundred thousand who are extending the limits of the empire in the same continent but the other side of the equator. The sword flashing in the sun attracts the attention of thousands, but it is the old rusty spade that does the best work. Britain has made much use of the sword and the cannon; it has also made better, more permanent and more sublime use of the plough and the spade.[63]

57 '... atal yr ysbryd daionus gredaf sydd o hyd yn ysbryd Prydain – ysbryd cyfiawnder, trugaredd, a gwroldeb, na wnai, pe yn gwybyd, bechu yn erbyn iawnder unrhyw wlad wanach na hi ei hun', *Tarian y Gweithiwr*, 8 Feb. 1900.   58 'Nid oes raid i neb ofni fod y Wladfa yn llai Prydeinig ei hianian', *Y Drafod*, 5 Jan. 1900.   59 *Cymru*, 105:18 (15 Apr. 1900) 197.   60 'Mae'r Cymry'n deyrngarol iawn i'r ymherodraeth y mae eu gwlad yn rhan ohoni. Y mae'n wir fod papurau newyddion Cymru wedi condemnio y rhyfel sydd wedi dwyn cymaint o alar i'n teuluoedd, oherwydd tybient y gallasem gael pob peth ddymunem wrth gerdded llwybr heddwch', ibid. 198.   61 '... gwaith distawach, ond mwy bendithiol', ibid. 200.   62 '... ffynnon bywyd a chysur i wlad fuasai'n anial a sychedig', ibid. 201.   63 'Gymaint yn well yw

Edwards continued by reflecting on how Wales could best further the work of the British empire. During the South African War *Cymru* carried a monthly digest of war developments and letters written by Welsh soldiers in action. Edwards also frequently praised Welsh troops for their bravery, conduct and contribution to the war effort. But Edwards emphasized that Wales' mission was also in part a religious one and, more importantly, one involving participation in imperial government. 'Before long I hope to see Welsh men going out, not only as missionaries for Christ, but as the rulers of countries', he wrote.[64] Noting that up to that time few Welsh had taken the 'difficult' Civil Service examinations, and fewer still passed them, he nevertheless hoped to live to see the day when 'Welshmen would start playing their part alongside English, Scots and Irish in ruling India, Egypt and southern Africa'.[65] To Edwards, this was inevitable due to the characteristics of the Welsh:

> the time will come for Wales to play its part in the civilisation and governance of the world. The tolerance of the Welsh and their love for elevating nations enables them to rule with a powerful meekness. Our schools, are they not, are preparing benefactors for the world.[66]

This marked a shift away from the earlier common belief that the Welsh role in empire was predominantly religious. Edwards believed Welsh people were particularly suited to govern, and were also ideal colonists. These themes often appear in his writing. In the 'Conclusion' to *Wales* (1901), his history of the country written for the 'Story of the Nations' series, Edwards looked outwards not inwards, and presented the Welsh as active participants and shapers rather than passive subjects of empire. He argued that 'the life of Wales, in the intense conservatism of its unbroken continuity, has not been selfish. The desire to give has been as strong as the desire to retain. No colonist throws himself more readily into the life of his adopted country, but the new country will have an Eisteddvod and a Sunday school.'[67] The Welsh would serve

gwneyd i'r anialwch flodeuo fel gardd na chodi pyramidiau anferth er cof am orthrymwyr. Ie, gymaint yn well yw gwaith y tair mil ar hugain sydd yn gwneyd yr argae na gwaith y dau can mil sydd yn yr un cyfandir, ond yr ochr arall i'r cyhydedd, yn estyn terfynau yr ymherodraeth. Y mae fflachiad y cleddyf yn yr haul yn tynnu sylw'r miloedd, ond yr hen raw rydlyd sydd yn gwneyd y gwaith goreu. Y mae Prydain wedi gwneud llawer o ddefnydd o'r cleddyf a'r fagnel; y mae hefyd wedi gwneyd defnydd gwell a mwy parhaus a mwy aruchel o'r aradr a'r rhaw', ibid. **64** 'Cyn hir gobeithiaf weled bechgyn Cymru yn myned allan, nid yn unig yn genhadon dros Grist, ond hefyd yn llyodraethwyr gwledydd', ibid. **65** '... yn dechreu cymeryd eu rhan gyda Saeson ac Ysgotiaid a Gwyddelod, i reoli yr India a'r Aifft a deheubarthau Affrig', ibid. **66** 'Ond daw yr amser i Gymru gymeryd ei rhan yng ngwareiddiad ac yn llywodraethiad y byd. Mae goddefgarwch Cymro, a'i gariad at godi cenedl, yn ei gymhwyso at reoli gydag addfwynder nerthol. Y mae ein hysgolion, ond odid, yn paratoi cymhwynaswyr i'r byd', ibid. **67** Edwards, *Wales*, 403–4.

their adoptive countries unquestioningly, but their Welshness, or at least ele-
ments of it, would be retained. It might be argued that in this respect
Edwards' thoughts, although rooted in loyalty to the British empire, also
reveal an ambition for an international role and reflect his belief in a 'Greater
Wales'. This separate Welsh transnational empire, based on the expatriate
Welsh as well as those at home, partly coincided with the geographic limits of
the British empire (including what some scholars have begun to term the
'British world'), but also went beyond them.[68] As Edwards insisted,

> [The Welshman's] conservative desire for independence is strong
> enough to send him to almost superhuman toil in inhospitable
> Patagonia, and to maintain Welsh newspapers and magazines, full of
> old-world poetry and half-legendary history, among the modern and
> practical organs of the opinion of the United States. But the remi-
> niscences of the old life are but a recreation of mind. In the struggle
> for American Independence, in the developing patriotism of the
> British Colonies, the Welshman has been among the foremost in
> devotion and energy. The first period of Welsh history ends with the
> poet's lament for its fallen princes; the second ends with the poet's
> vision of a future of more self-conscious life and of greater service.[69]

It can be argued, therefore, that to regard Edwards merely as a supporter
of the British empire misses the manner in which his analysis of Wales' contemporary and historical condition shaped his thinking about that imperial
polity. And in envisaging an imperial destiny for the Welsh as rulers as well
as servants, Edwards showed himself to favour the idea of empire, provided
it was run by people who were suitable for the role. Welsh characteristics
made its people superior to the English as instruments of empire, and Welsh
people could best fulfil their imperial role by remaining patriotic to Wales
first and foremost. 'Let us ensure our children become patriotic Welsh people;
by doing that we will make them stronger and better. It is the most patriotic
parts of our empire that give us the best rulers, the most successful generals, the most influential thinkers.'[70]

Empire was represented in Welsh journalism in news stories, editorial
polemics and missionary reports, and writers and editors implied a set of particularly Welsh roles in British overseas expansion. From William Rees' sym-

---

68 See Carl Bridge and Kent Fedorowich, 'Mapping the British world', *Journal of Imperial and
Commonwealth History*, 2:31 (May, 2003) 1–15; also available in Bridge and Fedorowich (eds),
The British world, 1–15. 69 Edwards, *Wales*, 404. 70 'Gadewch i ni gadw ein plant yn Gymry
gwladgarol; trwy hynny gwnawn hwy'n gryfach ac yn well. Y rhannau mwyaf gwladgarol o'n
hymerodraeth ni sy'n rhoddi y rheolwyr goreu, y cadfridogion mwyaf llwyddiannus, y med-
dylwyr mwyaf dylanwadol', *Cymru*, 105:18 (15 Apr. 1900) 201.

pathy for Continental nationalism, or the Liberal republicanism of Thomas Gee, through the cultural criticism of such missionaries as William Pryse, to the embracing of an ethnically-defined idea of participation in a British empire by T.E. Ellis and O.M. Edwards, leading sections of the press in Wales, in both English and Welsh languages, were preoccupied by the problems and possibilities of empire. In part, this stemmed from a concern to explore Wales' asymmetrical relationship with England and the other nations of the then United Kingdom by finding ways of expressing Welsh 'difference', the search for which led to the launching of many Welsh newspaper and magazine titles into an often uncertain market. But it was also a product of multiple and serial attempts to establish for Wales a distinctive place in the wider world and a clearly identifiable role in its affairs. In certain respects, this brio, some might say bravado, grew out of an ambition by journalists, who all too frequently regarded themselves as public intellectuals and social leaders, to punch above their weight in relation to their more powerful and media-savvy English neighbours. By so doing, however, they ensured that empire, in both its religious and secular forms, continued throughout the Victorian and Edwardian periods to provide the vocabulary and the dominant mental frameworks in which the 'Wales' signified by the press might position itself in a far broader, even global, context. The currents of 'imperial thinking' that coursed so powerfully through the press not only theorized Welsh difference, and offered alternative ways of 'being Welsh', both of which were intended to resist integration into an 'English' world, but they did so in a manner that paradoxically but unmistakeably sought imperial solutions to their perceived sense of powerlessness. From the cattle ranches of Patagonia to the 'benign' offices of British colonial administration, the anti-imperial response of the Welsh to the European monarchies, and even in some measure to English domination of the British state, over time legitimated and made possible other forms of direct Welsh involvement in the Western colonial moment.

5. Mutiny or freedom fight? The 1857 Indian Mutiny and the Irish press

JILL C. BENDER

The 'Devil's Wind', the 'Mutiny of the Bengal Army', the 'First Freedom Struggle', the 'Great Indian Mutiny' – a variety of names have been used to describe the Indian insurrection that shook the mid-nineteenth-century British empire to its core. The wide range of labels is significant, reflecting the diverse responses of those involved in and influenced by the violent uprising. Contemporaries and, subsequently, historians have provided different interpretations, some presenting the events of 1857 as a military mutiny, others as a nationalist uprising of the Indian people.[1] In Ireland the insurrection elicited particularly varied and often unpredictable responses, reflecting the island's ambiguous status within the empire. The Act of Union 1801 legislatively drew Ireland into the United Kingdom, yet economic and administrative integration was never complete. Indeed, Ireland's relationship with Britain occasionally proved more reminiscent of the ties existing between an imperial power and a colony.[2] This has led some academics to describe Ireland's history as that of a colony in all but name.[3] To many contemporaries however, the position seemed much more ambiguous. The diverse political, religious, and ethnic groups that made up the island's population

---

1 Early historians of the event include J.W. Kaye, Colonel G.B. Malleson, and T. Rice Holmes, who all presented it as a military mutiny. In 1909, V.D. Savarkar seized on the event as a means of generating support for Indian nationalism, publishing *The Indian war of independence of 1857*. A number of additional works coincided with the centenary, including S.N. Sen's *Eighteen fifty-seven* (Delhi, 1957). More recently, see Saul David, *The Indian Mutiny, 1857* (London, 2002). 2 David Fitzpatrick, 'Ireland and the empire' in Andrew Porter (ed.), *The Oxford history of the British empire*, iii: *the nineteenth century* (Oxford, 1999) 495. 3 In recent years, historians have applied colonial models to Ireland in order to explore its role in England's early-modern expansion into an Atlantic world. See for example David Beers Quinn, *Ireland and America: their early associations, 1500–1640* (Liverpool, 1991); Nicholas P. Canny, *The Elizabethan conquest of Ireland: a pattern established, 1565–1576* (New York, 1976); K.R. Andrews, N.P. Canny and P.E.H. Hair (eds), *The westward enterprise: English activities in Ireland, the Atlantic and America, 1480–1650* (Liverpool, 1978); N.P. Canny, *Kingdom and colony: Ireland in the Atlantic world, 1560–1800* (Baltimore, 1988). For an exploration of the role Ireland subsequently played in Britain's empire see Keith Jeffery (ed.), *'An Irish empire'? Aspects of Ireland and the British empire* (Manchester, 1996). For insights into how the colonial context has been applied to present-day Ireland see Stephen Howe, *Ireland and empire: colonial legacies in Irish history and culture* (Oxford, 2000).

each adopted their own views regarding the nature of Ireland's connection with Britain.[4]

As the first event truly to challenge the 'second British empire', the Mutiny provided an excellent opportunity for the Irish, nationalist and unionist,[5] Catholic and Protestant, to express and promote their own views. Further, the event coincided with a period of growth in the island's press industry, providing a medium through which these causes could be voiced. The repeal of taxes on advertisements and the abolition of the stamp on newspapers coupled with increasing literacy rates to set the press industry on the road to lower costs and potentially wider circulation.[6] As Marie-Louise Legg points out, newspapers reflected 'the self-awareness of Ireland as a country separate from Britain' and, throughout the nineteenth century, provided political movements with 'an important vehicle for their propaganda'.[7]

This chapter uses Irish press reports of the 1857 Indian Mutiny as a window through which to glimpse how the Irish perceived their own role within the mid-nineteenth-century British empire. In the face of an imperial crisis, did the Irish press encourage readers to rally behind the empire, or to support the empire's adversaries? Did contemporaries attempt to establish an affinity between Ireland and India? How did the different elements within Ireland respond to each other and to the various opinions expressed about the insurrection? Did the Mutiny modify attitudes towards race in Ireland in the same way that it did in Britain? Finally, what, if anything, does this tell us about Ireland's relationship to the empire?

As disseminators of political ideas as well as news on a local, national and international level, newspapers have the potential to provide insights into the society whose readership sustains them. However, when using newspapers as a historical source, it is important to be aware of the biases and motives of those individuals responsible for running each newspaper. Although most Irish newspapers remained relatively conservative in nature until the 1870s, the nineteenth century saw a significant increase in nationalist and Catholic-associated journals.[8] Indeed, by the time news of the Indian Mutiny reached Ireland in June 1857, there seemed to be a newspaper to suit just about any reader.

To examine the cross-section of different political, religious and regional views on the event, the analysis that follows focuses on five different con-

4 S.B. Cook, 'The Irish raj: social origins and careers of Irishmen in the Indian Civil Service, 1855–1914', *Journal of Social History*, 20 (1987) 507.   5 Throughout this chapter, the terms 'unionist' and 'conservative' refer to those individuals who favoured, or at least were hesitant to change, Ireland's mid-nineteenth-century political connection with Britain.   6 R.V. Comerford, 'Ireland, 1850–70: post-famine and mid-Victorian' in W.E. Vaughan (ed.), *A new history of Ireland*, iv: *Ireland under the Union: I, 1801–70* (Oxford, 1989) 376, 390–1.   7 Marie-Louise Legg, introduction to *Ireland: politics and society through the press, 1760–1922* microfilm series (Woodbridge, Conn., 2000).   8 Hugh Oram, *The newspaper book: a history of newspapers in Ireland, 1649–1983* (Dublin, 1983) 43, 77.

temporary journals. In particular, two Dublin-based newspapers with very different political and religious leanings, the *Dublin Evening Mail* and the *Nation*, provide the basis for the following research. The *Dublin Evening Mail* was founded in 1823 and became an instant success, built on a nasty 'diet of virulent anti-Catholic bigotry'.[9] Although the paper had apparently toned down its rhetoric and become subtler in its prejudices by 1857, the journal presented a very conservative-unionist and Protestant take on the Indian Mutiny. On the opposite extreme of the journalistic spectrum lay the *Nation*. Established in 1842 by Thomas Davis, Charles Gavan Duffy and John Blake Dillon, the *Nation* initially represented the journalistic arm of the Young Ireland movement. The nationalist journal was far from subtle in its agenda. In 1857, supporting the sepoys (Indian soldiers enlisted in the service of the British East India Company) from the start, the *Nation* seized on the Indian insurrection as a means of propagating its own anti-British, pro-Catholic, nationalist sentiments.

The *Freeman's Journal*, another Dublin-based newspaper, was initially founded in the eighteenth century as a Protestant paper. A change in ownership in 1854, however, set the journal on a course of 'constitutional nationalism and catholicity'.[10] Still, at the time of the Mutiny, only three years after the change in allegiance, the newspaper continued to be somewhat conservative. It thus offers an interesting contrast to the *Dublin Evening Mail* and the *Nation*. The pages of the *Belfast Daily Mercury* and the *Ulsterman* meanwhile provide an insight into how the Mutiny was reported in the north of the island. Calling for reform and the abolition of the East India Company regiments from the start, the *Belfast Daily Mercury* represented 'conservatively minded Protestant Liberals' in Ulster.[11] The *Ulsterman*, on the other hand, appeared to be Ulster's equivalent of the *Nation*, representing Catholic nationalists in the province. Like the *Nation*, the *Ulsterman* saw the Indian Mutiny as an opportunity for Irish nationalists to intertwine the sepoy insurrection with the Irish cause.

THE ORIGINS OF THE UPRISING

Officially, the British declared the uprising to be a military mutiny, sparked by the introduction of the Enfield rifle to India.[12] The Enfield represented a technological improvement in weaponry, simplifying the firing process by combining the bullet and the powder in a single cartridge. To ease passage and ignition, each cartridge was coated with pig or cow fat; unfortunately,

9 Ibid. 49.   10 Ibid. 65.   11 A.T. Harrison (ed.), *The Graham Indian Mutiny papers* (Belfast, 1980) 142.   12 Eric Stokes, *The peasant armed: the Indian revolt of 1857*, ed. C.A. Bayly (Oxford, 1986) 4.

this represented a religious insult both to the army's Muslims and to its Hindus. In response, on 10 May 1857, the sepoys at Meerut refused to use the new rifles, and initiated a violent rebellion. In the ensuing chaos, the suspect new ammunition provided a convenient explanation. However, many believed that the true origins of the insurrection ran deeper. Some criticized the advanced age and incompetent leadership of British officers in India. The decision to issue the new ammunition reflected an imperfect acquaintance with the customs of those under British rule and a weakness in British authority. Others blamed British missionaries in India, who were accused of pushing natives toward a conversion they were not yet prepared for and, consequently, destroying the trust established between the British and the sepoys serving in the military.

For the most part, press reports syndicated throughout Ireland varied little in their depiction of the progress of the fighting and military campaigns.[13] Editorials and articles on the subject used the raw news in different ways, however, offering an insight into local opinion. Exploring the possible origins of the conflict provided the Irish – nationalist or unionist, Catholic or Protestant – with an opportunity to shed light on and devote thought to their own specific situations. From the start, Irish unionists wrestled with the deeper implications of the Mutiny, questioning why such violence could occur and how similar situations might be avoided in future imperial endeavours. According to Irish nationalists, blaming the uprising on the new cartridges was ridiculous; the origins of the rising lay in a full century of British oppression in India.

While many unionist journals discussed the various explanations for the outbreak of the Mutiny, some approached the potential causes as 'questions for future consideration'.[14] Their primary concern was to ensure an effective response to the immediate threat of violence. In a letter to the editor of the *Dublin Evening Mail*, one correspondent compared the *raj* to a burning house:

> If a man's house is on fire, his object is to extinguish the flame, and to this end are all his efforts directed. When the fire is extinguished, he will naturally inquire into the causes which produced it. Our Indian empire is on fire – the flame is confined to the Bengal Presidency. Let us direct all our energies towards subduing it. This done, we shall have ample time and opportunity to consider and remove the causes which led to its ignition.[15]

According to the *Belfast Daily Mercury*, the solution – and for that matter, the cause – seemed almost obvious. The root of the problem lay in the 'imperfect

13 Harrison, *Graham papers*, 142. 14 *Dublin Evening Mail*, 19 Aug. 1857. 15 Ibid.

military organisation and command' exercised by the East India Company.[16] The journal called for the abolition of the Company regiments and the consolidation of native troops under the direct control of the British crown.

Although Catholic-nationalist newspapers in the north and the south of the island initially differed in their predictions,[17] they more or less agreed from the start on the origins of the violence. The *Nation* immediately dismissed the cartridge affair as 'absurd', suggesting instead that it was only a matter of time until a people as oppressed as the Indians should desire independence. Similarly, the Belfast-based *Ulsterman* recognized the cartridge issue as only the 'immediate cause'. Again, rebellion was seen as an inevitable result of oppression. 'Public testimony has shown that the English in India treat the natives as dogs; even dogs will turn and bite when they are too cruelly used.'[18]

Irish nationalists immediately claimed a sense of kinship with the sepoys. According to nationalists, the most obvious form of oppression suffered under British control was that of religious discrimination. In Ireland, the first half of the nineteenth century had witnessed political conflicts drawn more or less along religious lines. The Act of Union of 1801 had left the Catholic question unanswered and it was not until the Catholic Relief Act of 1829 that Catholics were granted the right to political participation. But as Oliver MacDonagh points out, the political tactics and organization adopted by Catholics in pursuit of emancipation did not disappear with the 1829 legislative victory.[19] Thus, the thirty years preceding the Indian Mutiny witnessed continued attempts by Catholics to improve their political standing, and Protestant efforts to maintain their existing position.[20] To nationalists, there appeared to be similarities in the political and religious uncertainties of Ireland and India. In the eyes of some Irish Catholics, the fear of religious conversion that led the Meerut sepoys to protest against the Enfield cartridges proved to be a very real and very dangerous threat.

At the time of the insurrection, missionary activity was relatively new to India. Initially, the East India Company had strictly prohibited all missionary activity, and even later the freedom to proselytise remained restricted to Protestants. The first Catholic missionaries did not appear in significant numbers until the 1830s, when anti-Catholic legislation was relaxed. For years, Catholics had eyed the Protestant orphanages and schools in India with suspicion.[21] The pages of the *Nation* suggest that even with the presence of

---

16 *Belfast Daily Mercury*, 30 June 1857.   17 The *Nation* anticipated the sepoys' success from the very start, commenting that even should they fail in their efforts Britain was bound to lose India. The *Ulsterman*, in contrast, felt that although the British would never succeed in fully 'eradicat[ing] disaffection and discontent', it was only a matter of time before the British would regain control. *Ulsterman*, 1 July 1857.   18 *Ulsterman*, 1 July 1857.   19 Oliver MacDonagh, 'Introduction: Ireland and the Union, 1801–1870' in Vaughan (ed.) *New history of Ireland*, iv, 1. 20 Comerford, 'Ireland, 1850–70', 385–6.   21 Anne Maher, 'Missionary links: past, present

Catholic bodies, suspicion remained intense when violence erupted in May 1857. Reports published in the newspaper maintained that orders had been given to deny the monthly allowance to wives of Catholic soldiers on military leave unless their children were sent to Protestant schools. Further, rumours abounded suggesting that, at the death of the parents, Catholic children in India would be placed in Protestant schools to be raised as Protestants. These fears were heightened by the story of Mrs Kirley, who had supposedly converted to Protestantism after the death of her husband. The journal devoted weeks to establishing the wishes of her late husband regarding the education of his children. The issue at stake was the Catholic children's future, their mother having already proved to be a lost cause, her conversion only important in that it proved 'how well-founded were the suspicions of Catholics as to the proselytizing tendencies of the Patriotic Fund officials'.[22] With Irish Catholics being targeted by evangelical Protestants in India, it seemed likely to some Catholic nationalists that the same missionaries were the cause of the Indian Mutiny. Catholic nationalists were not opposed to missionary activity *per se*, but rather to its Protestant manifestation. In an article reprinted from the *Wexford People*, the readers of the *Nation* were reminded not to forget the words of the Bishop of Almira: 'If our government were Catholic, I would promise that within twenty years India would be wholly Christian.'[23]

According to the nationalist press, a further parallel between Ireland and India could be found in terms of atrocities supposedly committed by the sepoys in India and British acts of brutality inscribed in the pages of Irish history.[24] Tales of children tossed into the air to be caught on the points of British bayonets, and of the slaughter of Irish women and children merely fifty years earlier, were re-told in the pages of the nationalist journals. In the eyes of the nationalist press, the British were now only experiencing for themselves the cruel practices that they had perfected in Ireland and subsequently taught the sepoys.

In addition to intertwining Irish history with Indian history, the Irish nationalist press attempted to compare the Indian present with the potential future of Ireland. Pointing to the sepoys' response to oppressive colonial rule, the *Nation* called for a similar reaction from the Irish: 'in the twinkling of an eye, without previous sign or signal of their intention, thirty thousand Sepoys have flung her [Britain's] authority to the winds, and at last, though late, stand embattled on the side of the people they have so long oppressed. Will such a day ever arise for Ireland?'[25] According to the journal, Ireland and

and future' in Michael Holmes and Denis Holmes (eds), *Ireland and India: connections, comparisons, contrasts* (Dublin, 1997) 30–1. **22** *Nation*, 19 Dec. 1857. **23** *Nation*, 24 Oct. 1857. **24** *Nation*, 8 Aug. 1857. **25** *Nation*, 18 July 1857.

India shared a history of British atrocities and Protestant proselytism – why
then should they not also share a future free from British rule? Throughout
Ireland, nationalists posted proclamations and manifestos calling for the Irish
to seize this moment of English distraction and weakness to launch an Irish
revolt. While the placards did not secure this goal, they did prove successful in antagonizing Protestants.[26]

IRISH PARTICIPATION IN BRITAIN'S INDIAN EMPIRE

The controversy among the Irish regarding the Indian Mutiny was by no
means limited to explaining the initial outbreak of violence. Irish participation in the British *raj* also provoked a multitude of questions regarding
Ireland's appropriate role in the crisis, and what it implied about Ireland's
relationship with Britain and her empire. That the Irish did participate is
undeniable, especially when one takes into account the sarcastic adage about
the British empire: 'The Irish fought for it, the Scottish and Welsh ran it,
but the English kept the profits.'[27] Indeed, by the mid-nineteenth century,
astounding numbers of Irish found themselves defending the empire's interests overseas.

Many of the most famous participants in the crisis – the Lawrence brothers, John Nicholson and Frederick Sleigh Roberts – were Irish Protestants
who had obtained influential positions in the service of the East India
Company and the British army. Irish contributions to the 'second British
empire', however, were limited neither to the actions of officers nor to those
of the Protestant faith. Irish involvement was essential to the British empire
in India due to the sheer number of Irish soldiers fighting in the ranks. By
1857 the Irish constituted over fifty per cent of the East India Company's
white soldiers.[28]

A number of factors motivated the Irish to seek the advantages offered by
the empire. Many of the ambitious and well-educated sons of the Irish gentry
and professional middle classes turned to service in India as a means by which
to climb the social hierarchy.[29] Some had family members who had served in
India, and the decision to follow suit seemed only natural. This was the case,
at least, for Frederick Roberts, a young Irish subaltern in 1857, who eventually went on to become a field marshal. Roberts' father had enjoyed a distin-

26 Harrison, *Graham papers*, 143.   27 Cook, 'The Irish raj', 509.   28 Patrick Cadell, 'Irish
soldiers in India', *Irish Sword*, 1 (1950) 79. The Irish constituted over forty per cent of the
combined East India Company's European regiments and the regular British army serving in
India throughout the 1850s. See Thomas Bartlett, 'The Irish soldier in India, 1750–1947' in
Holmes and Holmes (eds), *Ireland and India*, 16.   29 T.G. Fraser, 'Ireland and India' in Jeffery
(ed.), *'An Irish empire'?*, 77–8.

guished career in the service of the East India Company and Roberts, himself, later explained in a short memorandum: 'I had quite made up my mind to be a soldier, I had never thought of any other profession.'[30] Even for those without the education and upbringing of Roberts, military service in India provided an important employment opportunity. Troops were often well-paid and well-fed, and service held the promise of both promotion and prestige – all potentially enticing factors in an Ireland still recovering from the Famine and with a small industrial base limited to the Dublin and Belfast regions.[31]

Even for those lacking military ambition, imperial service provided avenues of opportunity. Most notably, with the introduction of open and competitive entrance examinations, the Indian Civil Service became a very real and desirable option for many. Irish universities responded enthusiastically, proving adept at preparing students for the test. Although changes were made at institutions throughout the island, Trinity College, Dublin responded most quickly and thoroughly, introducing chairs and courses in subjects pertinent to the examination as early as the 1850s.[32] According to the *Dublin Evening Mail*, the press played an influential role in the changes enacted by Trinity, pointing out the shortcomings in the educational system in the early years of the competitive examination. Further, the journal suggested that the curriculum changes were necessary to save the faltering university. 'Two summers ago we had to record the discreditable fact, that out of 14 candidates from Trinity College at a public examination, not one was successful. The repetition of such failures would soon have levelled the national University, surrounded as it was by Whig and Romish enemies, to the dust.'[33] Correct or not, the very idea that the alterations in curriculum had saved the university suggests that the public desired a stronger performance in the competitive examinations. The response to the academic changes indicates that students appeared willing to attend universities that prepared them for a future in India. Imperial service thus continued to be viewed by many university-educated Irish as a desirable occupation, at least one worth competing for.

Written in the late summer and early autumn of 1858, the letters of James Graham suggest that the violence of the Mutiny did little to alter the prestigious reputation of a career in the imperial service. However, the correspondence of the young Irishman, who held a position in the Commissariat at the time of the Mutiny, also indicates that scepticism regarding the benefits of an Irish education continued to exist. In letters home to his sister, Anne, Graham assessed the future prospects of his nephew. According to Graham, his nephew's classical education was entirely inappropriate for the service

30 Frederick Roberts, *Letters written during the Indian Mutiny* (London, 1924) xvii.   31 Cook, 'The Irish raj', 511.   32 Belfast established an Indian-language program that rivalled that of Trinity, while Cork and Galway both introduced additional courses. Ibid. 510–11.   33 *Dublin Evening Mail*, 5 Aug. 1857.

examinations, which tested knowledge in English, German, French, 'Hindustani', history and geography. While Graham considered the Irish schools to be superior in the teaching of English, he found them lacking in the necessary modern languages and the 'top-dressing which bring him [the scholar] up to the examination mark'.[34] When Irish institutions fell short, Graham did not hesitate to look to England. He expressed his opinion that his sister should send her younger children to be educated at English public schools, commenting that 'you have no idea what a gain it is in after life. They there make friends who have the power, and do assist them in their future career.'[35] According to Graham, English connections could get the mid-nineteenth-century Irishman that much further in his career aspirations.

The Mutiny provided Irishmen with greater military opportunities. The increased need for manpower dictated by the internal restructuring of the Indian army, coupled with the decreasing number of available soldiers due to death and injury, morbidly improved the opportunities for any surviving and healthy individuals. Despite Graham's low expectations for his nephew's chances at obtaining a position in the Indian service, he encouraged him to apply, suggesting that the timing might be advantageous.[36] In a similar vein, Frederick Roberts wrote to his family about his frequent promotions in the wake of the Mutiny. Although evidently excited by his personal advancement, he lamented to his mother: 'I believe I am promoted in the room of some of the poor fellows who have lost their lives by these gallant *Sepoys*! but I would far rather remain a 2nd Lieut. all my life than rise through such horrid means.'[37]

For those opposed to the imperial connection, the growing number of Irish defending the empire's interests overseas provided an entirely different opportunity. Recognizing Ireland as 'the great reservoir from which England has but too often and too easily recruited her armies', the nationalist press adopted enlistment – or perhaps more accurately, anti-enlistment – as a means to resist Ireland's connection with England.[38] The nationalist press in the north did not appear to adopt the anti-enlistment cause as enthusiastically as papers in the south, perhaps due to the smaller number of Catholics in Ulster. One of the strongest advocates of anti-enlistment on the island was the *Nation*. Almost from the first reports of violence, the journal strove to strike fear into the minds of those Irishmen contemplating enlistment, conjuring up the image of all that might go wrong at home while one was away fighting England's battles. According to the *Nation*, loved ones might lose their land to unjust English landlords, or relatives already forced to seek their livelihood in England might be sent home to starve or enter a workhouse should they so much as ask for a

34 James Graham to Anne Graham, 3 Aug. 1858, printed in Harrison, *Graham papers*, 111–12. 35 James Graham to Anne Graham, 17 Oct. 1858, printed in ibid. 116.   36 James Graham to Anne Graham, 24 Sept. 1858, printed in ibid. 114.   37 Roberts to his mother, 11 June 1857, printed in *Letters written during the Indian Mutiny*, 16.   38 *Nation*, 5 Sept. 1857.

much-deserved holiday.[39] Just in case such alleged treatment at home was not sufficient to dissuade Irish Catholics from enlisting, the *Nation* periodically published accounts of the horrors and discrimination faced by the Irish in India 'to damp the ardour of any would-be soldier'.[40] According to the nationalist press, England's abuse of Ireland, at home and abroad, would not cease should the Irish choose to support the empire's cause overseas.

Regardless of nationalist efforts to discourage Irish enlistment, the Irish continued to participate in defending the Indian *raj*. This left the nationalist journals with the difficult task of explaining why some Irish Catholics were choosing to fight alongside the English. If one was to believe the pages of the nationalist press, they could not be supporting the empire of their own volition. Instead, according to the *Nation*, the Irish serving in the Indian service were nothing more than victims of circumstance and English oppression. 'There never was a greater fallacy than to suppose that enlisting is, with the Irishman, the result of loyalty or of any political reasoning whatsoever. It proceeds from a love of military life, or from dislike to enter a workhouse. When employment fails, it is well known that the Irishman talks of "taking the shilling".' While the *Nation* admitted that occasionally the Irish undertook military service for reasons other than poverty, the journal argued that for the vast majority of Irish Catholics, the Indian Mutiny was not such an occasion.[41]

When the journal knew the names, families and backgrounds of Irish Catholics fighting for the empire, explanation became an even more complicated task. After all, how were journals like the *Nation* to support those Irish Catholics who were fighting for the very cause abhorred by nationalists? With many individuals in Ireland connected in some way to someone serving in India, condemning all individuals involved would alienate readers and thus threaten the nationalist cause as well as newspaper sales. As a result, the pages of the *Nation* occasionally reflect a tenuous balancing act, supporting individual Catholics in India while condemning Britain's presence in the territory. Such an effort is apparent in the journal's October 1857 memorial for one Irish casualty.

> We ask today of the readers of THE NATION, their prayers for the soul of Corporal HENRY DOWNEY – a noble hearted and true Irishman, who fell at Cawnpore on the 26th of June – a victim to English rapacity and thirst for dominion ... [The English] pretend that we have no tear for HENRY DOWNEY, because we curse the day he took their hire! They pretend that to predict and pray for the fall of their blood-brought Empire, is to forget that they will send our brothers whom they trepanned the first into the abyss!... We ask

39 *Nation*, 29 Aug. 1857.   40 *Nation*, 31 Oct. 1857.   41 *Nation*, 5 Sept. 1857.

then, that the readers of THE NATION offer up a prayer for the souls of HENRY DOWNEY and our Catholic fellow countrymen.

According to the *Nation*, Downey was 'one of a host of men in the ranks of England's legions' to be numbered among the journal's 'most faithful adherents – officers and privates – men who would not prove untrue to Ireland did she need their aid'.[42] Serving in India, thus, did not require checking one's nationalist sentiments at the door. It was possible to support Irish independence and to fight for the empire overseas.

Nicknaming the *Nation* and its nationalist compatriots the 'sepoy journals', unionist newspapers were noticeably disturbed by nationalist antics. From the *Belfast Daily Mercury* to the *Dublin Evening Mail*, Irish unionist newspapers praised those volunteering for service in India and condemned the anti-enlistment campaign waged by the 'Ultramontane' press.[43] However, despite their apparent support for the cause in India, even unionist journals occasionally faltered in their loyalty, expressing frustration with Ireland's ambiguous position in the British empire. When the government announced the possibility that the Irish militia might not be called on to defend the country in the absence of regular troops, the *Dublin Evening Mail* responded with sarcastic frustration. 'But surely that fastidious caution of "No Irish need apply", would be not only ludicrously, but disastrously out of place in this extremity.'[44]

IRISH RACIAL ATTITUDES

If the Mutiny sparked questions about Ireland's relationship with Britain and her empire, it also called into question the status of non-Europeans under Britain's imperial control. To many Britons, the insurrection signalled Indian rejection of assimilation to Western norms.[45] Optimistic early nineteenth-century humanitarian expectations were disappointed.[46] Indeed, the insurrection caused considerable damage to British-Indian relations, and the years that followed the Mutiny saw a significant hardening of British racial attitudes in India and at home. These changes were perhaps most evident in the massive restructuring of Britain's imperial presence in India that followed the Mutiny. In response to 1857, the British abolished the East India Company and con-

---

42 *Nation*, 10 Oct. 1857.   43 In particular, the *Dublin Evening Mail* praised the Roscommon Militia for volunteering for service, writing that the 'spirited conduct' of the men of Roscommon reflected how 'the disinterested advice of the *Nation* and its fellow-labourers in the cause of disloyalty has been received by the people'. *Dublin Evening Mail*, 9 Oct. 1857.   44 *Dublin Evening Mail*, 7 Aug. 1857.   45 John M. MacKenzie, 'Empire and metropolitan cultures' in Porter (ed.) *Oxford history of the British empire*, iii, 280.   46 Andrew Porter, 'Trusteeship, antislavery and humanitarianism' in ibid. 198.

solidated the Indian empire under the control of the British crown. The military structure in India also witnessed substantial change, aimed at improving British surveillance and diminishing the chances of another insurrection. The crown assumed direct control of the Company's regiments, while a new Indian army was established officered entirely by Europeans. The ratio of Indians to Britons in the army was significantly reduced.[47]

These changing attitudes also became apparent in Ireland, well before the violence had been suppressed. On 5 September 1857, the Reverend George Salmon, a well-respected mathematician and theologian who later became the provost of Trinity College,[48] preached a sermon on behalf of the Church Missionary Society in which he hinted at the changing perception of Indian natives. 'Fifty years ago it was urged that there was no pressing haste for the conversion of the Hindoos, because they were a civilized and a moral people, more mild and sober than most Europeans. This is not likely to be soon said again now.'[49] Salmon refused to abandon his humanitarian ambitions, however, and encouraged the missionaries not to let the Mutiny impede their religious efforts.

In the wake of the Mutiny distinctions were often drawn between Muslims and Hindus – some believed that Muslims has started the insurrection in an effort to re-establish the Mughal dynasty.[50] However, as Salmon's sermon indicates, suspicion attached to both peoples. Unionist journals generally did not distinguish between Hindus and Muslims, but depicted all sepoys as vicious murderers, foreshadowing images that would become established tropes in Victorian literature.[51] For many, the mutineers came to represent the most savage individuals, worse even than the 'Red Indians'.[52] As a result, unionist journals in both the north and the south of Ireland began to call for ruthless revenge against the sepoys. The *Northern Whig* argued that the mutineers should be punished mercilessly – 'the murderers should be traced, taken, and straight away hung by the neck until they are dead'.[53] In a similar vein, the *Belfast Daily Mercury* suggested that it was only through comprehensive retribution that the British might feel compensated for atrocities suffered at the hands of the mutineers.[54]

---

47 In the years leading up to the Mutiny the ratio of sepoys to Europeans was approximately 9:1. After the insurrection, it was thought that the ratio should be closer to 3:1. Harrison, *Graham papers*, xliv.   48 Henry Boylan, *A dictionary of Irish biography* (Dublin, 1998, 3rd edn) 389.   49 George Salmon, *The Indian Mutiny and missions: a sermon preached on behalf of the Church Missionary Society, on Sunday, September 5, 1857* (Dublin, 1862) 16.   50 Harrison, *Graham papers*, xlv.   51 See Jenny Sharpe, 'The unspeakable limits of rape: colonial violence and counter insurgency' in Patrick Williams and Laura Chrisman (eds), *Colonial discourse and post-colonial theory: a reader* (Harlow, 1993) 221–43.   52 *Dublin Evening Mail*, 11 Sept. 1857. 53 Harrison, *Graham papers*, 149; *Northern Whig*, 6 Feb. 1858.   54 *Belfast Daily Mercury*, 5 Sept. 1857.

According to the *Belfast Daily Mercury*, the only individuals worse than
the Indian sepoys were the writers of the 'sepoy journals' in Ireland. The
newspaper directly compared Irish nationalists to the Indian rebels. 'But what
shall we say of the Irish demons who gloat over such atrocities as we have
above indicated? Are they not worse than the Sepoys? Have they not fouler
minds and blacker hearts than any Sepoy?'[55] Like the *Belfast Daily Mercury*,
the *Dublin Evening Mail* frequently condemned the nationalist press, com-
paring the 'treasonous' behaviour of the *Nation* to that of the sepoys. The
Irish nationalists posed a particularly difficult quandary for the conservative
journals. While it was simple to call for immediate and harsh revenge against
those misbehaving miles away in India, what was one to do with perceived
traitors at home?

Occasionally conservative newspapers offered a united response to articles
in the *Nation*. One such example surfaced in the *Dublin Evening Mail* on 2
September 1857 and in the *Belfast Daily Mercury* just two days later. The
Nation article in question depicted a conversation in Hell, with only one
Catholic present – a soldier from Tipperary sent to Hell merely for 'taking
the Queen's shilling'. The soldier laments his decision, crying, 'O wisha wisha,
bad look to the day I ever took the Saxon shilling. To die like a haythin,
without priest or prayer; and what harm, if I fell in a good cause?' In
response, both the *Dublin Evening Mail* and the *Belfast Daily Mercury* denied
that the soldier provided an accurate reflection of Catholic sentiment. Instead,
both newspapers pointed to a quote from the *Freeman's Journal*.

> Any idea of jealousy between English and Irish interests seems quite
> to be lost in a feeling of intense indignation and disgust at the atroc-
> ities which would have disgraced even the most noble cause in which
> ever arms were taken. And though it might be supposed an East
> Indian question would have little sympathy here, the outrages com-
> mitted have completely divested the cause of the insurgents of the
> slightest sympathy; and, as far as regards the mercantile classes of
> this city, Protestants or Catholics, Liberals or Conservatives, we find
> but one feeling, that of patriotic indignation against the savages who
> have so outraged our countrymen and countrywomen, as well as those
> of the sister country, and an enthusiastic admiration of the heroic
> courage displayed by so many, of whom Ireland, as well as England,
> has cause to be proud.

According to the *Dublin Evening Mail* the words of the *Freeman's Journal* did
not just present a more accurate reflection of Catholic sentiments regarding
the Indian Mutiny, but also provided a much more 'honest' depiction of the

55 Ibid.

attitudes of Catholics and Protestants alike.[56] The *Belfast Daily Mercury* concluded its discussion of the *Nation*'s article with the suggestion that the ability of the nationalist journals to publish such sentiments was further proof
of the liberty granted by the imperial connection – no other government
would have been so tolerant.[57]

On 10 October 1857, the *Nation* ran an article in direct response to the
angry allegations of treason launched by the unionist press. The article, entitled 'The real "Irish Sepoys"', accused the 'British journals, with their piti-
ful mimics in this country' of resorting to name-calling for lack of a stronger
argument with which to explain British actions in India. Depicting the sepoys
as traitors and collaborators who had helped establish and maintain British
control in India, the *Nation* hinted that the term was more applicable to Irish
unionists.

> *'Sepoys' were those who in their own land were the upholders of foreign*
> *rule* ... 'Sepoys' were the natives of India who, for the hire of England
> – hire wrung out of the blood and tears of their own kindred – were
> used by England to slaughter their own fellow countrymen who dared
> to claim India for the Indians. *To what class of Irishmen will that*
> *description apply?*

The article went on to explain that the nationalist press had never supported
the atrocities committed by the sepoys against their own people, although the
nationalists claimed to expect little else from a people under British rule. It
was only when such violence was exercised *against* the British, rather than
for the British, that the nationalists claimed to have expressed their admira-
tion. The article concluded with the idea that, while, historically, the sepoy
may better represent the Irish unionists, the term had taken on new meaning since the Mutiny:

> the Indian Sepoy now stands before us in another light – in one
> which may make the 'Sepoy' a glorious and honourable title. He has
> arisen from his thraldom; he has returned to his allegiance to his
> country, he no longer strikes *for* his country's oppressors, but *at* them;
> he no longer upholds a foreign rule – he fights for his own 'Immortal
> Green,' and all the world admire and applaud him.[58]

The *Nation* thus claimed proudly to embrace such nicknames as the 'sepoy
journal'. However, its use of the term was not always consistent. The *Nation*

56 *Dublin Evening Mail*, 2 Sept. 1857.   **57** *Belfast Daily Mercury*, 4 Sept. 1857.   **58** *Nation*,
10 Oct. 1857.

had deployed 'sepoy' as a derogatory term to describe its political and religious opponents in September 1857, commenting that 'JOHN BULL, amid the comfort and quiet of London, displays a spirit of revenge and ferocity to the fullest extent as savage as that of the barbarian Sepoy.'[59] Even after the 10 October article explaining the new meaning of 'sepoy', the journal occasionally slipped, describing British 'barbarism' as 'British Sepoyism'.[60]

The nationalist press frequently turned to comparisons to explain and justify the actions of the sepoys as well as Irish support for them. According to the *Nation*, it had been less than a century since a similar popular rising against oppression had occurred in France. 'Just as the French revenged the iniquitous rule of their Kings and aristocracy, under which they had so long groaned, so now the Hindoo sought to wash away a century of British injustice and tyranny in the blood of his oppressors.'[61] According to the *Nation*, therefore, the rebellion in India was as legitimate as the French Revolution had been seventy years earlier – and deserved similar support. In the eyes of the nationalists, atrocities were understandable when driven by an admirable and passionate cause such as the fight for freedom.

In the previous century, both the possession of empire and the perceived differences between the French and the British had proven influential in the development of a British identity.[62] By embracing their similarities to France and opposing the British presence in India, nineteenth-century Irish nationalists appeared to further distance themselves from the British. The *Nation* consistently cited examples in which the French newspapers, *Univers* and *Le Nord*, condemned the British presence in India and brazenly supported the sepoys' cause. December 1857 saw the publication of *Des sentiments de justice et d'humanité de l'Angleterre dans la question indienne* in Paris. According to the *Nation*, the author of the pamphlet aimed to reveal the British to be 'quite as bad, if not worse' than the sepoys they were fighting against.[63] The *Ulsterman* even reported that French support for the Indian cause went further than press reports and pamphlets, extending to the battlefield. On 21 September 1857, the journal reported that a French general had joined the sepoys in their fight against the English. The French press reportedly had refrained from releasing the news until the general had avoided interception and safely reached his destination. Further, the *Ulsterman* suggested he was not alone. There were 'said to be fourteen Europeans in Delhi already, holding command in the rebel army'.[64]

Referring to the *Univers* and *Le Nord* as members of the 'Ultramontane' press and no better than the Irish sepoy journals, the unionist papers

59 *Nation*, 12 Sept. 1857.   **60** *Nation*, 21 Nov. 1857.   **61** *Nation*, 12 Sept. 1857.   **62** MacKenzie, 'Empire and metropolitan cultures', 273. See also Linda Colley, *Britons: forging the nation, 1707–1837* (New Haven, 1992).   **63** *Nation*, 26 Dec. 1857.   **64** *Ulsterman*, 21 Sept. 1857.

responded to the nationalist reports with their own examples of France's support for the British in India. In September 1857 the French Emperor Napoleon III donated £1,000 'in favour of the officers and soldiers cruelly afflicted in India'.[65] While the British accepted the sign of support, a letter published in the *Dublin Evening Mail* suggested that some found the amount a bit stingy: 'his Majesty has behaved very liberally; but could he do less, and will his pocket miss the thousand pounds ...?'[66] Any French support thus appeared to be both offered and accepted rather grudgingly.

CONCLUSIONS

The Indian Mutiny provided an opportunity for the Irish – of all political and religious sympathies, at home and abroad – to voice their opinions regarding Ireland's position in the empire. The fact that Irish newspapers adopted the Mutiny as a sustained topic of debate suggests that the various interpretations of the event, and of Ireland's role in its suppression, resonated with Irish audiences that had already developed their own, competing views about Ireland's place within the British empire. In many ways, the Indian Mutiny presented a new arena in which older arguments continued to be fought out – even debate about the supposed savagery of the sepoys was adapted to suit the different agendas of nationalists and unionists.

Ireland's response to the struggle was never as straightforward or as unified as any one journal or individual would have liked to suggest. The way in which one interpreted the cause of the violence, the way in which one chose to participate in the event and those to whom one looked for validation, all constituted a statement of some sort. However, to simply label Irish perceptions and responses to the Indian Mutiny as Protestant or Catholic, unionist or nationalist, at home or abroad, is to oversimplify the situation. Individuals such as Henry Downey, who personified the large number of Catholics fighting for the empire, and conservative journals such as the *Belfast Daily Mercury*, which, from the start, advocated change in the British presence in India, inhabited grey areas between the two extremes. A variety of factors came into play in each individual's response to the Mutiny. While religious and political beliefs could certainly be influential, so too were economic interests, humanitarian ambitions, family background, social standing and, more often than not, the simple necessity of daily survival. The decision whether to fight for or against the empire did not always come down to a matter of being Irish, but simply to individual circumstance.

To return to an earlier question – what does all of this say about how contemporaries perceived Ireland's role within the British empire at the time

65 *Dublin Evening Mail*, 9 Sept. 1857. 66 *Dublin Evening Mail*, 11 Sept. 1857.

of the Mutiny? The many shades of grey that marked the Irish response reflect Ireland's rather ambiguous position within the mid-nineteenth-century empire. Many Irish proved more than willing to support Britain's imperial endeavours and, by providing much needed manpower and strong military leadership, played an integral role in the maintenance of British rule in India. The enthusiasm with which Irish universities responded to competitive examinations for the Indian Civil Service, and the existence of attitudes of racial antagonism and cultural superiority, reflected a degree of pride in Ireland's position within the empire. However, other factors appear to tell a different story. Among nationalists, a belief in Britain's past oppression of Ireland always lurked just below the surface. The anti-enlistment cause, the apparent discrimination against those who chose to enlist, and the placards calling for the Irish to follow the lead of the sepoys, portrayed Ireland in a more subordinate light. For some, Ireland represented a conquered land, still undecided as to whether it should assert its independence or prove its equal position within the empire. At the time of the Indian Mutiny, contemporaries could have provided a no more clear-cut answer to the question of whether Ireland represented a part of the metropole or the periphery than can scholars in the twenty-first century.

6. The dog in the night-time: the *Freeman's Journal*, the Irish Parliamentary Party and the empire, 1875–1919[1]

FELIX M. LARKIN

To understand the slightly bizarre title of this essay, it is necessary to turn to one of the Sherlock Holmes stories of Sir Arthur Conan Doyle. In 'Silver Blaze',[2] Holmes famously directs the attention of a police inspector to the curious incident of the dog in the night-time. The inspector points out that the dog did nothing in the night-time. That, says Holmes, was the curious incident. In relation to the general theme of this collection of essays, the curious fact about the *Freeman's Journal* is that it was not much concerned with the British empire. Significant events in individual colonies and Dominions were, of course, reported in the paper and would sometimes occasion comment in its leader columns, but the *Freeman* neither espoused the cause of empire nor offered a critique of it. Furthermore, the paper failed to develop any significant imperial connections – journalistic or commercial. In short, like the dog in the Sherlock Holmes story, it did nothing – or at least very little – about the empire.

This essay will attempt to explain why this was so, first outlining the history of the *Freeman's Journal* and its position in the political life of Ireland in the late nineteenth and early twentieth centuries. Some analysis of the *Freeman*'s actual coverage of imperial affairs will then follow. Finally, the essay will focus on the careers of certain *Freeman* journalists – just to make the point that none of the paper's staff obtained work as correspondents or representatives of newspapers in the colonies and Dominions.

THE 'FREEMAN' BEFORE THE PARNELL SPLIT

The *Freeman's Journal* was published in Dublin continuously from 1763 to 1924 and was the foremost nationalist newspaper in Ireland in the nineteenth century. It had, however, a rather dubious connection with Dublin Castle

---

1 My thanks to Ian d'Alton, Deirdre McMahon and Simon Potter for reading and commenting on successive drafts of this essay, and to Philip Hamell for some helpful drafting suggestions. 2 In *The memoirs of Sherlock Holmes* (London, 1950 [1894]) 7–34.

during the editorship and later proprietorship of Francis Higgins, known as the 'Sham Squire', between 1784 and 1802. Higgins bequeathed the paper to his nephew Philip Whitfield Harvey, a native of Wexford and, by all accounts, an honourable man. Under Harvey's ownership, the *Freeman* gradually recovered its independence from government influence. He died in 1826 and was succeeded by his son-in-law, Henry Grattan, a son of the parliamentarian. Coincidentally, in its early years – before the advent of Francis Higgins – the paper had strongly supported the elder Henry Grattan.[3]

The *Freeman* was purchased in 1831 by its first Catholic editor, Patrick Lavelle, who was a valuable but over-zealous advocate of repeal of the Act of Union.[4] In 1841 it passed into the hands of the Gray family, who retained ownership for the next fifty years. Three generations of Grays were associated with the *Freeman* – starting with Sir John Gray, whose statue stands in O'Connell Street, Dublin and who is best known for his work as a member of Dublin corporation in bringing the Vartry water supply to the city. A Protestant, he too was a supporter of repeal of the Union, and later of the Irish Tenant League movement and of Church of Ireland disestablishment. He sat as MP for Kilkenny from 1865 until his death in 1875, and he had begun to ally himself with Butt's Home Rule party in the last year of his life.[5]

His son, Edmund Dwyer Gray, owned the *Freeman's Journal* from 1875 until 1888, and was also a Dublin city councillor and Home Rule MP.[6] A moderate, he initially opposed Parnell and threw the weight of the *Freeman* – unsuccessfully – against him. When, after the 1880 general election, Parnell was elected chairman of the Irish Party, Gray was one of eighteen MPs who voted against him.[7] Thereafter, however, he largely supported Parnell's leadership – partly because he accepted that Parnell was now invincible, but also because Parnell established in 1881 his own weekly newspaper, *United Ireland*, with the *Freeman*'s star reporter (and later MP), William O'Brien, as editor. The threat that the *United Ireland* might, if necessary, be turned into a daily organ to rival the *Freeman* copperfastened Gray's loyalty.

3 For details of the early history of the *Freeman's Journal* (henceforth *FJ*), see Brian Inglis, *The freedom of the press in Ireland, 1784–1841* (London, 1954). For information about Francis Higgins, see also W.J. Fitzpatrick, *The Sham Squire* (Dublin, 1866 [3rd edn]); Moira Lysaght, 'The Sham Squire', *Dublin Historical Record*, 2:25 (Mar. 1972) 64–74; and *Revolutionary Dublin 1795–1801: the letters of Francis Higgins to Dublin Castle*, ed. Thomas Bartlett (Dublin, 2004). 4 Brian Inglis, 'O'Connell and the Irish press, 1800–42', *Irish Historical Studies*, 29:8 (Mar. 1952) 15. 5 John T. Gilbert, 'Sir John Gray', *Dictionary of national biography* (London, 1908), viii, 452. See also T.O. Ruttledge, 'The Gray family of Claremorris, Co. Mayo', *Irish Genealogist*, 4:7 (1989) 551–62. For details of Gray's work on the Vartry water scheme, see Mary Mulvihill, 'An Irishwoman's diary', *Irish Times*, 15 Mar. 2003; I am grateful to my brother, Terence Larkin, for bringing this article to my notice. 6 George Barnett Smith, 'Edmund Dwyer Gray', *Dictionary of national biography* (London, 1908), viii, 448. See also Ruttledge, 'The Gray family'. 7 *FJ*, 18 May 1880.

O'Brien wrote of Edmund Dwyer Gray that he was 'the most enterprising newspaperman Ireland ever produced'.[8] Under his management, the *Freeman*'s production capacity was greatly expanded, its circulation increased threefold and it became highly profitable. So successful was it that Gray eventually turned it into a public company in 1887, with share capital of £125,000, though contriving to retain control for himself. He died at the early age of 42 in 1888, having converted to Catholicism in 1877[9] – presumably through the influence of his English-born wife Caroline (*née* Chisholm), a devout Roman Catholic.

THE 'FREEMAN' IN THE PARNELL SPLIT AND AFTERWARDS

Mrs Gray was effectively in control of the *Freeman* company at the time of the Parnell split: she owned about 45 per cent of the shares.[10] At first, the paper – with her approval – came out in favour of Parnell. However, once the anti-Parnellites launched their own daily newspaper, the *National Press*, in March 1891 and the *Freeman* began as a result to lose circulation and revenue, Mrs Gray wavered. Under the influence of her son – also named Edmund Dwyer Gray, then aged 21 and fearful for his inheritance – she resolved that the paper should switch sides. A change in the composition of the board of the *Freeman* company was necessary to achieve this. That required a special general meeting of the company, which was held on 21 September 1891. The new anti-Parnell board chosen by Mrs Gray included her son and the man soon to become her second husband, Captain Maurice O'Conor. The *Freeman* and the *National Press* later merged in March 1892, with Mrs Gray (now Mrs O'Conor) selling her shareholding as part of the deal: in simultaneous transactions, the *Freeman's Journal* bought the *National Press* newspaper and the *National Press* company bought Mrs Gray's shares. The young Edmund Dwyer Gray and Captain O'Conor both ceased to be directors of the merged company in 1893.[11]

The period from 1891 onwards was one of relentless decline in the fortunes and prestige of the *Freeman's Journal*. This decline had its roots in the divisions within Irish nationalism brought about by Parnell's fall, divisions

8 William O'Brien, *Recollections* (London, 1905) 182–3. A harsher judgment is suggested in Joyce's *Dubliners*: when, in the story 'Grace', one of the characters recalls Edmund Dwyer Gray 'blathering away' at the unveiling of his father's statue in O'Connell Street, Dublin; another comments that 'none of the Grays was any good'. See Harry Levin (ed.), *The essential James Joyce* (London, 1963) 473. 9 Archives Office of Tasmania, Hobart, NS 575/7, papers relating to Edmund Dwyer Gray's reception into the Catholic Church, 10 Sept. 1877. 10 *FJ*, 22 Sept. 1891. 11 Emmet Larkin, *The Roman Catholic church in Ireland and the fall of Parnell* (Liverpool, 1979) 236–9, 263, 269–75 and 283. See also Earnán P. de Blaghd, 'I was a teenage press baron: the problems of Edmund Dwyer Gray, Junior', *Dublin Historical Record*, 4:41 (Dec. 1987) 31–42.

which were replicated in the newspaper market. First, the damage inflicted by the *National Press* was huge. Then, after the merger, there was a long and bitter struggle for control of the *Freeman* between the rival anti-Parnell factions led by Tim Healy and John Dillon; this was resolved in 1896, largely in the latter's favour.[12] Moreover, from 1891 onwards, the *Freeman* faced strong competition from the *Irish Daily Independent*, later the *Irish Independent*. The *Independent* had been established as a pro-Parnell organ after the *Freeman* defected to the other side, but was purchased in 1900 by William Martin Murphy, an associate of Healy. He relaunched it in 1905 at half the price of the *Freeman* and in a more popular format.[13]

Thomas Sexton MP, the Irish Party's acknowledged financial expert, had become chairman and business manager of the *Freeman* company in 1893. In that capacity, he proved incapable of meeting the challenge of Murphy's new *Independent*. Already weakened by its tribulations in the 1890s, the *Freeman* was thus fatally undermined. The leaders of the Irish Party stepped in to save it in 1912, forcing Sexton to retire.[14] However, the paper continued to incur losses, and its parlous condition was exacerbated by the destruction of its premises during the 1916 Easter Rising. It was, therefore, impossible for the Irish Party stalwarts who ran the paper to keep it going once the party had been defeated in the general election of December 1918. It was sold off in October 1919.[15]

In its final years, from 1919 to 1924, the *Freeman* was the property of Martin Fitzgerald, a Dublin wine-merchant of moderate nationalist sympathies who became a member of the first Senate of the Irish Free State.[16] It appeared for the last time on 19 December 1924, and was subsequently absorbed by its rival, the *Irish Independent*.

THE 'FREEMAN' AND THE PARTY

One of the most interesting aspects of the *Freeman*'s history is the tension that arose from time to time between the paper and the politicians with whom

12 See F.S.L. Lyons, *The Irish Parliamentary Party, 1890–1910* (London, 1951) 38–45.   13 See chapter 7 below. See also Donal McCartney, 'William Martin Murphy: an Irish press baron and the rise of the popular press' in Brian Farrell (ed.), *Communications and community in Ireland* (Dublin and Cork, 1984) 30–8 and Patrick Maume, 'Commerce, politics and the *Irish Independent*, 1891–1919', unpublished paper read before the 24th Irish Conference of Historians, University College Cork, 20–22 May 1999; I am grateful to Dr Maume for making a copy of this paper available to me.   14 'Appendix II: press reaction to the Rising in general' in Owen Dudley Edwards and Fergus Pyle (eds), *1916: the Easter Rising* (London, 1968) 259–64.   15 F.S.L. Lyons, *John Dillon: a biography* (London, 1968) 389–90, 419, 457–8.   16 For biographical information on Martin Fitzgerald, see F.M.L., 'Appreciation: Kathleen Bowles', *Irish Times*, 24 June 1997. Mrs Bowles was Fitzgerald's daughter. See also Desmond Ryan, *Remembering Sion* (London, 1934) 256–69.

it was, in general terms, aligned. Examples include the *Freeman*'s opposition to Parnell in the late 1870s and its response to the Parnell split and its aftermath. Likewise, under Thomas Sexton, the *Freeman* often took an independent line – especially after Sexton had retired from parliament in 1896 and was out of touch, and increasingly out of sympathy, with his erstwhile colleagues at Westminster.[17] None of this, however, should obscure the essential fact that the paper was, during the last quarter of the nineteenth century and until after the general election of 1918, the semi-official organ of the Irish Party. Indeed, it was aptly described – in an anonymous memorandum in the Redmond papers, *c.*1916 – as 'a sort of political bulletin circulating amongst already staunch friends of the party'.[18] It is in this context that one must consider the *Freeman*'s attitude towards the empire.

T.D. Sullivan, the prominent Irish Party MP, was quoted in 1884 as saying: 'What the Irish party cared about was not Egypt or the Sudan, but about Ireland and their own countrymen, and in place of concerning [themselves] about Khartoum or Gordon they were thinking of Dublin, of Cork, and of Mullingar.'[19] Of course, this was not true of every member of the party, but it is a fair representation of the party's collective approach to the empire and to other foreign questions. Reinforcing that approach was the consideration that, as acknowledged by Parnell himself in 1877, there was 'an unwritten law, hitherto acquiesced in by the Irish members [of parliament], that no Irish may interfere in English and imperial concerns'[20] – a prohibition that was rarely transgressed. Redmond's support for the war effort in 1914 was a radical departure from well-established practice, and was recognized as such on both sides of the Irish Sea; it was without precedent for the Irish Party to identify so fully with the empire.[21]

The Irish Party's objectives were twofold: Home Rule and land reform. Nothing else mattered. Nor did the pursuit of Home Rule require the party to articulate a view on the future shape of the empire. Home rule was a modest measure of self-government. As a concept, it was closer to devolution than independence.[22] Certainly it fell far short of Dominion status. For

17 Lyons, *The Irish Parliamentary Party*, 39 n. 2. 18 National Library of Ireland, Dublin, John Redmond Papers, MS. 15,262 (1). 19 *FJ*, 2 June 1884, quoted in Alan O'Day, *The English face of Irish nationalism* (Dublin, 1977) 158. The speech from which this quotation is taken was given in Mullingar. 20 Letter from C.S. Parnell to the London *Times*, reproduced in the *Nation*, 11 Aug. 1877, quoted in F.S.L. Lyons, *Charles Stewart Parnell* (London, 1977) 66. 21 The *Freeman*, in a leader on the death of John Redmond, emphasized that his actions at the outbreak of the war in 1914 had been 'a break with the Irish tradition' and went on to say: 'He made up his mind that the aggression in Belgium and the passing of the Home Rule Bill had created a situation such as Ireland had not had to face [before].' See *FJ*, 7 Mar. 1918. 22 For one well-informed contemporary observer, Ireland under Home Rule would have been a 'mere semi-self-governing province'. See John Moynihan to Michael Moynihan, 21 May 1916, printed in Deirdre McMahon (ed.), *The Moynihan brothers in peace and war, 1908–1918: their*

that reason, and also because of the physical proximity to England, the Irish Party never really saw Ireland under Home Rule as comparable with Canada, South Africa, New Zealand or Australia. Moreover, it was not envisaged that Home Rule would negate Ireland's status 'as part of the metropolitan core of the empire'.[23] If England was the 'mother' of the empire, Ireland was the sympathetic maiden aunt – in cahoots with her sister's unruly children and always ready to join in their games, but not herself belonging in the nursery.[24] Hence the party's lack of any real interest in the empire, a lack of interest which was reflected in the *Freeman's Journal*.

This is not to say that the *Freeman* was anti-empire. Even if it had been inclined to pursue an anti-imperialist line (which it definitely was not), the Irish Party's alliance with the British Liberals would have inhibited it from doing so. Also, the task of administering the empire provided attractive employment opportunities for middle-class Irish Catholics, and the paper would not have wished to alienate that section of its readership. Quite simply, the *Freeman* had – like the Irish Party – political pre-occupations other than the empire that were more immediate. Events in the colonies and Dominions, when reported in the newspaper, were seen primarily through the prism of Ireland's Home Rule aspirations and – to borrow today's jargon – the story was 'spun' accordingly.

THE GRAY FAMILY AND THE EMPIRE

It is arguable that the *Freeman* might have had much greater interest in the empire if the Gray family had not sold out in 1892. The Grays had significant connections with the Antipodes. One of Sir John Gray's brothers, Moses Wilson Gray,[25] had emigrated to Australia in 1855, on the same ship that brought Charles Gavan Duffy into exile.[26] Like Duffy, Wilson Gray became a distinguished servant of the crown. He was a member of the legislative assembly of Victoria from 1860 to 1862. He then moved to New Zealand, and was a district judge there from 1864 until his death in 1875. Another of

new Ireland (Dublin, 2004).   23 Keith Jeffery, 'Introduction' in Keith Jeffery (ed.), *'An Irish empire'?: aspects of Ireland and the British empire* (Manchester, 1996) 1.   24 It is interesting to note in this context the recurrent depiction of the sisterhood of Britannia and Hibernia in British press cartoons of this period (see chapter 1 above). For two examples, see L. Perry Curtis Jr., *Apes and angels: the Irishman in Victorian caricature* (Newton Abbot, 1971) 25 and 41. Similar imagery is found in late-nineteenth century Ireland. See L. Perry Curtis Jr., *Images of Erin in the age of Parnell* (Dublin, 2000) 17; I am grateful to James H. Murphy, DePaul University, Chicago, for bringing this booklet to my notice and also for comments on the penultimate draft of this essay.   25 Carole Woods, 'Moses Wilson Gray', *Australian dictionary of biography* (Melbourne, 1972), iv, 287–8. See also Ruttledge, 'The Gray family'.   26 The name of the ship was the *Ocean Chief*.

Sir John Gray's brothers also settled in New Zealand, and one of his sons, the youngest brother of Edmund Dwyer Gray MP, emigrated to New South Wales.[27] Moreover, Edmund Dwyer Gray's wife – the woman who controlled the *Freeman* company at the time of the Parnell split – was the daughter and namesake of the English philanthropist, Caroline Chisholm, celebrated for her work with female emigrants to Australia.[28] She was caricatured as Mrs Jellyby in Charles Dickens' *Bleak House*.[29]

The last of the Grays associated with the paper – Edmund Dwyer Gray, junior – had actually visited Australia twice before reaching the age of 21 in April 1891.[30] In 1894, no longer a member of the *Freeman*'s board of directors, he emigrated to Australia and settled eventually in Tasmania, where he became a journalist and politician of note. He was the editor successively of three newspapers in Hobart, and was elected in 1928 to the Tasmanian parliament. He was treasurer and deputy premier of Tasmania from 1934 until his death in 1945, except for six months in 1939 when he served as interim premier.[31] Accordingly, it is likely that he would have had a strong focus on the empire had he remained in Ireland and he might also have encouraged some commercial links between the *Freeman* and the Australian newspaper industry; but that was not to be.

As editor of the Hobart *Voice*, Dwyer Gray wrote in 1926 about an incident indicative of the Irish Party's attitude to the empire.[32] In 1888, Cecil Rhodes had offered Parnell a donation of £10,000 on condition that the Irish Party would seek to retain representation at Westminster after Home Rule; Gladstone's unsuccessful Home Rule bill of 1886 did not provide for that. Rhodes' view was that, if Ireland had both Home Rule and its quota of MPs at Westminster, then the colonies could demand similar rights. Dwyer Gray's comment is worth quoting: 'Parnell was quite indifferent on the point, but

27 See Ruttledge, 'The Gray family'.   28 Judith Iltis, 'Caroline Chisholm', *Australian dictionary of biography* (Melbourne, 1966), i, 221–3. See also Margaret Kiddle, *Caroline Chisholm* (Melbourne, 1969 [3rd edn]). It is noteworthy that some Australian Catholic organizations are now pursuing the cause for beatification of Caroline Chisholm. I am grateful to Raymond V. Gray, of Towcester, Northants., for this information. Mr Gray is not related to the Gray family who owned the *Freeman's Journal*.   29 First published in book form in 1853. It had previously appeared in twenty monthly numbers, from Mar. 1852 to Sept. 1853.   30 He was in Australia when his father died in 1888, but returned soon afterwards and joined the editorial staff of the *Freeman's Journal*. He was again in Australia from early 1890 to Feb. 1891.   31 R.P. Davis, 'Edmund Dwyer-Gray', *Australian dictionary of biography* (Melbourne, 1981), viii, 390–1. When Dwyer Gray entered politics in Tasmania, he began using a hyphenated version of his name so as to gain higher placement on the ballot paper.   32 'Half told secrets', Hobart *Voice of Labour*, 27 Feb. 1926. See R.P. Davis, 'C.S. Parnell, Cecil Rhodes, Edmund Dwyer-Gray and imperial federation', *Papers and proceedings of the Tasmanian Historical Research Association*, 3:21 (Sept. 1974) 125–32. See also Lyons, *Parnell*, 442–4 and 587–9, and Donal McCracken, 'Parnell and the South African connection', in Donal McCartney (ed.), *Parnell: the politics of power* (Dublin, 1991) 125–36.

in any case £10,000 was a good persuader, and Parnell did what Rhodes wanted.'[33] The money was paid over, and became a matter of controversy after the split when Tim Healy accused Parnell of misappropriating part of it. Dwyer Gray was present at a meeting in London in March 1891 when Parnell – for reasons that were not obvious – refused a further donation of £10,000 from Rhodes, and on that occasion he learnt about the circumstances of the 1888 payment. Parnell's apparent indifference to the question of colonial representation at Westminster, and to Irish representation there after Home Rule, is consistent with the Irish Party's overall lack of concern with the empire.

REVIEW OF THE 'FREEMAN' IN 1900

In order to delve further into the *Freeman*'s attitude to the empire, it is perhaps appropriate to review the relevant contents of the paper over the period of a year. The year chosen is 1900, important in Ireland because of the reunion of the Irish Party after the Parnell split; in addition, there was a general election in early October. On the empire front, the outcome of the South African War remained uncertain, at least until mid-year, and the final steps were taken in the process that brought the Commonwealth of Australia into existence on 1 January 1901. Elsewhere, the Boxer Rebellion took place in China and US President William McKinley was elected for a second term.

What strikes one straightaway about the *Freeman* in 1900 is the marked paucity of reportage and comment on any imperial affairs other than the war in South Africa. There was, for example, no 'empire news' feature – whereas the paper carried a daily 'London Correspondence' column and had regular pieces entitled 'Paris Notes', 'American Notes' and 'The World of Rome' (about the Vatican). The Australian Commonwealth question was ignored except when something was happening in London – such as parliamentary debates on the enabling legislation. Coverage of the South African War was extensive in the first six months of the year. However, from the end of June onwards – after the relief of Mafeking and the capture of Pretoria – it was cursory. This was much the same for the British press, which also largely ignored the subsequent phase of guerilla warfare. Where the *Freeman* differed from comparable British newspapers – and this certainly showed its priorities – was that the war news was not gathered by a special correspondent engaged by the *Freeman*, but was taken (with attribution) mostly from the Press Association news agency.

The *Freeman* ran at least two leaders every day, commenting on the main stories of the day. Of the 312 issues of the paper published in 1900, some

33 Quoted in Davis, 'Parnell, Rhodes, Dwyer-Gray and imperial federation', 126.

113 had leaders about the war in South Africa: 75 of these, or almost 70 per cent, appeared before the end of June. The only other imperial matters mentioned in the leader columns were Australia (5 leaders),[34] India (1 leader on famine conditions, and 2 on the military situation on the north-west frontier) and elections in Canada (1 leader). Disregarding the leaders on the South African War, this gives a total of 9 leaders devoted to empire news in the *Freeman* in 1900 – hardly an impressive statistic. By comparison, the Boxer Rebellion and the US presidential election got 14 leaders and 11 leaders respectively.[35]

The *Freeman*'s leaders on the impending establishment of the Australian Commonwealth, though not numerous, demonstrate beyond doubt that the paper's interest was the Irish angle, not the empire. Their theme was the contrast between self-government in Australia and the denial of Home Rule in Ireland. Thus, on 15 May, the *Freeman* asked why the principles of self-government were 'to be kept for application in the southern seas or amid Canadian snows'. It added this rider: 'Have [these principles] no relation to a difficulty much more deep seated, much nearer home, and much more closely related with the vitality of the empire than any colonial question can be?'[36] That surely confirms that Ireland was – in the eyes of the *Freeman*, and of the Irish Party – in a different category from the colonies. Notwithstanding references to colonial examples of self-government, Home Rule for Ireland was seen as a refinement of governance within the imperial centre.

As regards the war in South Africa, the *Freeman*'s approach was complex. It was, of course, against the war, describing it as an 'unspeakable tragedy'[37] and 'the most unjustifiable war of modern times'.[38] However, it couched its opinions so as to position itself – and the Irish Party – alongside those elements in the British Liberal Party who also opposed the war. It is safe to assume that the paper hoped thereby to minimize the damage done by its anti-war stance to the prospects of a continuing alliance between the Liberals and the Irish Party. All this is evident in the following sentence from a leader on 9 July: 'The bitterest opponents of the present British policy in South Africa, and the harshest critics of British methods there, are to be found among Irish Home Rulers who accepted Mr. Gladstone's policy without reserve, and who were most eager to further that great man's desire for conciliation.'[39] Similarly, less than a month later, the paper was lavish in its praise of a speech by Sir William Harcourt, the Liberal MP, criticizing the war: for

---

34 In addition, there were two leaders on the Catholic Church in Australia.   **35** In the U.S. election, the *Freeman* favoured William Jennings Bryan (the Democratic party candidate) over the incumbent President, William McKinley (Republican).   **36** *FJ*, 15 May 1900.   **37** *FJ*, 28 May 1900.   **38** *FJ*, 1 June 1900.   **39** Gladstone had died in 1898. The reference to him here harks back to his policy of conciliation during and after the First Anglo-Boer War of 1880–1. The Gladstonian tradition of Liberalism was not in the ascendant in 1900.

the *Freeman*, his speech illustrated 'the difference between real Liberalism and sham'.⁴⁰

In arguing against the war, the *Freeman* was careful – and this required some ingenuity – to distinguish the war effort from the pursuit of legitimate imperial aims. In a leader on 31 May, it claimed that the blame for the war belonged not to the British nation, but 'solely to the capitalists and to Mr Rhodes'. It went on: 'The assumption of the uninformed, or misinformed, Irishman or Englishman that the war was inevitable, and the subjection of the [South African] Republic an absolute necessity of imperial policy, is absolutely without any foundation whatever.'⁴¹ In other words, the paper sought to attack the war while avoiding hostility towards the empire. Needless to say, it drew parallels between Ireland and the Boer republics – as in this sarcastic observation in a leader from early June: 'Clearly the conciliation of the Orange Free State has begun. The methods are familiar. They are those of Cromwell and Inchiquin brought up to date by latter-day gabblers about the rights of citizenship.'⁴² Earlier, in February, the *Freeman* had declared that '[British] success, if it could be attained, would only create another Ireland in the Transvaal'.⁴³

The foregoing is just a snapshot, but it is sufficient for the purpose of picking up the authentic voice of the *Freeman's Journal* on the subject of the empire. That voice presages many of the themes and pre-occupations of recent historiography on Ireland and the empire, and this phenomenon will be discussed in the next section of this essay.

'IRELAND AND EMPIRE' HISTORIOGRAPHY

A key issue in the 'Ireland and empire' historiography is the ambiguous status of Ireland – whether metropolitan or colonial, or a mixture of both. David Fitzpatrick states the problem as follows:

> The formal Union of the kingdoms of Ireland and Great Britain (1801–1922) masked a hybrid administration with manifest colonial elements, allowing variant interpretations of the character of Ireland's dependency. Was Ireland an integral part of the United Kingdom, a peripheral, backward subregion, or a colony in all but name?⁴⁴

40 *FJ*, 2 Aug. 1900. 41 *FJ*, 31 May 1900. 42 *FJ*, 5 June 1900. Murrough O'Brien, 1st Earl of Inchiquin, drove out the Catholic inhabitants of Cork, Youghal and Kinsale in 1644 and was later 'guilty of great atrocities' at Cashel, thereby earning for himself the sobriquet 'Murrough of the Burnings'. See J.S. Crone, *Concise dictionary of Irish biography* (Dublin, 1928) 174. As regards the reference to 'gabblers about the rights of citizenship', the pretext for the South African War was the denial of voting and other rights to the *uitlanders*, British immigrants in the Transvaal. 43 *FJ*, 2 Feb. 1900. 44 David Fitzpatrick, 'Ireland and the empire' in Andrew Porter (ed.),

More succinctly, Keith Jeffrey refers to 'the paradox that Ireland was both imperial *and* colonial' (his italics).[45] This paradox is reflected in the columns of the *Freeman's Journal*.

It has been noted already that the *Freeman* – and the Irish Party – viewed the empire essentially from a metropolitan perspective, and so did not focus on imperial concerns and did not make common cause with what the paper spoke of as 'our colonial cousins' and 'the distant peoples of the empire'.[46] The condescending tone here is itself significant. Nevertheless, as also noted above, the *Freeman* would point out the freedoms achieved in other parts of the empire in decrying that Ireland had been denied a lesser measure of autonomy. This tendency on the part of nationalist Ireland to contrast its situation with that of the self-governing Dominions is widely acknowledged in the 'Ireland and empire' historiography. However, little consideration has been given to the failure of the Irish Party – because it thought about Home Rule within the framework of the United Kingdom[47] – to look to the Dominions for detailed models of self-government that might be applied to Ireland.[48] One will find in the *Freeman* no analysis of the nature of Dominion autonomy, only generalized aspirations to such freedom.

Similarly, the historiography does not give due weight to the case advanced by the *Freeman* and others – especially after self-government in the Transvaal (1906) and the Orange River Colony (1907; formerly the Orange Free State) – that Home Rule would benefit the empire by securing Ireland's loyalty. The argument was that the attitude of indifference to the empire prevalent among Irish nationalists was a function of the denial of Home Rule and would change once Home Rule had been granted. South Africa provided the most spectacular precedent for this, but not the only one. Thus, the *Freeman* wrote in October 1916 that 'the free Dominions of the empire are [now] spilling their blood and spending their manhood in its defence because their liberties and their rights are recognized and respected'.[49] Again, in July 1918 the paper stated: 'In the present war, [England] has retained South Africa because she granted the Boers their freedom.'[50] This sentiment ran deep in Irish Party circles,[51] and the party's support of the

The Oxford history of the British empire, iii: *the nineteenth century* (Oxford, 1999) 494. **45** Jeffery, 'Introduction' in Jeffery (ed.), *'An Irish empire'?*, 1. See also Deirdre McMahon, 'Ireland and the empire-Commonwealth, 1900–1948' in J.M. Brown and W.R. Louis (eds), *The Oxford history of the British empire*, iv: *the twentieth century* (Oxford, 1999) 145. **46** Both phrases are taken from *FJ*, 26 Sept. 1918. **47** On the subject of the Irish party and federalism within the United Kingdom (and the possible implications of that for the empire), see Michael Wheatley, 'John Redmond and federalism in 1910', *Irish Historical Studies*, 127:32 (May 2001) 343–64. **48** In contrast, Lord Milner (for example) took the view that Irish self-government 'should be restricted to that of Quebec within Canada rather than of Canada within the empire'. Quoted in Fitzpatrick, 'Ireland and the empire', 506. **49** *FJ*, 19 Oct. 1916. **50** *FJ*, 19 July 1918. **51** As early as 1886, Thomas Sexton MP – later chairman of the *Freeman's Journal* company – had said in the House

war effort in 1914 – in the words of the *Freeman*, 'a break with the Irish tradition'[52] – was made possible by Home Rule having at last become law, though suspended for the duration of the war.[53]

In emphasizing Boer reconciliation with the empire post-1906, as in its sympathy for the Boer cause in 1899–1902, the *Freeman* betrayed a distinctly uncharacteristic colonial aspect. Its metropolitan outlook had broken down under what Keith Jeffrey calls 'the common perceived experience which Boers and Irish nationalists had as oppressed communities within the British empire'.[54] In the same vein, in April 1919 the paper compared 'Ireland in smouldering revolt' with 'all Egypt in a flame of protest [and] the fires of rebellion in the Punjab'.[55] However, other analogies with 'oppressed communities' revealed a somewhat different attitude – as in the following extract from a *Freeman* leader on 23 July 1919: 'If Sir Edward Carson and his gunrunners have the right to split up Ireland, then no answer is left to the imperialist in face of M. Bourassa's claim for French-Canadian independence or General Hertzog's for the separation of Dutch South Africa.' Moreover, in October 1917 the paper complained – in language that would not now be politically correct – that the British government was behaving 'as if Ireland was a nigger country under crown colony administration'.[56]

The obvious inconsistency in these remarks, together with the infrequency and overall thrust of the *Freeman*'s references to the empire, highlights another theme of the 'Ireland and empire' historiography. This is 'the *irrelevance* of the empire to some Irish concerns'.[57] That theme connects with the central thesis of this essay. References to the empire in the *Freeman's Journal* were largely rhetorical devices designed to serve the paper's agenda in relation to Irish politics. Its interest was Irish affairs, not the empire. The relative unimportance of imperial matters to the *Freeman* – and to the Irish Party – was summed up by the paper's leader-writer in March 1918: 'It was not, indeed, of empire that John Redmond was thinking in the lead he gave his nation in the fatal days of August 1914. He was thinking of freedom and nationality, and he was thinking above all of Ireland.'[58] These words recall the passage

of Commons on the second reading of the first Home Rule bill: 'Canada was discontented and rebellious till she got what she wanted, and when she obtained what she wanted she became contented and loyal ... [This] will be precisely and absolutely reproduced in the case of Ireland.' See *Hansard's parliamentary debates*, third series, ccvi, 701, 1 June 1886.   **52** *FJ*, 7 Mar. 1918. See footnote 21 above.   **53** See D.R. O'Connor Lysaght, 'The rhetoric of Redmondism, 1914–1916', *History Ireland*, 1:11 (spring 2003) 44–9.   **54** Jeffery, 'Introduction' in Jeffery (ed.), *'An Irish empire'?*, 6.   **55** *FJ*, 17 Apr. 1919.   **56** *FJ*, 17 Oct. 1917.   **57** Jeffery, 'Introduction' in Jeffery (ed.), *'An Irish empire'?*, 17, italics in original. See also Stephen Howe, *Ireland and empire: colonial legacies in Irish history and culture* (Oxford, 2000), esp. 65.   **58** *FJ*, 9 Mar. 1918. This passage may understate Redmond's personal commitment to the empire, but it reflects the views of his Irish Party colleagues generally (views which were, of course, articulated in the *Freeman's Journal*). John Redmond and his brother, William Redmond MP, both had Irish Australian wives from T.D. Sullivan quoted earlier. They were written just days after Redmond's death, by which time the policy of Home Rule and its advocates – both in parliament and in the press – were doomed to extinction. This gives them added piquancy.

THREE 'FREEMAN' JOURNALISTS

The fact that the empire did not seriously engage the attention of the *Freeman's Journal* may well have compromised the chances of its journalists getting work as correspondents or representatives of newspapers in the colonies and Dominions. There is no record of any having done so. Nor did any of the *Freeman* staff have experience of working in the colonies or Dominions. In this respect, the careers of three of the most eminent journalists on the *Freeman* between 1881 and 1924 – James M. Tuohy, William Henry Brayden and Patrick J. Hooper – can be regarded as typical. All three did undertake work for non-Irish, non-British newspapers, but that work was for papers in the United States. None of them was involved in any way with the empire press.

Tuohy was the *Freeman*'s London correspondent for over 30 years, from 1881 to 1912. This position was at least as important as that of editor because it gave easy access to Irish Party MPs when parliament was sitting and also because much of the foreign – including empire – news appearing in the paper was filtered through its London office. From 1889 onwards, Tuohy took on the further role of London correspondent of the *New York World*. He became its European manager in 1897, and continued in that capacity until shortly before his death in 1923. He was the friend and confidant of the editor and proprietor of the *World*, Joseph Pulitzer. The London *Times*, in its obituary of Tuohy, hailed him as the 'doyen of American correspondents in Europe'[59] – a remarkable accolade for an Irishman. Probably his greatest career achievement, however, was reporting – with five other *Freeman* journalists, working under his direction – the protracted debate in Committee Room Fifteen at Westminster in December 1890 on the question of whether Parnell should continue as leader of the Irish Party.[60]

and that undoubtedly influenced their thinking. Nevertheless, they approached imperial matters with a metropolitan perspective. Thus, Stephen Gwynn wrote of John that 'he felt acutely that the empire belonged to Irish nationalists at least as much as to English Tories'; see Stephen Gwynn, *The last years of John Redmond* (London, 1919), 15. Similarly, William could say in the House of Commons in 1907 that the British colonies 'were as much the heritage of Ireland as of England' and 'were no more British than Irish colonies'; see *Hansard*, fourth series, clxix, 484–6, 15 Feb. 1907, quoted in Terence Denman, *A lonely grave: the life and death of William Redmond* (Dublin, 1995) 65. **59** London *Times*, 8 Sept. 1923. See also *Who was who, 1916–1928* (London, 1929) 1059; I am grateful to James McGuire for bringing this reference to my attention. **60** See F.S.L. Lyons, *The fall of Parnell, 1890–91* (London, 1960) 120.

Brayden and Hooper were consecutive editors of the *Freeman's Journal*, and both had previously served under Tuohy in the London office. Brayden first became editor of the anti-Parnell *National Press*, but was appointed editor of the *Freeman* when it merged with the *National Press* in March 1892.[61] He held the post until 1916. Subsequently, up to his death in 1933, he was a correspondent for the Chicago *Daily News* and the Associated Press of America. He was heavily involved in army recruitment during the First World War – activity for which he was appointed OBE in 1920 – and he undertook some anti-Sinn Féin propaganda work for Dublin Castle in 1918–19.[62] Patrick Hooper was Tuohy's assistant from 1897 to 1912, when he succeeded him as London correspondent. He was editor from 1916 until the *Freeman* ceased publication in 1924. Like Tuohy and Brayden, he then became a correspondent for an American paper, the *Philadelphia Public Ledger*. He also pursued a political career as an independent member of the Irish Senate, and was vice-chairman of the Senate when he died in 1931.[63]

Both Hooper and Brayden are mentioned in James Joyce's *Ulysses*, the 'Aeolus' episode of which is set in the *Freeman*'s offices in North Prince's Street, Dublin.[64] That the *Freeman's Journal* should feature in *Ulysses* affirms its central position in Irish life at the beginning of the twentieth century. On the other hand, the identification of the press with Aeolus, the god of the winds, is a typically cruel piece of Joycean mockery.[65]

CONCLUSION

Finally, another *Freeman* journalist worthy of note in the context of this essay is Edward Byrne, editor from 1884 to 1891 and the last editor but one before

61 Brayden was aged 26 when he became editor of the *Freeman's Journal*. As Jacqueline Beaumont points out in her essay in this collection, it was not unusual for such a young man to be made editor of a major newspaper.   62 *Who was who, 1929–1940* (London, 1941) 155. For obituaries, see the *Irish Independent, Irish Press* and *Irish Times*, 18 Dec. 1933. For details of Brayden's propaganda work for Dublin Castle, see PRO, London, CO 904/168/1222–35, 1239–44 and 1265–70 (published on microfilm by Harvester Microform Publications in *The British in Ireland, part five: public control and administration, 1884–1921*, reel 91 [Brighton, 1985]); I am grateful to Brian P. Murphy for bringing these papers to my notice. I am also grateful to Brayden's son, Desmond Brayden, for permitting me to interview him in April 1999 (when he was aged 97).   63 William J. Flynn, *The Oireachtas companion and Saorstat guide* (Dublin, 1930) 177. For obituaries, see the *Irish Independent* and *Irish Times*, 7 Sept. 1931. I am grateful to Richard P. Hooper, grandson of Patrick Hooper, for making available to me his unpublished research on the Hooper family in Ireland.   64 James Joyce, *Ulysses* (London, 1969 [Paris, 1922]) 118–50. Patrick Hooper's father, Alderman John Hooper, editor of the *Freeman*'s evening newspaper, the *Evening Telegraph*, from 1892 to 1897, is also mentioned in *Ulysses*: Joyce accords him the doubtful distinction of having been one of Molly Bloom's lovers. See p. 652 of the 1969 edition   65 An occasional advertisement in the *Freeman's Journal* at this time (e.g. 10 Feb. 1900) was for Aeolus Cycles. Could this have been the source of Joyce's inspiration for

Brayden.[66] Staunchly pro-Parnell at the time of the split, he left the *Freeman* when the paper changed sides and became the first editor of the *Irish Daily Independent*. He resigned that position in 1896 on health grounds: a drink problem had incapacitated him.[67] Described by Tim Healy as 'a jaunty Galway man',[68] he was born in Tuam in 1847 and died there on 13 October 1899.[69] At the time of his death, he was about to go to South Africa – where war had just broken out – as a correspondent for T.P. O'Connor, the prominent London editor who was an Irish Party MP for a Liverpool constituency.[70] That was the closest any *Freeman* journalist got to having a professional link with the colonies or Dominions – albeit that Byrne did not live long enough to take up his appointment and so develop an imperial string to his bow. There is, therefore, a curious aptness about his untimely death. As a consequence, he just fails to be an exception to the rule in regard to the *Freeman*'s lack of involvement with the empire. Had he gone to South Africa, it might have been possible to represent his subsequent career as a small, discordant yelp from the otherwise silent dog in the night-time.

his identification of the press with the god of the winds? **66** Byrne's immediate successor was William J. McDowell. He was editor for six months only; Brayden displaced him when the *Freeman's Journal* and the *National Press* merged. McDowell had been on the *Freeman*'s staff since the mid-1880s, having previously worked on the Belfast *Morning News* (also owned for a period by the Gray family). Michael McDowell TD, currently Minister for Justice, Equality and Law Reform in the Irish government, is his great-grandson. For obituaries of William J. McDowell, see the *Freeman's Journal* and *Irish Independent*, 12 Apr. 1910. **67** Maume, 'Commerce, politics and the *Irish Independent*'. **68** T.M. Healy, *Letters and leaders of my day*, 2 vols (London, 1928), i, 339. **69** The most comprehensive obituary of Byrne was in the *Tuam News*, 20 Oct. 1899. See also Edward Byrne, *Parnell, a memoir*, ed. Frank Callanan (Dublin, 1981). **70** Boole Library, University College Cork, Cork, William O'Brien papers, box BF, William O'Brien to Sophie O'Brien, 23 Oct. 1899.

7. The *Irish Independent* and empire, 1891–1919[1]

PATRICK MAUME

This essay outlines the history of the first decades of the *Irish Independent*, including the paper's relationship with the London press and its role in promoting its proprietor's international business interests (whose relationship to the empire was symbolized by the 1907 International Exhibition). It also examines the paper's response to certain aspects of empire, including colonial conflict and the idea of a Dominion settlement to the Irish crisis. In its original form as mouthpiece for the Parnellite political project the *Independent*'s attitude towards empire was generally critical – tempered by expediency in relation to Parnellite links with Cecil Rhodes and by the paper's increasing financial dilapidation. Later, under the ownership of William Martin Murphy, it was primary a commercial undertaking, and took a more conciliatory attitude towards the perceived benefits of imperial connections – tempered by the political attitudes of its audiences and by resentment, shared even by Murphy himself, at the condescension and blunders of imperial statesmanship.

THE DEVELOPMENT OF THE 'INDEPENDENT'

The *Irish Daily Independent* and the *Evening Herald* were founded in December 1891 in Trinity Street on the site of the present-day Cuba boutique. The enterprise was sponsored by the Parnellite party in response to the defection of the *Freeman's Journal* papers, which originally backed Parnell but turned anti-Parnellite when their circulation was damaged by clerically-orchestrated boycotts and competition from the new anti-Parnellite daily *National Press*.[2] Parnell oversaw the formation of the company but died before the papers

---

1 Since 1998 I have researched the history of the *Irish Independent* between the foundation of the *Irish Daily Independent* in 1891 and the acquisition of Independent Newspapers from the Murphy family by Tony O'Reilly in 1973. My principal source has been the newspapers themselves; after working through the daily paper up to 1901 I switched to the *Irish Weekly Independent* because of time constraints. I have been partly financed by Independent Newspapers. 2 The *Irish Weekly Independent* (hereafter *IWI*), aimed primarily at farmers and emigrants, followed in 1892; it survived until 1960. It appeared on Thursdays; the *Sunday Independent* was not founded until 1905. In this period the two weeklies shared an editor.

appeared. The staff were Parnellite journalists who had resigned from the *Freeman* papers; the first editor of the *Independent*, Edward Byrne, had previously edited the *Freeman*.[3] The papers' appearance was brought forward to assist John Redmond in the December 1891 Waterford City by-election.

The group boasted that it would not be dominated by a single proprietor (as the Gray family had dominated the *Freeman*): the *Independent* was 'The People's Paper', 'Parnell's final legacy'.[4] Shareholders' clubs were formed to allow working-class Parnellites to invest in the papers; leaflets reminded businessmen that they were the best medium for advertising in Parnellite-dominated Dublin.[5] The papers faced a clerically-organized boycott in rural districts; one priest told parishioners who wanted the *Independent* to get it from a post office in Hell.[6] Nevertheless, the *Independent* established itself as the journal of record on the speeches of Parnellite leaders, persecution of Parnellites (it printed book-length reports of election petition hearings in Meath which unseated two anti-Parnellite MPs for clerical intimidation), anti-Parnellite factional disputes between Dillonites and Healyites (including rowdy shareholders' meetings over control of the *Freeman's Journal*) and the Parnellite culture of commemoration (voluminous reports of the annual October Parnell anniversary processions highlighted the participation of *Independent* staff).[7]

Parnellite advocacy of 'independent opposition' and claims that the anti-Parnellite majority had sold out to the Liberals drew the support of those who rejected constitutionalism as futile. Within the Parnellite organization, parliamentarians coexisted uneasily with Irish Republican Brotherhood (IRB) separatists. This was reflected among *Independent* personnel. The IRB leader Fred Allan was manager, and many separatists worked on the printing and delivery staff. The *Independent* offices became the IRB's unofficial Dublin headquarters. Two IRB men acquitted of killing a suspected informer after witnesses mysteriously retracted their evidence were given jobs; an *Independent* editorial praised Allan for saving them from imprisonment or death. The police believed M.A. Manning, editor of the *Weekly Independent*, and several prominent *Independent* journalists were IRB men; they noted that, at the 1898 opening of the Empire Music Hall, Manning, James O'Donovan (who succeeded Byrne as editor in 1897) and another *Independent* journalist ostentatiously remained seated when the queen was toasted.[8]

3 Edward Byrne, *Parnell: a memoir*, ed. Frank Callanan (Dublin, 1993). 4 *Independent*, 18 Dec. 1891; 25 Aug. 1893. 5 *Independent*, 16 Jan. and 7 Mar. 1892; 'A few facts for advertisers from the Irish General Election of 1892', leaflet in author's possession. 6 *Independent*, 18 and 24 Aug. and 5 Sept 1892. 7 *Independent*, 7, 8, 10 and 11 Oct. and 3 Dec. 1892; 17 May 1893; 30 Mar. 1894. 8 *Independent*, 13 and 26 Jan. 1894; Leon Ó Broin, *Revolutionary underground: the story of the Irish Republican Brotherhood, 1858–1924* (Dublin, 1976) 56–7, 85. Ó Broin mistranscribes O'Donovan's initial 'J' as a 'T', and gives Manning's initials as 'M.J.'.

Throughout the life of the 1892–5 government, the *Independent* emphasized the shortcomings of Chief Secretary John Morley's administration of
Ireland, tensions between Liberals and nationalists and the limitations of
Gladstone's second Home Rule bill. Parnellite politicians and authors of
Independent editorials criticized the bill in minute detail, stopping just short
of outright opposition.[9] The plight of evicted tenants (whom anti-Parnellites
had predicted would be reinstated by a Liberal government if Parnell was
defeated) under 'Morley the Grabber's Friend', and the hanging of the moon-
lighter John Twiss for murder (the *Independent* vigorously maintained his
innocence) were cited to prove that Liberals were as bad as Tories.[10] Home
Secretary Asquith ('a plaster of Paris Cromwell') was a particular target for
his refusal to release Irish Americans jailed for dynamite offences. The 1895
Liberal proposal to please British Nonconformists with a statue of Cromwell
outside the Houses of Parliament provoked a vigorous Parnellite campaign.
Although the plan was defeated on a free vote, the *Independent* claimed that
if the anti-Parnellites had any spirit the government could never have proposed this crowning insult.[11]

The *Independent* declared that Parnellites *were* the Irish nationalist party;
by throwing over Parnell at Gladstone's dictation the anti-Parnellites had
become a wing of the Liberal Party. Gladstone's retirement over increased
naval expenditure ('taxing Ireland and throwing the money into the sea') without carrying Home Rule, the lukewarm stance of his successor Lord Rosebery
on Home Rule and the Conservative-Unionist landslide in the 1895 general
election were hailed as proof of Parnell's foresight in resisting the Liberal
'English wolves'.[12]

After the fall of the Liberal government, Parnellism found itself at a loose
end. The paper optimistically noted Britain's diplomatic isolation, and predicted a major war that might give Ireland new possibilities. Diplomatic crises
were noted under the heading 'England's difficulty', hinting that they might
be Ireland's opportunity.[13] William Redmond predicted that the next war
would substitute 'La Marseillaise' for 'God Save the Queen'.[14] President
Grover Cleveland's 1895–6 confrontation with Britain over a Venezuelan debt
crisis aroused short-lived expectations of conflict; the *Independent*'s outspoken support for America in the Spanish-American War reflected hope that
Cuba – 'the Ireland of the West' – might set a precedent for intervention in
Ireland. The *Freeman's Journal* meanwhile supported Spain as a Catholic
country, leading to a prolonged slanging-match during which the *Independent*

9 *Independent*, 19, 24, 27 July and 1 Sept. 1893; 27 Feb. and 17 Aug. 1894; 10 May 1895. 10
Independent, 31 Oct. and 4 and 24 Nov. 1893; 17 Aug. 1894; 12 Jan. and 8, 11 and 13 Feb.
1895. 11 *Independent*, 8 Feb., 31 May, 14, 26 and 29 Aug. and 1 Sept. 1893; 3, 17, 18 and 19
June 1895. 12 *Independent*, 11 June 1892; 3 and 7 Mar. 1894; 5 Jan., 29 July and 13 Sept.
1895. 13 *Independent*, 4 Nov. 1895. 14 *Independent*, 10 Oct. 1895.

posted photographs of Cuban concentration camp victims in its office windows.[15] This support extended (with occasional hesitation) to the inglorious
American colonial campaign in the Philippines. The *Independent* responded
to calls for nationalist reunion by declaring that the anti-Parnellite leaders'
betrayal disqualified them from public life; the only acceptable reunion would
be a Parnellite triumph.[16] Pro-unity Parnellites, notably the MP Timothy
Harrington (editor of the weekly *United Ireland*), suggested the *Independent*'s
position reflected fears of a merger with the *Freeman* which would make
Independent editorial staff redundant.

The papers suffered chronic financial problems; they were undercapitalized
and business considerations took second place to politics.[17] Several Parnellite
MPs (who received no parliamentary salaries) were nominally employed by
the paper, receiving large salaries that stood in marked contrast with the low
wages paid to other employees.[18] In 1897–8 the paper was re-launched under
pressure from creditors (notably the London-based Linotype Company, whose
nominee J.F. Hosker replaced Allan as manager). A syndicate was formed to
supply extra capital, dominated by the Parnellite MP and *Leinster Leader* proprietor J.L. Carew. New printing techniques (including coloured ink) were
employed. Increased reliance on syndicated news material and popular fic-
tion were, however, criticized by advanced nationalists, who also sympathized
with the numerous employees (including IRB activists), who were fired in
order to reduce costs.[19] Arthur Griffith called the reformatted paper 'our
Anglo-Jewish contemporary'.[20] D.P. Moran nicknamed it 'Snippy Bits', a
mocking reference to its reliance on overseas press agencies and syndicated
society gossip.

In 1900 the paper lapsed into insolvency, almost taking John Redmond
with it. The vast cost of running the *Independent* helped force the Parnellite
leader into a humiliating temporary alliance with Tim Healy. The *Independent*
was bought up by William Martin Murphy, who merged it with the Healyite
Daily Nation edited by W.F. Dennehy, founder of the *Irish Catholic*. Dennehy
maintained that Irishmen should accept the empire as inevitable and proclaim
their loyalty to it, and campaigned to have Catholic chaplains appointed on
British Royal Navy vessels.[21] Manning, who remained editor of the *Weekly
Independent*, opposed this as encouraging Irish Catholics to join up.[22] The

15 *Independent*, 19, 21 and 23 Dec. 1895; 11, 21, 25 and 26 Apr., 3, 7 and 23 May and 4 July
1898. 16 *Independent*, 14, 15 and 28 Jan. and 3 May 1895; 3 July 1896. 17 *Independent*, 9
Feb. and 23 Dec. 1892; 23 and 31 July 1895. 18 *Independent*, 23 Nov. and 18 Dec. 1899; 15
Feb. 1900. 19 Ó Broin, *Revolutionary underground*, 100. 20 *United Irishman*, 14 Oct. 1899; 24
Mar. 1900. 21 *IWI*, 20 Sept. 1902; 11 and 18 July 1903; W.F. Dennehy, 'Nationality within
the empire', *New Ireland Review* (Mar. 1905) 10–16 and (May 1905) 159–65. He may have
found it prudent to moderate this view in the pages of the *Independent and Nation*. 22 *IWI*,
2 and 20 July 1901.

Weekly Independent also mounted strong opposition to the South African War,
though this may have reflected readers' perceived attitudes and the influence
of old staffers from the Parnellite era. Manning stepped down as *Weekly
Independent* editor when he became town clerk of Kingstown/Dun Laoghaire
in 1902, but continued to write for the *Evening Herald*. He disgusted former
separatist allies by presenting the township's loyal addresses to Edward VII
in 1903 and 1907.[23]

The merged paper existed to promote the political fortunes of T.M. Healy,
and it highlighted the presence of land-grabbers in O'Brien's United Irish
League and the dilemmas of the party leadership over Liberal opposition to
denominational education. Financial considerations remained secondary; in
1916 Murphy described the paper as 'a bottomless pit' in terms of its running costs under Dennehy between 1900 and 1904. In 1904, with Healyite
politics at a discount, Murphy considered selling the paper, but after being
advised that there was room in the Irish market for a popular halfpenny daily
modelled on the Northcliffe press, Murphy decided to remodel the paper and
seize this opportunity himself. A new company (the present-day Independent
Newspapers) was established; initially private, it went public in 1928. Murphy
took Northcliffe's advice on the relaunch, but denied repeated rumours that
Northcliffe funded the paper. Murphy himself provided all the capital for
the enterprise. He also denied claims that Englishmen were being brought in
to staff the paper, claiming that not a single Englishman had been hired
(although existing English employees, such as the manager W.T. Brewster,
remained).

The most up-to-date machinery was bought from America; new premises
were secured on Middle Abbey Street. A new editor (T.R. Harrington, formerly chief reporter) was sent to London to study the latest newspaper techniques. Harrington later reflected on the scale of Murphy's worldwide oper-
ations at the time.

> We used to call each morning on Mr. Murphy in his office at
> Poultney Hill, discuss the programme for the day ... Mr. Chapman
> [the works manager] and I used then to attend to various matters ...
> involving the expenditure of thousands of pounds. Mr. Murphy him-
> self, with his London manager, was concentrating ... on a big con-
> tract for which they were tendering [i.e. in his construction and rail-
> way business] ... he was always cool, clear, and precise, though he
> mentioned to me about that time that he had 'several ships at sea and
> was hoping they would reach port' ... He added that he never lost
> an hour's sleep over them, though, perhaps, tens of thousands of
> pounds were involved.

23 *IWI*, 1 Feb. 1902; 25 July 1903; *Irish Times*, 7 Dec. 1908.

According to Murphy, the relaunch cost £50,000 before the new paper even appeared.[24]

The first daily *Independent* was issued from Abbey Street on 2 January 1905. Northcliffean techniques of news selection and compression, vigorous marketing and new styles of advertising introduced from 1908 by the advertising manager T.A. Grehan soon made an impact. The *Freeman* responded by cost-cutting to maintain dividends, retaining its traditional format and continuing to report Irish Party leaders' speeches in full. The *Independent* soon claimed a circulation of 30,000; from 1910 it published audited circulation figures, an innovation proposed by Murphy himself. Circulation was stimulated by the elections of 1910 and the controversies surrounding the Home Rule bill. The Larkinite boycott of Independent Newspapers (especially during the 1911 rail strike and the 1913–14 lockout) had only a temporary effect; during the First World War circulation rose to over 100,000. By 1915 the *Independent* was making £15,000 per annum; by 1919 £40,000.[25] Murphy's political hostility to the Irish Party was held in check by Harrington. In its early years the new *Independent* editorially proclaimed loyalty to the Irish Party while criticizing aspects of its policy and distancing itself from the dissidents led by Healy and William O'Brien. Nevertheless, critics claimed its news coverage, slanted against the Irish Party, played a significant role in undermining Redmondism. The paper grew more critical after the 1914 attempt at a partition-based compromise on Home Rule, and went into open opposition after mid-1916.

THE 'INDEPENDENT' AND EMPIRE

During the life of the 1892–5 Liberal government, the Parnellite *Independent* incorporated imperial issues into its denunciations of Liberal hypocrisy. Criticism of the British annexation of Uganda reflected the belief that colonial rule would encourage Protestant missionaries and hinder Catholic evangelization. Concern for the implications of annexation for the indigenous African population was a secondary consideration.[26] Massacres of Africans by British colonists in Matabeleland were denounced as 'awful and unprovoked ... greedy, murderous and cruel'.[27] When Bishop William Alexander of Derry, a shareholder in Cecil Rhodes' Chartered Company, justified the killing of Matabele by reference to Joshua's slaughter of the heathen in the Promised Land, the *Independent* denounced him as a hypocrite.[28] The paper welcomed British reverses on the North-West Frontier in 1897, suggesting the troops

---

24 *IWI*, 5 Jan. 1935. 25 Frank Callanan, *T.M. Healy* (Cork, 1996) 484. 26 *Independent*, 28 Nov. 1892; 2 June and 5 Nov. 1894. 27 *Independent*, 2 and 5 Jan. 1894. 28 *Independent*, 6 Jan. 1894.

were weakened by 'diseases of a loathsome character'.[29] Some ambivalence was visible in its Indian coverage however. When an Irish officer commanded the force which recaptured Chitral in 1895 it hailed a gallant fellow-countrymen before regretting a 'triumph for Jingo plunder'.[30]

Criticism of empire continued under the Salisbury government. The *Independent* responded to unionist glamourization of imperial strength by echoing the prophecies, made by British radicals and pessimists, of imperial overstretch and diplomatic isolation. Jingo predictions that China might become a second India were derided; British apprehensions over Russian expansion into Manchuria were noted with glee. Queen Victoria's Diamond Jubilee in 1897 was dismissed as asking the Irish to honour 'an estimable English lady who cares nothing for their country'. The *Independent* suggested that the money spent on the celebrations should instead have been used to relieve the latest Indian famine, and noted the colonial premiers' assertions of autonomy during their visit to London for the jubilee.[31] The imprisonment of the Indian nationalist Tilak was cited as proof that the *raj* was 'as despotic as Russia', maintained by force rather than the popular 'loyalty' asserted at the jubilee.[32] 'The Imperialists had their jubilee in 1897' proclaimed one Parnellite MP after Orange celebrations provoked rioting in Rutland [Parnell] Square and a police baton-charge. 'We will have ours in 1898'. The *Weekly Independent* marked the 1798 centenary with a widely praised, if loss-making, weekly supplement printed on green paper.

William Redmond received stacks of hate mail when he asked a Parnellite convention to cheer for the Afridi tribesmen defending their homes against British aggression.[33] When Redmond followed this up during the Fashoda crisis by declaring that if war broke out between Britain and France the Irish people would fight for France, one Tory newspaper remarked that his supporters, whom he called the Irish people, were a mob of skulking cattle mutilators, and suggested that if war did break out Redmond should be hung immediately.[34] The *Independent* retorted that cattle mutilators were morally superior to the abortionists, baby farmers, child molesters and practitioners of unnatural vice whose activities filled newspaper reports of British police courts. It added that an Anglo-French war would 'make many republics' from the empire.[35]

As the government's preparations for a new Sudan campaign became apparent (see chapter 2 above), the *Independent* hoped it would encounter the same fate as the Italian army at Adowa, and speculated that the European powers might join forces to attack the overstretched empire, 'most ruthless

29 *Independent*, 2 Sept. 1897.   **30** *Independent*, 26 Apr. 1895.   **31** *Independent*, 25 Sept. 1896; 15 Mar., 1 Apr. and 6 July 1897.   **32** *Independent*, 3 and 30 July and 16 Sept. 1897.   **33** *Independent*, 13 and 14 Oct. 1897.   **34** *Independent*, 22 Oct. 1898.   **35** *Independent*, 25 Oct. and 3 Nov. 1898; 31 Jan. and 3 Mar. 1899. The paper regularly contrasted Irish sexual virtue with newspaper reports of British vice, which it reprinted for readers' edification and titillation.

and hypocritical of the world's despoilers'.[36] The Parnellite journalist and MP J.J. O'Kelly, who had visited the Sudan in the early 1880s, supplied a regular commentary. Expressions of hope that Kitchener might share the fate of Gordon gave way to reminders that it was not surprising that modern weapons should rout brave men armed only with swords and spears.[37] The 'wholesale butchery' of wounded Dervishes after Omdurman was portrayed as being as bad as the behaviour of the lowest savages and, like the *Manchester Guardian* in England, the *Independent* opposed the proposed government grant to the British commander.[38] Explicit connections were also drawn with past British behaviour in Ireland. Kitchener's actions (including the desecration of the Mahdi's grave) were compared with the horrors of Elizabethan Ireland.[39] Similarly, in 1899, descriptions of British troops burning villages in West Africa were compared to Irish experiences in 1798.[40]

At first glance the *Independent*'s coverage of events in southern Africa seems to fit the same pattern, and it reprinted Labouchere's denunciations of the conquest of what became Rhodesia.[41] Sympathy for the African population of Rhodesia was limited and confused, however, as demonstrated when the defeat of Jameson's attempt to overthrow the Kruger government in the Transvaal Republic was followed by a Matabele uprising. The paper endorsed the rebellion, but also simultaneously complained that, by allowing the colony's available defence forces to launch the Jameson Raid, the jingoes had left settlers at the mercy of savages.[42]

The *Independent* denounced the Jameson Raid as unprovoked aggression and contrasted Boer leniency towards the raiders with the harsh treatment of Irish American dynamiters in British prisons. The paper even suggested Kruger should be asked to demand the dynamiters' release in exchange for Jameson. It hoped the raid had burst the 'British Empire bubble' and Germany would replace Britain as suzerain of the Transvaal. An advertisement claimed proudly 'President Kruger Reads the *Weekly Independent*'.[43] The *Independent*'s position was complicated, however, by its involvement with Rochfort Maguire, a leading associate of Rhodes who was also related by marriage to Bishop Alexander. Maguire had played a prominent and highly discreditable role in Rhodes' dealings with the Matabele chief Lobengula. He was Parnellite MP for West Clare 1892–5 and assisted the 1897 refinancing of the *Independent*. In January 1898 – several months after his com-

---

36 *Independent*, 17 and 28 Mar. 1895.   37 *Independent*, 20 Apr. and 9 June 1896.   38 *Independent*, 6 Sept. 1898; *IWI*, 22 Feb. 1899.   39 *Independent*, 5 Sept. 1898.   40 *Independent*, 3 Jan. 1899.   41 *Independent*, 2, 11 and 29 Jan. and 25 Oct. 1894. Despite Labouchere's opposition to Parnell the *Independent* regularly reprinted items from his paper *Truth*, as his criticisms of Liberal Imperialists could be deployed against John Dillon's continued alliance with the Liberals.   42 *Independent*, 31 Mar., 2 and 3 Apr. and 29 July 1896.   43 *Independent*, 2, 3, 4, 7, 8 and 10 Jan., 29 and 30 Apr., 3 and 19 June 1896.

plicity in the Jameson Raid was exposed – he was offered a Parnellite by-election candidacy in a marginal Dublin Unionist seat; Maguire declined but contributed £250 to the campaign.[44] Hence the *Independent*, while denouncing the Jameson Raid, alleged Rhodes was being attacked to screen Chamberlain, and praised Rhodes' courageous role in conciliating the rebellious Matabele.[45] It remarked that the Liberal MPs loudest in their denunciations of Rhodes had savaged Parnell at the bidding of the Nonconformist conscience, and bitterly contrasted English public support for Rhodes with Irish treatment of Parnell.[46] The *Independent* even proclaimed that such great men as Rhodes and Parnell should not be judged by conventional morality, and fantasized that Rhodes secretly aimed to lead a Boer-supported South African Republic.[47]

Like most other Irish nationalist papers, the *Independent* was outspoken in its support for the Boer republics in the crises leading to the outbreak of the South African War. It subsequently joined in nationalist rejoicing over repeated British military defeats. Between editions, news from the front was signalled by hoisting coloured lights above the *Independent* offices in Trinity Street. Telegrams from the front and pictures of the rival leaders were projected onto a screen in the office windows. News-hungry crowds spilled into Dame Street, where they were attacked by an 'Anti-Boer Society' of Trinity College students, in turn resisted by squads of *Evening Herald* newsboys.[48] It is hardly surprising that, as Donal Lowry points out below, the police asked the paper to end these displays.[49] When Trinity celebrated the relief of Mafeking by decorating Burke's statue, the *Independent* fumed that Burke would have defended the Boers as he had the American colonists.[50]

The paper justified its reproduction of the London *Daily Telegraph*'s war coverage by stating that though the political views expressed were alien to Irish nationalists, the *Telegraph*'s stories must be accurate because the military authorities were attempting to suppress them.[51] Rudyard Kipling's poem 'The absent-minded beggar', published for the benefit of soldiers' womenfolk and children in Britain, was accompanied by a verse parody hailing the 'sturdy-minded beggar' Kruger and proclaiming that when British troops returned many graves would be 'left behind them'. 'Shade of Parnell!' exclaimed Griffith.[52]

44 *Independent*, 25 and 30 Apr. and 25 July 1895; 14 Feb. 1896; 21 Apr. and 8 July 1897; 1 Jan. and 2 Apr. 1898; obituary, *IWI*, 25 Apr. 1925. See Anthony Thomas, *Rhodes: the race for Africa* (London, 1996) 190–9, 202–3. 45 *Independent*, 26 Aug. 1896. 46 *Independent*, 9 May 1896. 47 *Independent*, 18 Apr. and 8, 9 and 25 Aug. 1898; 4 May and 20 and 22 July 1899. 48 *Independent*, 13, 14 and 20 Oct. 1899. 49 See also Donal McCracken, *Forgotten protest: Ireland and the Anglo-Boer War* (Belfast, 2003) 45. 50 *Independent*, 19 Dec. 1899. 51 *Independent*, 3 and 4 Nov. 1899. 52 *Independent*, 31 Oct. and 1 Nov. 1899; *United Irishman*, 28 Oct. and 4 Nov. 1899.

Queen Victoria's 1900 Irish visit was officially announced as symbolizing royal gratitude for the valour of Irish soldiers with the British forces in South Africa, and was accompanied by the formation of the Irish Guards and the granting of permission for Irish soldiers to wear shamrock on St Patrick's Day. The visit was roundly denounced by the *Independent*, which campaigned against Lord Mayor Pile's successful campaign to persuade Dublin Corporation to present a loyal address to the monarch. This editorial line was endorsed by correspondents such as the young W.T. Cosgrave (who declared Victoria personally responsible for all Ireland's misfortunes during her reign, including the Famine) and Anna Parnell (who suggested that nationalists who did not wish to be identified with 'the robber hordes in South Africa' should wear shamrock dipped in ink until the desecration of the national emblem had been expiated 'by a Boer victory or other means').[53]

After the occupation of the Boer republics (which led to a marked decrease in the war news carried by the *Independent*, since most British war correspondents returned home) the *Independent* continued to attack British mistreatment of Boer civilians. It publicized the sufferings of Boer women and children in concentration camps, highlighted British reprisals against Boer prisoners and civilians and republished Continental cartoons depicting Chamberlain and Kitchener as mass-murderers. Chamberlain, it suggested, would be immortalized in children's stories as 'Glasseye', more terrifying than Bluebeard.[54] The trial and execution of the Australian officer 'Breaker' Morant and an associate for killing Boer prisoners were greeted with the comment that these 'two Australian devils' were only the tip of an iceberg of atrocities.[55]

Again, attitudes towards non-European peoples were ambiguous at best. Celebrating Boer guerrilla leaders like De Wet, the paper claimed that 'The physical superiority of the Boers gives no chance to the inferior [English] race ... leaving the British soldier degraded forever in the eyes of the loathsome nigger.'[56] The paper responded to British complaints about the killing by Boers of black prisoners by declaring that the British had broken the laws of war by using 'savage' troops against 'civilized' opponents, and that the Boers were justified in eradicating this threat to the white population. The *Independent* rejoiced that the 1902 Treaty of Vereeniging ensured that the Boers 'will not be insulted by any admission of their debased and treacherous subjects, the Kaffirs, to civic rights'.[57] When Chamberlain visited South Africa after the war the paper printed racist cartoons of Africans who met with him.[58] Those who rebelled against British authority sometimes received more sympathetic coverage, though even the cartoonist Frank Rigney, far

---

53 *Independent*, 12 Mar. 1900. 54 *IWI*, 18 Jan. and 8 Feb. 1902; cartoon supplement, 15 Mar. 1902. 55 *IWI*, 12 Apr. 1902. 56 *IWI*, 1 Feb. and 8 Mar. 1902. 57 *IWI*, 31 May and 7 June 1902. 58 *IWI*, 10 Jan. and 7 and 21 Mar. 1903.

2 Cartoon by Frank Rigney from the *Irish Weekly Independent*, 5 April 1906.
Reproduced courtesy of the National Library of Ireland

more nationalistic than the editorial staff (he was subsequently active in Irish American radical nationalist circles), portrayed them as resembling blackface minstrels. The paper later jeered at the Anglo-Japanese alliance, suggesting that after this pact with 'an inferior Asiatic race', Britain would soon be reduced to allying on equal terms with 'Hottentots' and 'Eskimos'.[59]

THE 'INDEPENDENT' AND EMPIRE UNDER WILLIAM MARTIN MURPHY

From 1904 the *Independent* was embroiled in controversy over Murphy's plans to hold an International Exhibition in Herbert Park, South Dublin (modelled on that of William Dargan in 1852), with the intention of positioning himself as leader of the Irish business community. Separatists and Irish Irelanders complained that the exhibition would promote imports, though much of their opposition reflected Murphy's success in securing the king as patron and the unionist politics of many of the Dublin businessmen involved. The *Independent* had attacked Queen Victoria's 1900 visit and criticized Edward VII's coronation, but it strongly supported the 1903 royal visit and thereafter praised the king as a friend of Ireland. When a 1903 meeting addressed by Lord Mayor Harrington was disrupted by Griffith, Maud Gonne and their allies, who demanded an immediate mayoral repudiation of the impending royal visit, the *Independent* denounced them as 'hooligans'.[60] Similar disruption of a meeting convened by Murphy to stimulate support for the Exhibition almost lost Eoin MacNeill his job after the *Independent* denounced him as 'a civil servant masquerading as Robert Emmet'.[61] When the Irish Party leadership subsequently opposed the presentation of an address to the visiting monarch by Dublin Corporation, the *Independent* denounced them for capitulating to

> such ridiculous separatists as the so-called 'National Council' – the latest mixum-gatherum of hysterical females, shoneen mystics, and ignorant hobbledehoys. The fact that the 'Brats' Brigade' suggests any line of policy should be sufficient reason why self-respecting Irishmen should adopt the very reverse.[62]

Similar opposition to an address during the king's 1904 visit was denounced as the work of 'obscure organs of churlishness', though the issue of the *Weekly Independent* that welcomed the visit simultaneously denounced Younghusband's incursion into Tibet as naked aggression and massacre.[63]

59 *IWI*, 22 Feb. 1902. 60 *IWI*, 23 May 1903. 61 *IWI*, 2 Apr. 1904; Michael Tierney, *Eoin MacNeill: scholar and man of action*, ed. F.X. Martin (Oxford, 1980) 72. 62 *IWI*, 11 July 1903. 63 *IWI*, 30 Jan. and 7 May 1904.

British newspapers saw the Exhibition as proof of Ireland's increasing prosperity and contentment within the empire. Murphy and the *Independent* retorted to Irish Ireland criticisms and an attempted boycott by arguing that the exhibition would provide employment and allow Irish manufacturers to learn from the best new overseas products; opponents were accused of trying to make Ireland turn her back on the modern world. 'We are to ignore the time spirit which is infusing into progressive peoples a sentiment of international solidarity, and are bidden to take an antiquated and unamiable provincialism as our ideal.'[64]

Edward VII opened the exhibition in 1907 and offered Murphy a knighthood, which he declined on political grounds. The event helped considerably in winning Murphy acceptance among Dublin's traditionally Protestant and unionist-dominated business community, and in bringing about his election to the committee, and eventually the presidency, of the Dublin Chamber of Commerce. When Edward VII died, the *Independent* mourned him as a great and beloved monarch and friend of Ireland; Murphy organized the reception committee for George V's 1911 visit.[65]

Murphy's railway contracts in East Africa also attracted political controversy. During the January 1910 election Redmondites in Healy's North Louth constituency claimed Healy had repaid Murphy for the support of the *Independent* by using political influence to get the contracts. Murphy and Healy denied this; Healy stated that while Murphy was a friend Harrington was hostile, and that he did not consider the *Independent* friendly.[66] Its Dundalk correspondent was his bitter local enemy T.F. McGahon, proprietor of the *Dundalk Democrat*.[67] Controversy over Murphy's East African interests recurred during the 1912 labour enquiry. Larkin accused Murphy of neglecting workers who contracted tropical diseases on the railways. Murphy replied that they were paid high salaries to take such risks, and the *Independent* published a letter from a Clontarf employee of Murphy's tram company praising his generous treatment while ill with typhus.[68]

Murphy's proprietorship also exerted an influence over the line taken by the *Independent* on Irish Home Rule and, in particular, the idea of Dominion status as a solution to Ireland's unsatisfactory constitutional position. After 1906 fresh contrasts were drawn between the granting of self-governing Dominion status to a South Africa dominated by Boers who had recently fought Britain, and the continued repression of a relatively peaceful Ireland.[69] In 1914 the *Independent* took advantage of an unsuccessful pro-German revolt by Boer hardliners to point out that South Africa would have been lost if it

---

64 *IWI*, 12 Mar. 1904. 65 *IWI*, 14 May 1910. 66 *IWI*, 9 July 1910; 18 Feb. 1911. 67 *IWI*, 21 Jan. 1910. 68 *Independent*, 4 Oct. 1913. 69 *Independent*, 24 Aug. 1907; 21 Aug. 1909.

2 Cartoon by Frank Rigney from the *Irish Weekly Independent*, 24 August 1907.
Reproduced courtesy of the National Library of Ireland

had been treated like Ireland. It highlighted reports that the rebels had cited Carson as a model.[70]

In 1912 the *Independent* took up the case (put forward by Erskine Childers in his book *The framework of Home Rule*) that Gladstonian Home Rule would not provide a lasting solution, and that the answer lay in Dominion status. This reflected the views of Murphy himself, who had been impressed by Childers' book and feared that an Irish parliament with restricted fiscal powers would place political advantage above financial prudence, and escape responsibility by blaming Westminster.[71] The *Independent* also complained that the continuing fiscal authority of the Westminster parliament, combined with a reduction in the number of Irish MPs, would increase Ireland's vulnerability to damaging financial legislation. Murphy shared the widespread middle-class nationalist view, encouraged by the Childers Commission Report of 1896, that Irish economic development had been stunted by British over-taxation. The Parnellite *Independent* had made much of the report, and the new paper attacked the 1909 Lloyd George Budget, the 1911 National Insurance Act and wartime tax measures on similar grounds.

After the Home Rule bill made its first passage through parliament (and hence could no longer be amended) the paper laid aside advocacy of Dominion status for the time being and issued regular appeals to Ulster unionists to stop bluffing and join nationalists in improving the bill by agreement. It kept up its fire on the government over such issues as the embargo imposed on Irish cattle to halt the spread of foot and mouth (where the *Freeman* was inhibited by its links to the Irish Party and hence to the government). The 1913 lock-out added to the paper's dissatisfaction. While the strikers' complaints about the government's deployment of the police to protect the employers' property are well-known, Murphy and the *Independent* were also discontented with the government's handling of the crisis; they believed the police had not been backed up properly and the government had tried to appease the strikers for fear of losing labour votes in Britain.[72] Most of the British newspaper comment reprinted in the *Independent* came from Conservative journals – most pro–Home Rule Liberal and Labour papers backed the strikers.[73] The *Independent* complained that if these papers really supported Home Rule they should not meddle ignorantly in an Irish dispute.

By October 1913 the *Independent* had begun to recall old suspicions that nationalists could not rely on Asquith and his lieutenants. It grew increas-

---

70 *Independent*, 6 Mar. 1915.   71 *Independent*, 9 Mar. and 25 May 1912.   72 National Archive of Ireland, Dublin, T.R. Harrington Papers, 4/5 Murphy to Harrington, 1 May 1916.   73 See the Murphy profile in the *Standard*, reprinted *Independent*, 24 Nov. 1913; see also *Independent*, 13 Oct. 1913 (citing the *Globe*) and 8 Oct. 1913 (citing the *Morning Post*).

ingly concerned at official hints, especially from Churchill, that the government might raise 'an Offa's Dyke between the North-East corner and the
rest of this country'.[74] Murphy reacted with particular fury to the Liberal
government's adoption of a compromise based on partition in March 1914,
making an unprecedented personal intervention to ensure that the paper kept
up the attack. He subsequently directed Harrington to throw the paper
behind the nascent Irish Volunteers.[75] The editorial tone grew still more
heated when stray bullets from the Bachelor's Walk shootings hit the paper's
subsidiary offices at the southern end of O'Connell Bridge.

Nevertheless, from the outset of the First World War the *Independent*
repeatedly argued that Ireland's economic and political interests lay with
the empire, urged readers to enlist for overseas service and reminded them
that war loans would be less costly than a German victory. Employees were
also encouraged to join up. When the *Freeman* accused the *Independent* of
covert anti-war sympathies because of its criticisms of Redmond, Harrington
retorted that although Murphy rarely intervened in the editorial affairs of
the paper he had expressly endorsed the decision to back Redmond's stance
on recruiting, regretting only that Redmond had not acted sooner.[76] In 1913
the paper had co-operated with Sir Roger Casement's campaign to relieve
distress in Connemara and seek a German liner service for Queenstown;
however, when Casement allied with the Germans the *Independent*
denounced him as insane.[77] The sinking of the *Lusitania* was condemned in
graphic terms, mourning the fate of 'the innocent victims of the red-handed
sea-fiends ... [which] shocked the civilised world – in which Germany can
no longer be included ... [it was] as if a band of assassins had descended
on the town of Cavan and slaughtered the entire population'.[78] Gordon
Brewster, the paper's chief cartoonist and son of W.T. Brewster, celebrated
Allied prowess and ridiculed the Central Powers in front-page cartoons for
the *Weekly Independent*; some were reproduced in recruiting literature. His
brother, R.G. Brewster, enlisted at the outbreak of war and was killed in
action in 1918.[79]

Although the paper grew increasingly critical of Redmond's political tactics, Harrington restrained Murphy, fearing that all-out conflict with Redmond
might damage circulation.[80] When denouncing the 1916 Easter Rising, however, the paper insisted that Birrell and Redmond must share with Carson
the blame for provoking the insurrection. The *Independent* also campaigned

74 *Independent*, 9 and 10 Oct. 1913; *IWI*, 22 Nov. 1913.   75 T.M. Healy to Maurice Healy,
17 Mar. 1914, quoted in Callanan, *Healy*, 503; see also *Independent*, 5 Nov. 1914.   76
Independent, 1 Oct. 1914.   77 *IWI*, 21 Feb. 1914; *Independent*, 5 and 10 Oct. 1914; 9 Jan., 6
Mar. and 11 Dec. 1915; 1 Jan. 1916; 8 Feb. 1922.   78 *IWI*, 15 May 1915.   79 *IWI*, 17 Aug.
1918; *Independent*, 5 Oct. 1914.   80 *Independent*, 10 Dec. 1914.

against the partitionist compromise offered by Lloyd George and endorsed by Redmond.[81] When the proposals failed because of the conflicting expectations of Redmondites and Ulster unionists, the *Independent* openly denounced Redmond and resumed its campaign for all-Ireland Dominion status, a cause also advocated by an isolated Murphy at the Irish Convention of 25 July 1917–5 April 1918. Although Murphy privately favoured conscription if accompanied by immediate Dominion status, the *Independent* joined the 1918 anti-conscription campaign.[82]

Murphy increasingly despaired of the government, lamenting that recruiting had been mismanaged and no effective constitutionalist alternative had emerged.[83] The paper bitterly contrasted the Indianization of the Indian Civil Service with the purge of nationalist security risks from its Irish counterpart.[84] As late as 1919, however, the *Independent* still hoped for concessions from Lord French. It hailed the defeat of Germany as vindicating its support for the war effort, and commented scathingly on the Irish Party's belated embrace of Dominion status 'when whipped to it by the *Independent* newspapers'.[85] Throughout the War of Independence it joined the Northcliffe press and elite groups such as Horace Plunkett's Irish Dominion League in advocating Dominion status, which it appealed to Ulster to accept 'as a business proposition'.[86] The paper also drew scathing comparisons between the government's behaviour in Ireland and German atrocities in Belgium.[87] The Government of Ireland Act was dismissed as an 'Irish Partition and Plunder Scheme'.[88] Again, connections were made with events taking place elsewhere in the empire in order to advance an essentially Irish domestic political agenda. Britain was accused of spreading anarchy worldwide through its 'Amritsar policy', a reference to the recent massacre of Indians by British troops. More significantly, comparisons continued to be made between Ireland and the self-governing settler Dominions. 'England recognises that the Colonies [i.e. Dominions] cannot be kept in leading-strings forever … Only in Ireland is the demand for self-government branded by England as a crime.'[89]

During the War of Independence the *Independent* found itself threatened by both sides. It suffered government censorship for criticising the security forces, and the destruction of its printing presses by the IRA in December 1919, as retribution for having denounced the attempted assassination of Lord French.[90] The chief photographer, Matt Rice, was repeatedly threatened by Black and Tans for his records of their misdeeds, although he was protected

81 E.g. *IWI*, 24 June 1916. 82 *IWI*, 5 Aug. 1916; 25 May 1918. 83 Harrington papers, 1052/4/46 Murphy to Harrington, 19 Oct. 1918. 84 *IWI*, 6 and 13 July 1918. 85 *IWI*, 14 June 1919. 86 *IWI*, 30 July 1921. 87 *IWI*, 14 Aug. 1920; 29 Jan. 1921. 88 *Independent*, 1 Mar. 1920. 89 *Independent*, 4 June 1920. 90 *Independent*, 16 Jan. 1920; 28 Apr. 1922.

by fellow-journalists, some of them loyalists. Some staff members belonged to the IRA, with an active cell among the printers.[91]

William Martin Murphy died in 1919 and was succeeded by his son, William Lombard Murphy, a surgeon who served with the Royal Army Medical Corps at Salonica and who remained proprietor until his death in 1943. The Murphys consciously promoted the image of their founding father as a farsighted entrepreneur and statesman, and retained a strong anglophilia. The Dominion basis of the Treaty settlement was hailed as having vindicating Murphy's position.[92] Opponents had their own memories of the *Independent* group's history. During the Spanish Civil War, Frank Ryan claimed that its stories of Republican atrocities in Spain were the product of a constant 'imperialist' ethos, echoes of its 1914 accounts of German atrocities in Belgium.[93] The paper's attitude to empire was, however, inevitably influenced by the events of 1916–23 and the sheer passage of time. During the 1930s younger editorial writers praised Gandhi,[94] compared British repression of the Arab Revolt to the Black and Tans and predicted Britain would compromise with the Mufti of Jerusalem as it had with Michael Collins.[95]

The ambivalence of the *Independent* towards empire in the paper's first three decades was shared by large sections of the Irish nationalist population. Its Parnellite incarnation was often fiercely critical of empire, hovering between British radical anti-imperialism and straightforward declarations that any enemy of Britain was a friend of Ireland. This critique, however, was opportunistic and unsystematic; its ability to take advantage of nationalist support for the Boers was hindered by former Parnellite coquetries with Cecil Rhodes, while discontented separatists within the crumbling Parnellite party contrasted its cries of 'Independence from British dictation' with its increasing dependence on British creditors and news agencies. Murphy's *Independent*, despite such individual vagaries as the separatism of Frank Rigney, was more favourable to the empire. The Murphy paper aimed at a market composed of those who enjoyed or aspired to a middle-class consumerist lifestyle. In this context, for the *Independent* as for British Liberal commentators, membership of an empire reformed around liberal principles of self-government could be justified as a legitimate commercial proposition bringing mutual benefits. This acceptance, however, was modified by suspicion that the imperial government was too short sighted and narrow-minded to develop Irish resources and treat Irish nationalists as equals.

91 Hugh Oram, *The newspaper book: a history of newspapers in Ireland, 1649–1983* (Dublin, 1983) 139–40. **92** *Independent*, 14 Jan. 1922; *IWI*, 10 and 17 Dec. 1921. **93** Fearghal McGarry, *Ireland and the Spanish Civil War* (Cork, 1999) 52, 94. **94** *IWI*, 10 May 1930; 31 Jan. 1931. **95** *Independent*, 10, 27, 28, 30 and 31 Jan. and 1 Feb. 1939.

Murphy, whose business interests spanned the empire, distanced himself from 'unamiable provincialism' (i.e. separatism) and what he saw as the irresponsible opportunism of the Irish Parliamentary Party. Nevertheless, he and his paper came to see Home Rule as insufficient, and campaigned for Dominion status as the only way to reconcile Irish self-respect with the constraints and opportunities of empire.

8. 'The view from Fleet Street': Irish nationalist journalists in London and their attitudes towards empire, 1892–1898

IAN SHEEHY

From its earliest years one of the central charges made against the Irish Home Rule movement was that a separate Dublin parliament would spell the demise of the British empire. In his March 1880 election manifesto Disraeli claimed that the Liberals, having previously failed to 'enfeeble' the colonies through a policy of 'decomposition', had seized upon Home Rule as the weapon with which to shatter the empire. In presenting Home Rule as inimical to a united empire the Tory chief was playing on a seemingly widespread fear. That very month Justin McCarthy, the Irish Party MP, well-known novelist and London Irish journalist, had deplored in the periodical press how English public opinion, enslaved by the belief that Home Rule meant 'the dismemberment of the empire', refused to even accord the Irish issue a proper debate.[1]

Opponents of Gladstone's Home Rule bill of 1886 also accused the Liberal leader of seeking the break-up of the British empire. Some Unionists focused on the effect that Home Rule would have on the colonies of settlement, arguing that such an act of separation would scupper growing hopes of closer relations between them and Britain. Others, including liberal intellectuals like W.E.H. Lecky and Goldwin Smith, were more concerned with the consequences for British rule in India, believing that the encouragement Irish Home Rule would give to Indian nationalists might prove fatal. To Lord Randolph Churchill, Irish autonomy simply meant the end of the empire, for it effectively represented an admission by the British of their incapacity to govern other peoples. 'We cannot hold our supremacy over our colonies if we cannot govern this country', he said at Belfast in February 1886. 'Mr Gladstone asks for time, like Macbeth before the murder of Duncan. Mr Gladstone, before he plunges the knife into the British Empire, reflects; he hesitates.' Many Unionists felt that the solution to the Irish question in fact lay within the empire, namely in the adoption of the Indian model of arbitrary government, of rule by force rather then consent. Taking their cue from the Tory leader Lord Salisbury and his infamous Hottentot parallel of May 1886, they asserted

---

1 John Morley, *The life of Gladstone*, 2 vols (London, 1908), ii, 160–1; Justin McCarthy, 'The common-sense of Home Rule', *Nineteenth Century* (Mar. 1880) 406–7.

that, like Indians and Africans, the Irish were a race incapable of self-government.[2] Whatever their specific concern, Unionists persistently hammered the general point home. 'Mr G could hardly recite the Lord's prayer in public now without laying himself open to the charge of inciting the disruption of the Empire', wrote Edward Hamilton, Gladstone's former private secretary, in July 1887.[3]

Whilst the Unionists' dire warnings would not have perturbed the Fenian element within the Home Rule movement, many constitutional Irish nationalists responded vigorously to charges of imperial disintegration. Speaking to the Commons in June 1874 Isaac Butt, the Irish Party leader, averred that Home Rule would maintain the 'integrity of the Empire', since Westminster would retain 'exclusive control' over imperial affairs. Rather than being an act of severance (or the first step towards independence), said Butt, Home Rule would make the Irish people loyal to Britain and its empire, bringing unity to the latter, for it would represent a 'new compact carried ...on the free sanction of the Irish people'. Ireland would become what she had never been under the Union: one of the empire's strengths. Indeed, Butt's federal scheme of Home Rule, whereby Irish MPs were to remain at Westminster, was designed to allow Ireland to continue to play a full part in an empire which she had helped create and people.[4] Other nationalist publicists followed Butt's lead and presented Home Rule as a source of imperial strength and vitality. In his 1880 article McCarthy sought to correct the erroneous assumptions of English public opinion by arguing that Home Rule would 'really tend to reconcile England and Ireland, and make them, for the first time since the Union, friendly and willing co-partners in one great Imperial system'.[5]

Nationalists had one thing in common with British unionists: they too believed that the empire supplied the model for Irish government. However, for them the answer lay with white settler colonies like Canada and Australia, and they repeatedly sought to bolster their assertions by citing these examples (doing so more often than is sometimes acknowledged).[6] This was because there

2 L.J. Jennings (ed.), *Speeches by Lord Randolph Churchill*, 2 vols (London, 1889), ii, 4–5, 13; Tom Dunne, '"Les trahison des clercs": British intellectuals and the first home-rule crisis', *Irish Historical Studies*, 23 (1982/3) 154–66; Donal McCartney, *W.E.H. Lecky: historian and politician, 1838–1903* (Dublin, 1994) 114–30. 3 British Library, London, Edward Hamilton papers, Add. MS. 48646 Hamilton diaries, entry for 5 July 1887. 4 *Hansard*, 3rd series, ccxx (1874) 700–17. Other nationalists in the 1870s and 1880s, such as the young John Redmond and F.H. O'Donnell, also stressed the importance of combining Home Rule with continuing Irish representation at Westminster so that Ireland would not be cut off from the empire and its Irish inhabitants. In Redmond's case this commitment to the empire was long-lived, becoming prominent during his time as Irish Party leader from 1900 until 1918. See Paul Bew, *John Redmond* (Dundalk, 1996) 12–13, 30–9 and F.H. O'Donnell, *A history of the Irish Parliamentary Party*, 2 vols (London, 1910), i, 48–52. 5 McCarthy, 'The common-sense of Home Rule', 421. 6 Stephen Howe, for example, in his recent work *Ireland and empire* (Oxford, 2000) says that due to the limited

had been discontent among these communities during the first half of the nineteenth century, until the granting of 'responsible' self-government to Canada
in the 1840s and the Australian colonies in the 1850s had seemingly turned
them into loyal members of the empire. The Canadian parallel was especially
popular with nationalists. As well as removing the deep discontent there (which
had erupted into armed revolt in the 1830s), internal self-government had also
seemingly healed the cultural-religious divisions between Catholic French
Canadians and Protestant British settlers which had contributed to the earlier
strife and which found such strong echoes in Ireland. Thus, Butt in 1874 and
McCarthy in 1880 (and again in an 1882 article) employed the example of
Canada to show how self-government in Ireland would lead to domestic harmony and imperial loyalty.[7] Then, in the midst of the Home Rule crisis of
1886, the nationalist historian R. Barry O'Brien expounded the 'lesson of
Canada' in detail for the *Freeman's Journal*. 'Home Rule, and Home Rule only,
made Canada loyal and contented', he concluded before echoing Butt's 1874
speech in his closing words: 'Home Rule, and Home Rule only, will make
Ireland loyal and contented – the strength, and not the weakness, of the
Empire.'[8] By then the imperial arguments and examples of the nationalists had
been taken up by the Gladstonian Liberals. Gladstone himself had been a leading supporter of self-government for the white colonies since mid-century, and,
as recent studies have stressed, he came to see Home Rule as very much within
this tradition of imperial pacification and unity through Westminster sponsored
reform, glancing at the colonial parallels, especially Canada, during his
Commons speeches of 1886.[9] Moreover, he and his Irish allies received a welcome fillip from the fact that most political leaders in the white colonies shared
their vision of Home Rule as conducive to imperial unity. This included the
arch empire-builder Cecil Rhodes, who saw a federal Home Rule scheme as
the first step towards a grander imperial federation.[10]

autonomy enjoyed by the white colonies, nationalists made little attempt to draw comparisons
between them and Ireland (pp 44–5). However, the historical evidence does not support this
claim. In contrast to Howe, David Fitzpatrick does note how both Irish and Liberal Home
Rulers drew attention to the example of Canada. See David Fitzpatrick, 'Ireland and the empire',
in Andrew Porter (ed.), *The Oxford history of the British empire*, iii: *the nineteenth century* (Oxford,
1999) 506.   **7** *Hansard*, 3rd series, ccxx (1874) 700–17; McCarthy, 'The common-sense of
Home Rule', *Nineteenth Century*, 406–7 and 'Home rule II', *Nineteenth Century* (June 1882)
865–7.   **8** R. Barry O'Brien, 'Articles on Ireland', *Freeman's pamphlets*, *No. 8* (Dublin, 1886)
45. Another nationalist who in 1885–6 highlighted the Canadian precedent in order to prove
Ireland's capacity for Imperial loyalty was O'Brien's close friend, Sir Charles Gavan Duffy,
who had himself gone from being a Young Ireland rebel in the 1840s to a successful colonial
politician in the 1870s. See R. Barry O'Brien, *The life of Charles Stewart Parnell* (London, 1910,
2nd edn) 333–60.   **9** H.C.G. Matthew, *Gladstone, 1809–98* (Oxford, 1997) 468–71, 501; E.F.
Biagini, *Gladstone* (London, 2000) 25–8, 76–89, 103–4; *Hansard*, 3rd series, ccciv (1886) 1045–9,
1081 and vol. cccvi, 1228–30; Dunne, '"Les trahison des clercs"', 144–6.   **10** O'Brien, *Life of
Parnell*, 426–30.

Although the views expressed in this long running debate on Home Rule and the empire were often passionately held, they also reflected the increasingly prominent place that the empire was beginning to occupy within British politics and society.[11] Disraeli's Crystal Palace speech of 1872 and the Royal Titles Act of 1876, which proclaimed Queen Victoria the Empress of India, was part of this process. External threats also concentrated British political minds on the empire. The United States, Germany, France and Russia were all growing rapidly in economic and military power during the second half of the nineteenth century. By the 1880s rivals were undertaking ambitious programmes of navy building, and consolidation at home was being succeeded by expansion abroad. In the face of global recession they had substituted protectionism for free trade, with their new acquisitions being absorbed into their commercial systems. A small number of mighty states were seemingly set to divide the earth between them (a lesson pressed home by Social Darwinists in these decades). For Britain the signs were clear – industrial, naval and imperial supremacy could no longer be taken for granted.

The resulting renewed commitment to empire – the so-called 'new imperialism' – had two main features. Firstly, and most prominently, it involved calls for closer ties between Britain and the white settler colonies, or Dominions, of Canada, Australia and New Zealand. Only an integrated empire could match the challenge of larger land-based rivals. Dominion manpower, markets and raw materials could be drawn into an imperial economy building on possibilities offered by recent advances in communications (underwater telegraph cables) and shipping (increased capacity and refrigeration capabilities). These ideas were accompanied by a new vision of a 'Greater Britain', a concept first advanced by Sir Charles Dilke in his 1868 work of that name. Dilke argued that a British people, linked by their superior civilization,

11 There is a growing body of work dealing with this phenomenon, on which the discussion contained in the following paragraphs has been based. For accessible surveys see T.O. Lloyd, *The British empire, 1558–1995* (Oxford, 1996, 2nd edn); Lawrence James, *The rise and fall of the British empire* (London, 1994); P.J. Marshall, '1783–1870: an expanding empire' and Ged Martin and Benjamin E. Kline, 'British emigration and new identities' both in P.J. Marshall (ed.), *The Cambridge illustrated history of the British empire* (Cambridge, 1996); Andrew Porter, 'Introduction: Britain and the empire in the nineteenth century' in Porter (ed.), *The Oxford history of the British empire*, vol. iii. For more detailed studies see Andrew S. Thompson, *Imperial Britain: the empire in British politics, 1880–1932* (Harlow, 2000); Andrew S. Thompson, 'The language of imperialism and the meanings of empire: imperial discourse in British politics, 1895–1914', *Journal of British Studies*, 2:36 (Apr. 1997) 147–77; Wallace G. Mills, 'Victorian imperialism as religion – civil or otherwise' in Roger D. Long (ed.), *The man on the spot: essays on British empire history* (Westport, Conn., 1995) 21–43; E.H.H. Green, 'The political economy of empire, 1880–1914' in Porter (ed.), *The Oxford history of the British empire*, vol. iii; and the essays collected in Carl Bridge and Kent Fedorowich (eds), *The British world: diaspora, culture, identity* (London, 2003), also available as a special number of the *Journal of Imperial and Commonwealth History*, 2:31 (May 2003).

common language and culture, attachment to parliamentary government and reverence for the rule of law, remained a single nation although spread across the globe. As a result, in Alfred Milner's words, 'every white man of British birth' would feel at home in any of the settler colonies – commonly seen as 'sister nations' in a British 'family' of 'kith and kin'. The historian Sir John Seeley's *The expansion of England* (1883) meanwhile argued that it might be desirable to place this scattered British nation under the authority of a single, perhaps federal, imperial state.[12]

The attraction of strengthening the links between Britain and the Dominions was felt by sections of both main parties from the early 1880s onwards. There were always fewer Liberal proponents than Conservative ones – after all, the Liberals' imperial tradition was one of decentralization – but a future chief of the party, Lord Rosebery, advocated closer union, and Joseph Chamberlain, the leading imperialist of his age, began his political career in the Liberal ranks. It was, however, the imperial dimension of Home Rule that contributed in no small measure to Chamberlain's break with the Liberals over the Irish issue in 1886, with Chamberlain sharing the fear that Home Rule was an act of separation which would have a deleterious effect on the white colonies. His concern for the Ulster Protestants has also been seen as an early example of his belief in a 'greater' British race. In 1893, he depicted Home Rule as a fatal signal of British imperial weakness in a hostile world.[13]

One product of the idea of Greater Britain was the Imperial Federation League (established in 1884), which lobbied for British and Dominion representation in a central imperial parliament (either Westminster or a legislature separate from it) in London. While the League attracted the support of Rosebery and others, it foundered on the difficulties of reconciling Dominion self-government with the realities of an imperial assembly that would almost inevitably be dominated by a demographically preponderant Britain. Even more modest plans for constitutional links between the Dominions and Britain failed to generate support – Chamberlain's 1897 proposal for an imperial council that would exercise a degree of executive control over the empire's foreign policy elicited little enthusiasm. Consequently, many advocates of greater imperial unity turned to what they considered more concrete policies, seeking to secure imperial tariff preferences or defence agreements. While they believed that such schemes would lay the foundation for a subsequent restructuring of imperial political relations, they hoped that they would prove more palatable in the Dominions in the short term.[14]

12 Deborah Wormell, *Sir John Seeley and the uses of history* (Cambridge, 1980). 13 James, *Rise and fall of the British empire*, 315–16; Thompson, 'The language of imperialism'. 14 Thompson, *Imperial Britain*, 25–32; A.J. Stockwell, 'Power, authority and freedom' in Marshall (ed.), *Cambridge illustrated history of the British empire*, 149–51; Green, 'The political economy of empire', 346–68.

While the Greater Britain project was the primary manifestation of the 'new imperialism', a second, more direct, reaction to the changing international environment was also emerging. By the mid-1880s, German and French ambitions in Africa were becoming clear, encouraging British policymakers to attempt to safeguard Britain's perceived strategic and commercial interests (especially in relation to India) by making further territorial acquisitions. An unstable Egypt was annexed in 1882, Bechuanaland in South West Africa in 1884, and administrative control was established over the Niger Delta from 1886. Many of these steps were taken as ad hoc responses to pressing threats, without an overall expansionist master plan, but a climate of opinion favourable to expansion had been created by Disraeli and by the anti-liberal writings of intellectuals like J.A. Froude and Fitzjames Stephen.[15] Through them the ideas underpinning a more aggressive imperial policy had become familiar enough. They included the belief that British interests were paramount, so that the ultimate sanction of force was justified, and that subject peoples were unfit for self-government, so that legitimate authority rested on power rather than consent – the example of India being to the fore.

These ideas appealed to Tories in particular – while not opposed to continued British rule over existing tropical colonies, Liberal-radical opinion generally remained wedded to the Gladstonian policy of avoiding further imperial conquests and emphasized the need for a just and humane colonial policy. Some Liberals were however willing to accept a more forceful assertion of British interests and, if necessary, the extension of the empire. Rosebery was again prominent here, speaking in 1893 of how it was Britain's duty to impress its 'superior' civilization on as much of the world as possible lest other, lesser, nations did so instead.[16] This split in Liberal opinion was to seriously weaken the party by the turn of the century.[17]

The 'new imperialism' also reflected the shift in thinking about race that characterized the second half of the nineteenth century. The earlier view had been that human nature was uniform across the world and that it was only cultural differences which placed tropical peoples at a lower level of development, so that in time they would attain the British level of civilization. From mid-century, though, this gave way to the belief that such peoples were racially inferior and so inherently incapable of achieving equality with Europeans. A key factor in this change was colonial revolt in India (1857) and Jamaica (1865) – much British opinion saw these rebellions as decisive rejections of British values by the subject peoples involved, and as proof that

15 Dunne, '"Les trahison des clercs"', 144–6; McCartney, *Lecky*, 64–84.   16 See the extract from Rosebery's speech reprinted in Jane Samson (ed.), *The British empire* (Oxford, 2001) 191. 17 Fergus D'Arcy, 'Charles Bradlaugh and the Irish question: a study in the nature and limits of British radicalism, 1853–91' in Art Cosgrove and Donal McCartney (eds), *Studies in Irish history presented to R. Dudley Edwards* (Dublin, 1979) 232–51.

British civilization was unsuited to African and Asian peoples.[18] Further justification for continued British rule was provided by the application of Darwin's theory of natural selection to human society. Certain races, said Social Darwinists, had evolved clear advantages over others and so were most likely to prevail in the international struggle for survival. The powerful European could see his very strength as evidence that he was right to absorb the territory of the weaker African or Asian. Advocates of the idea of Greater Britain also drew on such racialist thinking, arguing for the superior qualities of a 'British' or 'Anglo-Saxon' race locked in a struggle with Teutonic and Slav rivals.[19] By the end of the nineteenth century, such ideas had begun to penetrate popular culture as well as political and intellectual circles.[20]

It was within this wider atmosphere of a growing debate on empire, then, that the Home Rule controversy was played out. Both sides in the struggle were clearly seeking to turn the increasing public attachment to, and interest in, the empire to their advantage. The unionists looked to utilize both aspects of the 'new imperialism' within their overall theme of imperial disintegration. As seen earlier, not only did they try and exploit the campaign for closer ties with the white colonies by describing Home Rule's disastrous effects upon this project, but they also evoked the new racial ideology by stressing Irish incapacity for self-government and drawing parallels with other subject peoples.[21] Irish and Liberal Home Rulers of course refuted these comparisons with Indians and Africans. As Stephen Howe has noted, for Irish nationalists this strategy blended a genuine belief that, like other Europeans, the Irish were superior to black peoples with a natural recognition that identifying with the latter could only harm the Home Rule cause given that British majority opinion deemed Africans and Asians unfit for self-government. Besides, like most radicals, Irish Home Rulers were not necessarily opposed to continued colonial rule in existing dependencies, though they too tended to resist further expan-

---

18 See Andrew Porter, 'Trusteeship, anti-slavery and humanitarianism' in Porter (ed.), *Oxford history of the British empire*, iii, 198. 19 Marshall, 'The empire under threat', 59–60. 20 John M. Mackenzie, 'Introduction' in Mackenzie (ed.), *Imperialism and popular culture* (Manchester, 1986) 1–16; John M. Mackenzie, *Propaganda and empire: the manipulation of British public opinion, 1880–1960* (Manchester, 1984); John M. Mackenzie, 'Empire and metropolitan cultures' in Porter (ed.), *Oxford history of the British empire*, iii, 270–93; Thompson, *Imperial Britain*, 19–23. 21 The question of whether unionist stereotypes of the Irish were directly analogous to racial prejudice against Indians and Africans in that they were part of a wider anti-Celtic racism is too large a debate to be entered upon here. The argument that this was the case has been forcefully made by L.P. Curtis Jnr in two works, *Anglo-Saxons and Celts: a study of anti-Irish prejudice in Victorian England* (London, 1968) and *Apes and angels: Irishmen in Victorian caricature* (Washington and London, 1997, 2nd edn). The main ripostes to Curtis have come from R.F. Foster, *Paddy and Mr Punch: connections in Irish and English history* (London, 1993) 171–94, 286–91, and Sheridan Gilley, 'English attitudes towards the Irish, 1789–1900', in Colin Holmes (ed.), *Immigrants and minorities in British society* (London, 1978) 81–110.

sion.[22] It was, therefore, to the white colonies that they turned for their imperial analogies. In citing the success of self-government in these places Irish
Home Rulers could hope to benefit from the pride in British 'civilisation'
which was behind the Greater Britain concept. But Irish attempts to exploit the
idea of Greater Britain did not end here. As early as 1880, for example, Justin
McCarthy, in his immensely popular *A history of our own times*, looked to work
contemporary ideas of imperial federation in the interests of Home Rule.
According to McCarthy, several forces were making for independence in white
colonies like Australia and Canada. These included their lack of input to imperial foreign policy and their sheer distance from Britain. But, he said, this
threat could be countered through a federal system in which Britain and the
colonies would send representatives to a central parliament in London. This
body would deal with all imperial questions, leaving local legislatures to treat
domestic concerns, thereby allowing the colonies to retain their rights of self-
rule while at the same time creating a more equal and unified empire.
'Consolidation into the Empire' is how McCarthy described this process. The
implications of such a federal framework for Ireland were obvious. If adopted,
it would enable her to combine Home Rule with participation in, and loyalty
to, the empire. The bogey of separation would be laid to rest.[23]

If the empire was an important enough issue in the 1880s to compel Irish
Home Rulers like McCarthy to address the imperial aspects of their cause, then
this was even more the case in the 1890s, as expansion in Africa proceeded
apace, imperially-minded pressure groups such as the Navy League were established and Colonial Secretary Joseph Chamberlain schemed to unite Britain
and the Dominions through a policy of imperial tariff preference.[24] The popular appeal of empire also seemed to be strengthening. 'We are [faced] by the
new school of Imperial democracy,' said the *Speaker*, a Liberal weekly, in 1894.
'We cannot ignore the fact that there is growing in the democracy the determination to keep our race and our flag in the van of the world's progress, and
not to shrink from the responsibilities and efforts which this determination
must impose upon them.'[25] Mass circulation newspapers, such as Alfred
Harmsworth's *Daily Mail*, were particular keen to tap this enthusiasm for
empire.[26] Empire seemed to be becoming a vote-winner. The sweeping Unionist
Party victory at the 1895 election seemed to confirm this, with the most strik-

22 Howe, *Ireland and empire*, 44–9.   23 Justin McCarthy, *A history of our own times*, 4 vols
(London, 1878–80), iv, 184–205. McCarthy also noted how the possible reconstruction of the
empire along federal lines would benefit Ireland in his 1880 article 'The common-sense of Home
Rule' (see note 1 above).   24 For further details see works cited in note 11 above.   25 Mackenzie,
'Introduction' in Mackenzie (ed.), *Imperialism and popular culture*, 1–13; *Speaker*, 10 Mar. 1894.
26 Stephen Koss, *The rise and fall of the political press in Britain*, 2 vols (London, 1981 and 1984),
i, 369–74; Simon J. Potter, *News and the British world: the emergence of an imperial press system,
1876–1922* (Oxford, 2003), ch. 5.

ing example being the defeat of a sitting working class member in Bethnal Green by an Indian politician advocating Unionist and imperialist views.[27]

For Irish Home Rule politicians and publicists in the 1890s, a renewed need to associate their cause with imperial loyalty and unity must have seemed pressing. After all, the 1895 election did not simply demonstrate the growing ascendancy of the 'new imperialism'. The heavy Liberal defeat also meant the shelving of Home Rule under a Unionist government, while Liberal commitment to Home Rule also seemed to be waning. The late Liberal government had refused to confront the Lords after their rejection of the 1893 Home Rule bill, and, in early 1894, Gladstone had been succeeded as leader by Lord Rosebery, whose support for Home Rule was suspect but who, as we have seen, was deeply committed to both aspects of the 'new imperialism'. In the subsequent Queen's Speech, Home Rule was conspicuous by its absence. A year later and it had again gone missing, this time from the election manifestoes of many Liberal candidates.[28]

Exploiting the rising imperial spirit through an even closer identification of Irish self-government with a strong empire therefore offered a way both to keep the Irish issue in the political foreground, at a time when it was slipping from view, and to restore the electoral fortunes of Home Rule. Even the Parnellite minority recognized that Irish nationalists had to do more to win over a sceptical British public, with their leader, John Redmond, arguing in these years that this was the only way to overcome a hostile House of Lords.[29]

However, if Irish Home Rulers were to benefit from the 'new imperialism', they still had to reconcile such an undertaking with their nationalist faith. One of the chief Irish Home Rulers to attempt this task was the London-based T.P. O'Connor, and it is on him that the latter part of this essay concentrates. A prominent figure within the anti-Parnellite majority of the Irish Party, and the leader of the Irish in Britain through his long-standing presidency of the Irish National League of Great Britain, he was well placed to assess the changing currents of British political life. Not only had he lived in London for over twenty years, but he was close to the Liberal Party – being a strong Radical as well as a nationalist – and was also a well-known Fleet Street editor. Having made his name with the tremendously successful *Star* in the late 1880s, O'Connor owned and edited two papers between 1893 and 1898: a radical evening title, the *Sun*, and a weekend paper, the *Weekly Sun* (which had begun life as the *Sunday Sun* in 1891).[30]

27 Mackenzie, 'Introduction' in Mackenzie (ed.), *Imperialism and popular culture*, 2–4. 28 T.W. Heyck, *The dimensions of British radicalism: the case of Ireland, 1874–1895* (Urbana, Illinois, 1974) 29–30, 216–18. 29 See Bew, *John Redmond*. 30 For more on O'Connor's political and journalistic career, see L.W Brady, *T.P. O'Connor and the Liverpool Irish* (London, 1983); John Goodbody, 'The *Star*: its role in the rise of popular newspapers, 1888–1914', *Journal of Newspaper and Periodical History*, 2:1 (spring 1985); and Ian D. Sheehy, 'Irish journalists and litterateurs in late Victorian London, c.1870–1910' unpublished DPhil thesis, University of Oxford,

Being at the helm of two London journals would have given O'Connor a not inconsiderable insight into the popular political mood. Significantly, then, an examination of his writings in the 1890s, especially in the *Sun*, shows a concerted effort to turn the 'new imperialism' to the advantage of the Home Rule cause by asserting that a self-governing Ireland was vital to the health and harmony of the empire. However, he did so on his own terms, so that in certain important respects his imperial vision was shaped by his nationalism (and his radicalism). Parts of the 'new imperialism' were embraced rather than the whole. In this joining of Home Rule with imperial sentiment O'Connor helps underline an important historical point, one also brought out by the case of the 1880s nationalist publicists: that the imperial loyalty of the Irish Party was not confined to the party's early and late periods, under Isaac Butt and John Redmond respectively, but was a notable feature throughout its existence.

Of course, we must be wary of T.P.'s 1890s imperial writings for several reasons, not least the obvious electoral motives involved in his approach. There was also the fact that focusing on the empire was in his interest as a newspaper owner and editor, particularly given how, from 1894, he ran into financial trouble on the *Sun* just as Harmsworth was beginning to make the empire a valuable commercial asset in Fleet Street.[31] Nevertheless, enough personal conviction can be detected in O'Connor's 1890s protestations of imperial loyalty to make them worth noting. Already, in 1888, he had made clear his identification with the empire, writing in an article on Gladstone of how future generations would remember the Liberal leader for 'adding to the stability and glory of our own Empire'.[32] Another possible objection is that, as a London resident with strong radical links, T.P. was somewhat unrepresentative of the party as a whole. Whilst being in the imperial capital rather than Ireland must indeed have played its part – bringing a more intense exposure to the 'new imperialism' – it should be remembered that John Redmond, whose commitment to the empire would later become pronounced, retained Ireland as his base. Alternatively, critics of the Irish Party in the early 1900s, such as Sinn Féin, would have seen O'Connor as all too representative of the party, his London focus and imperial loyalty graphically illustrating its anglicized state.[33]

Analysis of T.P.'s writings certainly helps to correct what has often been a neglected subject, namely the response to empire of Irish constitutional nationalists in the late nineteenth century. Recent works treating Ireland in an imperial context have not tackled this issue in detail.[34] Although the 'galvanic' effect

2003.   31 Brady, *O'Connor*, 130.   32 T.P. O'Connor, 'The candour of Mr Gladstone', *Contemporary Review* (Sept. 1889) 361–9.   33 Patrick Maume, *The long gestation: Irish nationalist life, 1891–1918* (Dublin, 1999) 9–10.   34 Howe in *Ireland and empire* suggests that nationalist politicians paid little attention to colonial Home Rule parallels (see note 6 above). Keith Jeffery (ed.), *'An Irish empire'? Aspects of Ireland and the British empire* (Manchester, 1996) does not include an essay on the topic.

of the South African War on Irish nationalism, including its constitutional strain, has been recognized, the question of more general attitudes to empire and the 'new imperialism' among Irish Home Rulers has been analysed less exhaustively.[35] The following observations are an attempt to redress this imbalance.

The elevation of the supposedly lukewarm Home Ruler Rosebery to the Liberal leadership provided one of the first occasions for O'Connor to give strong voice to his combination of Home Rule nationalism and imperial loyalty. Writing in the *Sun* in March 1894, he remarked that Rosebery's enthusiasm for empire was deemed in some quarters to preclude a similar concern for Ireland. '[Gladstone's] place has been taken', said O'Connor, 'by a statesman whose survey of the Empire at large is supposed by some not to have left him time or leisure or taste to concentrate his sympathies on the sufferings of Ireland.' Dismissing this contention, T.P. argued that, on the contrary, he had no misgivings about Rosebery's commitment to Ireland. Far from threatening Home Rule, the new Liberal leader was bound to support it because of the stability and unity such a measure would bring to the empire. 'I know', wrote O'Connor, 'that ... Lord Rosebery has steadily adhered to the opinion that not only for the sake of Ireland, but for the safety and dignity of the Empire, Home Rule is necessary and inevitable; and therefore I have really never had any serious apprehensions.'[36] Rosebery's professed ideal was a strong, united British empire and this, asserted T.P. that same month, was the best guarantee of his adhesion to Home Rule, since the latter was indispensable to the attainment of the former. 'And if Lord Rosebery is the man I take him to be', he wrote, 'he will not regard the Irish question as a millstone. For the solution of the Irish question lies at the very base of his chief and supreme object in life – the worthy and glorious ideal which he once declared in an eloquent and memorable passage to be worth living and dying for – the ideal of a truly united British Empire.'[37] Here O'Connor would have had in mind the effect of Home Rule in securing the imperial loyalty not only of the Irish in Ireland, but also of the Irish in the Dominions. There was also the fact that much non-Irish political opinion in these countries supported Home Rule too, and its continued denial might cause colonial political leaders to question their own positions within the empire, for the principle of autonomy on which the settler empire was based could be seen to be under threat. Either way, O'Connor had made a distinct effort to impress on his audience the conviction that a united empire and a Home Rule Ireland were two sides of the same coin.

His apparent confidence in Rosebery was of course not borne out by events, for, under Rosebery's stewardship, the Liberal party steadily disentangled itself

---

35 See, for instance, R.F. Foster, *Modern Ireland, 1600–1972* (London, 1989) 433, 444–8, 456; and David Omissi and Andrew S. Thompson (eds), *The impact of the South African War* (Basingstoke, 2002) for the effect of the South African War on Irish nationalism. 36 *Sun*, 11 Mar. 1894. 37 *Sun*, 7 Mar. 1894.

from its Irish undertakings. One suspects, though, that T.P. was only too aware of the new leader's indifference towards Home Rule and was trying to offset this, and keep Ireland in the foreground, by showing Rosebery – and the *Sun*'s readers – that an imperial emphasis should not mean a downgrading of Home Rule. From this viewpoint, O'Connor's March 1894 articles were an exercise in damage limitation. Perceiving that the recent defeat of the Home Rule bill was to be compounded by the accession to the leadership of a man whose political priorities lay elsewhere, he was essentially fighting a rearguard action to try and salvage some kind of standing for the Irish issue.

T.P. continued his attempt to prove that the new dispensation would in fact have a positive effect on nationalist hopes by claiming that not only would Rosebery uphold Home Rule but that he would also considerably improve its electoral prospects, since his imperial reputation meant he was admirably qualified to convey the imperial, or English, dimension of the Irish question to English audiences. 'I have held that Lord Rosebery's Premiership had an especial advantage', wrote O'Connor on 13 March, 'in that he was the very best man to bring this English – this Imperial side of the controversy – before the minds of Englishmen'. And this was something Rosebery had already begun to do in his recent speech to the House of Lords, having outlined the benefits that Home Rule would bring to the empire in addition to pacifying Ireland itself. For example, it would help ensure a peaceful and profitable relationship with the United States, converting the Irish population there from enemies into friends. Rosebery also touched on the point above regarding Home Rule's compatibility with the principle of autonomy that was assumed to underpin the empire. 'Lord Rosebery', wrote O'Connor, 'defended ... Home Rule as a part of a great scheme of Imperial decentralization on which the safety and unity of the Empire depend.'[38] If Rosebery presented Home Rule in this fashion, said T.P., as a measure designed to bring strength and harmony to the empire, he would undoubtedly win over enough Englishmen to make it a reality. Thus, O'Connor was confident that linking Home Rule to the dominant force of the 'new imperialism' would be an advantageous move in British electoral terms.

But, crucially, while he might perceive the value of an imperial approach with regard to British voters and the Liberals' agenda, T.P. had to ensure it was integrated with his nationalist (and radical) politics, for certain features of the 'new imperialism' – most notably the 'Greater Britain' ideal – had the potential to run counter to his Home Rule agenda. Moreover, there was also the question of whether O'Connor's embrace of a more strongly imperial stance involved genuine ideological commitment as well as a sharp awareness of the political usefulness of the 'new imperialism'. Both issues were addressed to a considerable extent in an article of 7 March 1894, wherein T.P. unfolded

38 *Sun*, 13 Mar. 1894.

his own vision of what the British empire should be and how a Home Rule Ireland could play its part within it. It is the most personal of all O'Connor's attempts at this time to blend the Irish issue with a markedly imperial outlook. Though hardly novel, his idea of empire was clear enough.

Concentrating on the settler colonies, O'Connor proclaimed his belief in a decentralized empire comprised of self-governing 'nations', whose freedom and equality within the imperial system would secure their loyalty to it. 'I want to see every nationality in this great and mighty Imperial fabric equally loyal, equally proud, because equally free,' he stated.[39] Such a conception was obviously in keeping with the long-standing Gladstonian policy of colonial autonomy and this Liberal influence was certainly at work. Yet, more interestingly, it is apparent that T.P.'s vision of empire was one that suited his Home Rule nationalism, and that this had entailed the eschewal of several fundamental, but uncongenial, aspects of the 'new imperialism'. For example, O'Connor's definition of empire depicted the 'white' colonies as 'nations' when, as we have seen, imperial enthusiasts in Britain, and much opinion within the colonies themselves, were stressing how they were part of the civilization, or family, of 'Greater Britain'.[40] T.P. would have known that Irish nationalists were unlikely to accept such an overtly 'British' framework, especially when the Gaelic Revival was beginning to assert Ireland's separate cultural identity. An empire based on distinct 'nations' was much more appealing to nationalist susceptibilities. A similar motive was apparent in O'Connor's emphasis on the equality and 'freedom' of the empire's members. This was probably a reference to the need for Irish self-government to be as full as possible and as such was designed to reassure those nationalists who feared a constrictive measure of Home Rule that would leave Ireland in a subordinate position. This prospect had been raised the year before by Parnellite criticism of the Home Rule bill, so that T.P.'s focus on 'freedom' was something of a riposte, as well as a gentle reminder to the Liberals not to make such a mistake.

It also sidelined another facet of the 'new imperialism', namely the various schemes for central imperial bodies, either executive or legislative, that Chamberlain and others were promoting, and which the colonies felt might sap their autonomy. Of course, constitutional nationalism could be reconciled with more formal systems of imperial government – Butt and McCarthy had earlier proposed federal Home Rule plans and Cecil Rhodes saw such an idea as the foundation for a truly imperial parliament – but O'Connor appeared to have shied away from this. His vision of the British empire was therefore one that a Home Rule Ireland would have had little difficulty fitting into, its principles of nationhood and local independence dovetailing perfectly with

---

39 *Sun*, 7 Mar. 1894. 40 To some extent, T.P. here anticipated the ideas expressed by the imperial theorist Richard Jebb in his later, influential *Studies in colonial nationalism* (London, 1905).

the Irish cause. Although he might have sought to endorse the spirit of the 'new imperialism', its details were very much modified to suit his own nationalist purposes.

That a Home Rule Ireland would enthusiastically uphold an empire constructed along such lines, T.P. had no doubt. Once Ireland had self-government, he said in this same article, its people would combine national patriotism with imperial patriotism. A Home Rule Ireland would be a willing partner in the imperial enterprise, with Irishmen taking pride both in their own work for the empire and the imperial accomplishments of earlier generations of their countrymen. 'Side by side with the sanction and final consecration in an Irish Parliament of the great principle of national aspiration and national patriotism', trumpeted O'Connor, 'I want to see grow up the noble and exalted patriotism of the children, the heirs, and the creators of a mighty empire.' He wanted Irishmen no longer to recoil from stories of their involvement in the empire, and instead to 'glory in them and to recount them and imitate them among the generations of the race that are to come'. 'The Irish question', he concluded, 'is the obstacle which stands before Ireland and her growth into the full stature of Imperial struggle and Imperial glory.'[41]

In making such a ringing declaration of imperial loyalty O'Connor naturally had one eye on his British readers. Countering the long-standing fear that Home Rule would bring separation by arguing that it would in fact create support for empire in Ireland was part of his attempt to turn rising public concern for the empire to the advantage of the Irish cause. However, on another level political conviction was arguably also at work. O'Connor's statements have a very direct, personal, quality, which strongly suggest that he was speaking the faith that was in him. It shows that alongside his Home Rule nationalism he possessed an overarching commitment to the empire. Although an understandable outcome for someone who had lived in London for over two decades, and had become close to the Liberals, such vows of imperial attachment still help to establish the essential continuity of the Irish Party's imperial loyalty between the 1870s and the First World War.

An objection might be raised here that the eruption of the South African War in 1899 would cast Irish nationalists, including the Irish Party, in anything but the role of imperial loyalists, with constitutional nationalists joining more 'advanced' elements in a vociferous pro-Boer stance. Whilst there is not space here to examine this issue fully, it is important to note that in taking such a position O'Connor, Redmond (Irish Party leader from 1900) and others were being, in David Fitzpatrick's words, 'perfectly consistent'.[42] This was because opposing the war against the Boer republics did not contravene the kind of empire in which O'Connor and Redmond believed. On

---

41 *Sun*, 7 Mar. 1894.   42 Fitzpatrick, 'Ireland and the empire', 506; Maume, *The long gestation*, 28; Foster, *Modern Ireland*, 433.

the contrary, it could be presented as very much upholding their idea of an empire of self-governing 'nations', with support for the Boers a defence of colonial autonomy and individuality against an unjustified attempt by the imperial centre to impose its will. Earlier, T.P. had made it clear in the wake of the Jameson Raid that he was against the enlargement of the empire through unregulated private adventuring. 'The day has gone by when the British Empire is to be extended at the will of the adventurer,' avowed T.P., 'whether for the purpose of satisfying the ambition of individuals or the greed of commercial speculators.'[43] His opposition to the South African War then demonstrated that even when it came from the imperial government he could still resist such expansionism. In his opposition to the latter O'Connor was following a well-trodden radical path. But his assertion of the right of a distinct people like the Boers to self-government in the face of an aggressive British empire obviously also stemmed from his Irish nationalism. It is another example of how that nationalism was important in determining T.P.'s response to the different strains of the 'new imperialism'.

Another notable juncture at which O'Connor's 'imperial' approach was marked was, understandably, after the disastrous general election of 1895. If the outlook for Home Rule was cloudy following the advent of the Rosebery premiership, then matters became even bleaker after an election in which not only the electorate but also the Liberal Party had seemingly cast the Irish issue aside. T.P.'s response was a spirited reiteration of the ideas and arguments he had been employing during the previous few years as he made another attempt to benefit from the rising imperial feeling of the British public. He sought to rebuild the popularity and profile of Home Rule by again identifying it with a stronger, more united, empire. In August 1896 he contributed an article to the *Contemporary Review* entitled 'Home rule and the Irish Party'. Here, he claimed that, although Home Rule appeared to have been firmly rejected, there were in fact currents at work which would restore its primacy and virtually guarantee its realisation. 'I firmly believe,' he wrote, 'that at this moment there are some forces working for Home Rule which are silently bringing it to the front again, and are making its ultimate success not only possible but not very remote.' The most powerful of these forces was the recent 'growth in Imperial sentiment'. 'In both England and Ireland', wrote T.P., 'a curious change, amounting to a transformation, has been ... going forward with regard to the question of England's Imperial position ... A sense has grown up of the greatness [and] the needful defence of the Empire much more vivid and real than existed even a few years ago.'[44]

How, T.P. asked, would this imperial trend benefit Home Rule? The answer was a familiar one. Just as he had argued that Rosebery's concern for

43 *Sun*, 20 Jan. 1896. 44 T.P. O'Connor, 'Home rule and the Irish Party', *Contemporary Review* (Aug. 1896) 182.

empire would cement his commitment to Home Rule, so he claimed that the British public's attachment to empire would lead them to accept Irish self-government because they would come to see that 'if the Empire is to be rendered ... greater, it can only be done by the settlement of this Irish problem'. Primarily, they would recognize that a contented Home Rule Ireland would put an end to the difficulties caused by the Irish vote both in the colonies and in the context of Anglo-American relations. Further, increasing public knowledge of the empire would make people even more familiar with the important lesson taught by the Dominions: that stability and loyalty came through self-government. All colonial statesmen, stated O'Connor, could testify to the 'effective and successful application of the principle of local self-government which underlines the demand for Home Rule'. In this way an empire-conscious public would be brought round to accepting Home Rule, viewing it as a necessary step towards the greater goal of imperial strength and harmony. 'A contented and self-governed Ireland,' he declared, 'is the true point of departure for a great, a solid, and a united Empire.' In this article O'Connor's certainly made his own commitment to the empire strikingly apparent. Moreover, he again showed how Home Rule for Ireland was simply the embodiment of those principles of freedom and equality on which the British empire should be based. The empire's 'expansion and safety' would be found in the 'content of all its component parts by equal liberties'.[45] T.P.'s vision of a decentralized empire of 'nations' was thus very much intact.

He also touched on this vision that same month in the *Sun*, arguing that the Liberals should seek to restore their fortunes by ensuring that the empire was 'as frequent and as fond an ideal of one political party as of the other; and that the difference between the Liberals and the Conservatives should be that we can only think of a strong and united empire when we feel that liberty is extended to all its parts'.[46] Although this statement illustrates something of his imperial beliefs, it also underlines O'Connor's awareness of the empire's potency as an electoral weapon (indeed, he clearly felt that the Tories had the advantage here). It therefore captures neatly the combination of motives which led T.P. to seek to intertwine his Home Rule nationalism with a strong commitment to empire during the 1890s. That his version of the 'new imperialism' was shaped in several important respects by his nationalism should not detract from the depth and sincerity of his imperial attachment. When the empire was faced with its greatest challenge yet in 1914, O'Connor's support was total. But, as his 1890s writings reveal, it was not a support forged for the first time by the advent of a world war. Rather, it was the culmination of an imperial loyalty stretching back for over three decades. And, crucially, his example helps show that the same can be said of the Irish Party and its backing for the Allied cause in 1914.

45 Ibid. 183–5.   46 *Sun*, 3 Aug. 1896.

9. Nationalist and unionist responses to the British empire in the age of the South African War, 1899–1902

DONAL LOWRY

At the beginning of the twentieth century, any reader of the Irish press would have been left in little doubt about the prominence of imperial concerns in Irish life. Newspapers were filled with accounts of the British empire's largest military campaign since 1815. However, the South African War (1899–1902) also exposed the empire to unprecedented criticism on a global scale, not only from its enemies but from supporters as well. In Ireland, pro-Boer elements in the press were closely monitored for inflammatory or seditious sentiments by Dublin Castle and its agents – significantly, Ireland was the only part of the United Kingdom where the police intervened to shut down a newspaper due to its stance on the war.

Historians have generally agreed that the South African War proved to be a turning point in the history of modern Irish nationalism. As Roy Foster has noted, the 'galvanic effect' of the conflict channelled moderate Irish opinion into an anti-imperial mould, boosting membership of the Gaelic League and other cultural nationalist organizations. According to Foster, it proved to be 'in this area as in others nearly as crucial an event as the death of Parnell' – 'the radicalization of Irish politics in the early twentieth century arose out of opposition to the Boer War'.[1] Donal McCracken has drawn similar conclusions from his detailed study of networks of Irish pro-Boers, at home, in the USA and on the battlefields of South Africa, where two 'Irish' brigades, of symbolic rather than numerical significance, fought for the Boers against the British.[2] Stephen Howe, in an otherwise persuasive critique of colonial and post-colonial approaches to Irish history and culture, is less convincing in his claim that the war had a minimal impact on those who would later fight in the Irish War of Independence (1919–21).[3] The conflict cer-

1 R.F. Foster, *Modern Ireland, 1600–1972* (London, 1989 edn) 433, 444, 448, 456.   2 See Donal P. McCracken, *The Irish pro-Boers, 1877–1902* (Johannesburg, 1989); *MacBride's Brigade: Irish commandos in the Anglo-Boer War* (Dublin, 1999); 'The Irish Transvaal Brigades', *Southern African-Irish Studies*, 2 (1992) 54–65; 'Irish settlement and identity in South Africa before 1910', *Irish Historical Studies*, 110:37 (1992) 148–9. For Irish nationalist attitudes towards the British empire, see also H.V. Brasted, 'Irish nationalism and the British empire', in O. MacDonagh (ed.), *Irish culture and nationalism* (1983) and chapter 6 above.   3 Stephen Howe, *Ireland and*

tainly played a central role in unifying the Irish Parliamentary Party under John Redmond, after the bitter divisions caused by the fall of the nationalist leader, Charles Stewart Parnell. Significantly, Redmond's first parliamentary speech as leader of a reunified party was in support of a motion condemning British policy in South Africa.

This evidence seems to support Senia Paseta's claim that 'the effect of the Boer War on Irish nationalism was vital', a view shared by Patrick Maume, who argues that '[o]ne motive for the Easter Rising [of 1916] was the fear that nationalists would die of ridicule if the First World War repeated the Boer War experience' of a highly vociferous but ultimately limited nationalist response.[4] The war had an equally important impact on Irish unionism. Alvin Jackson has identified the war as 'a personal and imperial watershed' for the younger generation of unionists who would lead Northern Ireland in its early decades. Writing of Sir James Craig (later Lord Craigavon and founding prime minister of Northern Ireland), Jackson notes that the struggle 'recruited him into a freemasonry of military-minded Irish Unionists who emerged from their wartime experiences with a revivified imperial zeal and aggression'.[5]

To some extent however, most of these accounts have underestimated the variety of attitudes that existed in Ireland towards the South African War and, by implication, the empire. There was not a simple split between pro-Boer and pro-British elements. While some Irish Party MPs took a strong anti-war line, the party was afflicted by divisions similar to those apparent in the British Liberal Party. The Irish Party had contained such individuals as James Rochfort Maguire and John Morrogh, who facilitated the relationship between Parnell and Cecil Rhodes.[6] Irish pro-Boers and advanced nationalists thus used the conflict to highlight what they regarded as the decadence and venality of the party. Significantly, too, Irish local councils had been reformed by 1898, and had become more representative of their constituents. These bodies had already been active in erecting monuments to the 1798 uprising, much to the annoyance of the government and the ascendancy elite they had displaced. The South African conflict provided them with a further opportunity to make their mark. These diverse and dissonant voices can be traced through the Dublin, Belfast and provincial press, offering an insight

empire: colonial legacies in Irish history and culture (Oxford, 2000) 57. **4** Senia Paseta, 'Nationalist responses to two royal visits to Ireland, 1900 and 1903', *Irish Historical Studies*, 34 (1999). See also Paseta, *Before the revolution: nationalism, social change and Ireland's Catholic elite, 1879–1922* (Cork, 1999) 151 and Patrick Maume, *The long gestation: Irish nationalist life, 1891–1918* (Dublin, 1999) 29. **5** Alvin Jackson, 'Irish unionists and empire', in Keith Jeffery (ed.), *'An Irish empire'? Aspects of Ireland and the British empire* (Manchester, 1996) 132. **6** Donal McCracken, 'Parnell and the South African connection', in Donal McCartney (ed.), *Parnell: the politics of power* (Dublin, 1991) 125–36.

into the impact of the war on Irish nationalist and unionist cultures, as well as wider attitudes towards the British empire.[7]

With the partial exception of some separatist and socialist organs, all Irish national and local newspapers of any significance were largely dependent for coverage of the war on identical reports syndicated from international news agencies. Nevertheless, initial press reactions to the conflict were predictably varied, with moderate nationalist, separatist, socialist and unionist papers all adopting familiar editorial positions. Media interest in the war was intense throughout the conflict, but two particularly concentrated periods of coverage can be discerned. Between August 1899 and spring 1900, war become imminent and then a reality. The initial disasters for imperial arms of 'Black Week' in December were followed by the taking of the Boer capitals of Bloemfontein and Pretoria. Advanced nationalists were then further demoralized by the apparent success of Queen Victoria's visit to Ireland. However, a second bout of 'Boer fever' occurred in the summer of 1900, when it became apparent that the Boers were not beaten after all, and that a prolonged, destructive guerrilla campaign was likely.

Advanced nationalists were quick to recognize that the escalating crisis in South Africa represented a major challenge for the British empire. A particular important role was played here by Arthur Griffith, founder of Sinn Féin and later president of the Dáil at the time of Britain's withdrawal from southern Ireland in 1922. Griffith had singularly strong feelings for the Boer cause, having worked as editor of the *Middleburg Courant*, and even had the Transvaal national anthem translated into Irish. These sentiments provided a particular edge to his editorship of the advanced nationalist weekly, the *United Irishman*.[8] Griffith was also the founder of the Irish Transvaal Committee, which became a focal point for advanced nationalist opposition to the war. Griffith claimed to provide readers with the most accurate account of South African events – in April 1899 he wrote scornfully of the dangers of 'imbibing draughts of detailed wisdom on the Transvaal from the fresh and watery leading columns of the [unionist] *Irish Times*, with occasional sips from the British South African *Independent* [probably a reference to Cecil Rhodes' earlier subsidization of the Irish Party] and the old unreliable *Freeman*['s *Journal*]'.[9]

---

7 For the longer-term impact of the war in Ireland see Donal Lowry, '"The world's no bigger than a kraal": the South African War and international opinion in the first age of "globalization"' in David Omissi and Andrew Thompson (eds), *The impact of the South African War* (London, 2002) 278–82; and '"Ireland shows the way": Irish-South African relations and the British empire/Commonwealth, *c*.1902–61' in Donal P. McCracken (ed.), *Ireland and South Africa in modern times* (Durban, 1996) 89–95.   8 Calton Younger, *Arthur Griffith* (Dublin, 1981) 12; P.A. McCracken, 'Arthur Griffith's South African sabbatical', and 'The quest for the *Middelburg Courant*', in D.P. McCracken (ed.), *Ireland and South Africa*, 227–62, 282–9.   9 *United Irishman*, 27 May 1899, quoted in McCracken, *The Irish pro-Boers*, 45.

Equally uncompromising was James Connolly, the Irish syndicalist leader and socialist editor of the *Workers' Republic*. Connolly saw the war as an opportunity to overthrow British power in Ireland, or at the very least achieve national prominence for his tiny movement. He, too, would become active in the Irish Transvaal Committee, and was preparing at this time a plan to seize key buildings in Dublin while the British were tied down in South Africa, anticipating the Easter Rising of 1916.[10] Writing in August 1899, he took a firmly Hobsonian[11] view of the crisis in the Transvaal, dismissing the *uitlander* franchise issue as a spurious justification for aggression[12], although he betrayed his hazy knowledge of the region's mineral resources when he attributed the war to the presence of diamonds rather than gold. He told his readers that the war vindicated 'the truth of the socialist maxim that the modern state is but a committee of rich men administering public affairs in the interest of the upper class'.[13] He went on to emphasize the lessons the conflict contained for Irish workers, stressing the ruthlessness of the British ruling class in launching a war of aggression, which should dissuade those who believed that a peaceful realisation of socialist objectives was possible. '[T]he capitalist class is a beast of prey, and cannot be moralized, converted, or conciliated, but must be extirpated.' Even before formal hostilities began, he highlighted the revolutionary opportunities in Ireland offered by England's difficulties in South Africa. Troops were being taken from Ireland for service in the Transvaal, he reminded his readers, and the Irish working class would be able to take advantage of this, were it not for the pusillanimous Irish Party and 'their good friends the [Royal Irish] Constabulary [who] may be trusted to keep this country quiet'.[14] By November, even though for the British the worst was yet to come on the battlefields of South Africa, Connolly was already optimistic about the ultimate significance of the struggle.

> I think [that this war] is the beginning of the end. This great, blustering British Empire; this Empire of truculent bullies, is rushing headlong to its doom. Whether they ultimately win or lose, the Boers have pricked the bubble of England's fighting reputation. The world knows her weakness now. Have at her then, everywhere and always and in every manner. And before the first decade of the coming century will close, you and I, if we survive, will be able to repeat to our children the tale of how this monstrous tyranny sank in dishonour and disaster.[15]

10 Younger, *Arthur Griffith*, 12.   11 See Introduction above.   12 See chapter 10 below.   13 See McCracken, *The Irish pro-Boers*, chs. 2, 4–6 for the various phases of the war and Irish opinion.   14 *Workers' Republic*, 19 August 1899.   15 *Workers' Republic*, 18 November 1899.

Connolly's views were echoed by other advanced nationalists. Hovering between Home Rule and separatism at the time, Patrick Pearse, soon to become editor of the Gaelic League journal, *An Claidheamh Soluis*, later recalled the Irish nationalist response to the South African War as a foretaste of an unyielding struggle against the British empire that would end in the streets of Dublin. The inveterate Fenian and later publisher of *Irish Freedom*, Tom Clarke, had spent part of his early childhood in South Africa and seriously considered fighting alongside the Boers. He, like Pearse, Connolly and Major John McBride, onetime second-in-command of the Irish Transvaal Brigade, would later be executed for their part in the 1916 rising.[16]

Advanced nationalists also arranged public protests against the war. James Connolly was the first to organize a pro-Boer street protest, in Foster Place, off College Green, Dublin, on 27 August. This proved to be a much larger gathering than the usual weekly socialist rallies, and the crowd that assembled to chant 'Long live the Boers' became the focus of widespread national press attention. A typically vitriolic anti-British letter composed by Maud Gonne, leading pro-Boer agitator, was read aloud. Gonne was experienced in press propaganda, having assisted her French lover Lucien Millevoye in editing the anti-Dreyfusite *La Patrie*. She also played a crucial role in helping to subsidize Griffith's *United Irishman* and the Irish Transvaal Committee.[17]

An even more substantial protest occurred on 1 October in the heart of Dublin, when a large crowd, said to number 20,000, assembled in Beresford Place, closely and not too discreetly observed by the Dublin Metropolitan Police. The authorities were anxious about the scale of the gathering and the sentiments expressed. The meeting was chaired by the veteran Fenian, John O'Leary, and the platform included Griffith, Michael Davitt, T.D. Sullivan (nationalist MP and balladeer), the poet William Butler Yeats and Patrick O'Brien MP, who unfurled a large Transvaal *Vierkleur*. Maud Gonne told the crowd of her sense of 'terrible humiliation to think that regiments with Irish names had gone out to fight the Transvaal'. She called for a boycott of British army recruiting in Ireland and hoped that the Irish soldiers already there would change sides and fight for the Boers.[18] A message from the mayor of Kilkenny proposed that a gift of two maxim guns named 'Wolfe Tone' and 'Parnell' should be sent to the Boers. The deeds of the late Fenian Alfred Aylward in fighting the British at the battle of Majuba in 1881 were recalled to great cheering.

Moderate nationalists were also opposed to the war, but rather than inciting rebellion in Ireland they focussed on the hollowness of the *uitlander* cause in the Transvaal, and restricted their disloyalty to supporting Irish volunteers

---

16 P. MacAonghusa (ed.), *Quotations from P.H. Pearse* (Cork, 1978) 10; McCracken, *The Irish pro-Boers*, 68. 17 McCracken, *The Irish pro-Boers*, 46; Foster, *Modern Ireland*, 449, n. xxxvii. 18 *United Irishman*, 7 October 1899. See also Liz Curtis, *The cause of Ireland: from the United Irishmen to partition* (London, 1994) 178.

fighting for the Boer cause in South Africa. The *Freeman's Journal* was fairly representative of the mainstream nationalist press when it argued that President Kruger's recent concessions to the *uitlanders* would satisfy neither 'the Jingoes of Johannesburg [n]or the Jingoes of London'. Its sister paper, the *Weekly Freeman*, together with the *Cork Examiner*, dismissed the *uitlanders* as 'interlopers'. On 4 October, the *Kilkenny Journal* went further by offering prayers for a Boer victory.[19] Within days of the outbreak of hostilities, the *Galway Observer*, a recognized organ of the Irish Party, endorsed the formation of an 'Irish Corps' in the Transvaal forces, numbering perhaps little more than six hundred, downplaying the role played by thousands of Irishmen fighting in British and colonial forces.

> Whatever may be the outcome of the war we have no doubt our countrymen will give a good account of themselves if they get a chance. Since Fontenoy an Irish Brigade has not had an opportunity of crossing swords with the British, on equal terms, and no doubt many of them will feel that now is the time to "remember Limerick and '98". The Irish people fortunately for them, can enter the ranks with a free conscience ... They will only be doing what their forefathers did before them on the battlefields of Ireland.

Significantly perhaps the paper also contrasted the assumed support given to the Boers by the Irish in southern Africa with the sentiment of Scots resident in the region, whose interests were 'sure to be on the side of the British'.[20] A fortnight later the paper noted the decision of Michael Davitt, leader of the Land League, to boycott the House of Commons in protest against the war. It also reported, under an over-dramatic but telling headline, 'The War in Galway', the sensation caused by the arrest of a local pro-Boer, Michael Joyce, for posting Irish Transvaal Committee bills. He was released, the paper reported, although only after the police had torn down the bills in a 'rather high-handed action'. The paper added that the bills 'only cautioned Irish youths against enlisting in the English army' and warned them to 'remember 98, the penal laws and the famine'.[21]

Similar sentiments were expressed during the opening weeks of the war by local county councils and boards of poor law unions, whose resolutions were published in the Irish nationalist press. A resolution passed by Limerick borough council became the most famous exemplar of this type:

> That we consider it a great sign of National weakness and decay that the various organisations in Ireland have not in a more determined

19 See McCracken, *The Irish pro-Boers*, 45.   20 *Galway Observer*, 14 October 1899.   21 *Galway Observer*, 28 October 1899.

manner expressed their sympathy with the plucky Boer farmers in their fight against the English, and this especially when the Englishmen themselves are protesting against the contemplated slaughter at the instance of Chamberlain and the other English Captalists, and we express a hope that if a war takes place it may end in another Majuba Hill.[22]

In October 1899, the Tipperary board of guardians similarly passed a resolution applauding the men of the Irish Corps in the Boer forces 'who truly represent Irish national opinion, notwithstanding the fact that some thoughtless, ignorant and dispirited young Irishmen are always to be found bearing arms for England'.[23]

As the war unfolded, it continued to provide a stimulus to unrest in Ireland. Newspapers carried reports of attacks on loyalists. The students of Trinity College, Dublin, widely assumed to be pro-British, as well as off-duty soldiers, were favourite targets, and these scuffles often turned into heated confrontations with the police. Assaults, leading to arrests and court proceedings, were frequent. Widely reported in the press, these incidents became focal points for further unrest.

Dublin Castle was conscious of the prominence in the pro-Boer and anti-recruiting movements of those with considerable journalistic experience, including Gonne and Connolly, subsequently joined by Alice Milligan and Anna Johnston, former editors of the *Shan Van Vocht*. Even the relatively moderate Redmondite *Irish Daily Independent* came under government scrutiny. The newspaper had erected a magic lantern display in its office window that depicted Boer leaders and South African scenes, and this had attracted large crowds. Under their ever vigilant assistant commissioner, James Mallon, and with the approval of the under secretary for Ireland, the Dublin Metropolitan Police decided to act. Two police superintendents visited the office and persuaded the manager to remove the display.[24]

In spite of these moves, pro-Boerism continued to spread in the provincial press, as rumours began to circulate of imminent imperial defeat. Sometimes nationalist press coverage could be relatively restrained. In November 1899, the *Galway Observer* carried a substantial review of Mrs Lionel Phillips' *South African Recollections*, by W.F. Regan, their London correspondent. Regan mildly suggested that Mrs Phillips, shocked by conditions in which the Jameson raiders had been held, should realise the conditions that Davitt and others had endured in British gaols.[25] More representative of the heady nationalist fervour of this period was the *Sligo Champion*:

22 McCracken, *The Irish pro-Boers*, 47. 23 See Terence Denman, '"The red livery of shame": the campaign against army recruitment in Ireland, 1899–1914', *Irish Historical Studies*, 29 (1994) 212. 24 McCracken, *The Irish pro-Boers*, 51. 25 *Galway Observer*, 25 November 1899.

History does not record a more diabolical or more audacious scheme of plunder than that in which England is now engaged in South Africa ... The sympathy of every just and upright man in the world will go forth to the brave Boers in their manly struggle for the independence as a Nation. May God strengthen their arms and send them a speedy recovery from all reverses.[26]

Another provincial pro-Boer highlight was provided by a meeting in Cork City on 12 November, where Maude Gonne and Mayor Daly of Limerick made particularly inflammatory speeches, widely reported in the press. The momentum of the pro-Boer campaign depended on news of British reverses, in ready supply during the early stages of the war due to British defeats at Stormberg, Magersfontein and Colenso. Even moderate nationalists rejoiced. 'In two brief months', the *Freeman's Journal* crowed, 'the bravery of the little peoples has destroyed the military prestige of the British Empire, demoralized their troop of enemies, and amazed the world with the spectacle of what men who prefer death to the destruction of their nationality can accomplish.'[27]

In the middle of this excitement, it was announced that Joseph Chamberlain, the colonial secretary, widely regarded in Ireland as the chief assassin of Home Rule and instigator of the war against the Boers, was to visit Dublin to receive an honorary doctorate from Trinity College on 18 December. The visit provided the press and the pro-Boer agitation with a new focus. The Irish Transvaal Committee organized a protest meeting in Dublin on the eve of the visit, in spite of a government proclamation. The driver of the carriage carrying Maud Gonne, Griffith, O'Leary and the party hierarchy lost his nerve on seeing so many policemen drawn up in Beresford Square. Connolly took the reins immediately and drove through the police cordon, shouting 'Up the Boers!' and 'Up the Republic!' as he broke the police line. The police escorted the carriage to a nearby station, where the occupants were cautioned. On their release, Connolly and his crew led a procession across the centre of the city, where a very large crowd had gathered. Street fighting broke out between the police (some mounted and using the flat of their sabres) and a crowd that had been inflamed by the seizure of a child's Boer flag. Leading nationalist MPs arrived, including Willie Redmond and Michael Davitt, who condemned both Chamberlain and his government. Order was eventually restored, but the event was reported in great detail by the nationalist press, including the *Freeman's Journal*, the *Irish Daily Independent* and, of course, the *United Irishman*.[28]

26 *Sligo Champion*, 18 October 1899, quoted in McCracken, *The Irish pro-Boers*, 51.   27 *Freeman's Journal*, 16 October 1899, quoted in McCracken, *The Irish pro-Boers*, 62.   28 See McCracken, *The Irish pro-Boers*, 62–7; Ruth Dudley Edwards, *James Connolly* (Dublin, 1981) 33–4.

The war certainly permeated popular culture, even if the contexts in which references to it were made were sometimes frivolous. In April 1900, for example, at the Limerick Quarter Sessions, Judge Adams presided over the case of John McEvilly, who was attempting to recover the sum of £4 10s. from John Higgins who had taken a large quantity of horse manure from his yard. In a reference to the gold of the Transvaal and its beleaguered president, the judge enquired of the plaintiff 'What was the value of the manure, Kruger?'[29]

Elsewhere the nationalist press was heartened by news of continuing Boer successes, with the exemplary role of the Irish Transvaal Brigade adding continuing interest. The editor of the *Limerick Leader* claimed in January 1900 that 'The Boers were fighting for what we have lost'.[30] Like the *Galway Observer*, the paper praised those Irishmen who were fighting for the Boers, and attacked what it regarded as cynical British attempts to increase recruiting by praising the valour of Irishmen in the imperial forces.

> The Irishmen of the Brigade are of the same stock as the Irishmen who have done the bulk [sic] of fighting for England in South Africa … But whilst the Irishmen sacrificing their lives for Cecil Rhodes and the capitalists, in as unjust a war as ever was waged, are [supposedly] "the first [sic] infantry in the world", the Irishmen who essay a blow for the freedom of a brave race in the eyes of the British are no better than sots and cowards. It was ever thus.[31]

The *Cork Examiner* proved equally predictable. In April 1900, T.D. Sullivan wrote to the editor to highlight the death in action of General de Villebois-Mareuil, the 'French Colonel' who had volunteered to fight for the Boers, who possessed the 'heart of a lion' and whose death had 'touched' Europe. Sullivan called on all popularly elected bodies, including municipal corporations, county and district councils and boards of guardians to send messages of sympathy to Villebois-Mareuil's family. He went on to condemn the war as a 'shocking tragedy, a hideous crime … being perpetrated before our eyes', and to attack those Irishmen fighting for the British imperial cause.

> Let us show that the agents of English tyranny, be they Irish, Scotch, Welsh, English, Canadian or Australian, have neither sympathy nor appreciation for a people who have been suffering from English oppression for hundreds of years [and that we can] honour the memory of gallant men who gave their lives to resist the onward march of the most unscrupulous, covetous and piratical empire of which there is record in human history.

29 *Limerick Leader*, 13 April 1900. 30 *Limerick Leader*, 17 January 1900. 31 *Limerick Leader*, 21 May 1900.

The same paper noted the appointment as Transvaal commandant-general of General Louis Botha, who had 'shown his appreciation of the Irish' by marrying Annie Emmet, a kinswoman of Robert Emmet.[32]

The Irish Transvaal Committee and its supporters sought to exploit every opportunity to keep the growing anti-war sentiment alive. At the beginning of 1900, the South Mayo by-election following the resignation of Davitt provided an important opportunity to do so. With the recent amalgamation of William O'Brien's United Irish League (UIL) with the Irish Party it was widely expected that the UIL candidate, John O'Donnell, would be elected unopposed. However, Griffith seized the opportunity to announce in the *United Irishman* that Major John MacBride, second-in-command of the Irish Transvaal Brigade, and a native of the county with powerful local connections, would be standing against O'Donnell. The conspiratorial Irish Republican Brotherhood, whose relationship with the Irish Transvaal Committee was not always a harmonious one, provided Griffith with funds to run the election campaign on MacBride's behalf. The *Connaught Telegraph* endorsed MacBride, but surprisingly, Davitt, then on his way to South Africa to report on the war at first hand, gave his support to O'Donnell. In the resultant, bitter campaign, Griffith did not hesitate to blacken the character of his opponents in the *United Irishman*:

> Just as the Gold of the Jews was lavished and continues to be lavished by the French Dreyfusites in assailing the French army ... so, even in the Irish West, the same foreign and filthy money is being lavished in assailing the Irish Transvaal Committee in the person of the heroic young Mayoman Major John MacBride[33]

MacBride lost, and Griffith and the Irish Transvaal Committee were incensed, with Griffith blaming Davitt for his supposed 'betrayal' of the national cause. The fortunes of Griffith and his comrades appeared to be mirrored by those of their Boer heroes, whose army now seemed to be everywhere in retreat. General Cronje was defeated at Paardeberg and the much-publicized siege of Ladysmith was lifted.

The pro-Boer cause, and with it, the attention of the newspapers, was given new focus, however, by the announcement that Queen Victoria would pay a visit to Ireland from 4 to 26 April.[34] She would pay tribute to the gallantry of her Irish soldiers in South Africa by announcing the creation of a regiment of Irish foot guards, and that Irish regiments would in future be allowed to wear shamrock on St Patrick's Day. The *Freeman's Journal*, unconvinced by this appeal to Irish martial sentiment, dismissed it as a celebration

32 *Cork Examiner*, 13 April 1900. 33 See McCracken, *The Irish pro-Boers*, 72. 34 See Paseta, 'Nationalist responses', 488–96, for an analysis of the impact of the visit.

of 'Irish mercenary valour in the odious and unjust anti-Boer war'.[35] William Butler Yeats wrote to the press attacking the visit of 'the official head and symbol of an empire that is robbing the South African Republics of their liberty, as it robbed Ireland of hers'.[36] Feelings ran high. In April, for example, three Limerick women who had arrived at their factory wearing union jack badges were reported as having been assaulted and had to be escorted back to their homes by police.[37] Nevertheless, there was considerable ambiguity in attitudes towards the monarch, even among nationalists, and this was especially true in Dublin, even if the *United Irishman* kept up its attacks throughout the visit.[38] Advanced nationalists, and some members of the Irish Party, were infuriated by John Redmond's declaration that the Irish people would be honoured by the right to wear shamrock bestowed on Irish regiments and that Irish people would show respect to the queen during her visit.[39]

On 13 April, following a series of inflammatory articles, culminating in an abusive piece by Maud Gonne on 'the Famine Queen', the police raided the *United Irishman* and suppressed the paper. The Irish Transvaal Committee was deprived of its mouthpiece at a crucial moment. The visit also sparked off what must surely have been the only physical confrontation during the war between editors based in the United Kingdom. Ramsay Colles, editor of the unionist *Irish Figaro*, wrote an article attacking Gonne's disloyalty and likening her to Herodotus, the 'father of lies'. Griffith arrived at Colles' office, armed with his South African *sjambok*, and the encounter ended with both parties claiming to have 'thrashed' the other. Griffith was brought before a magistrate following the incident, who sent him to prison for two weeks for refusing to be bound over to the peace. The feud did not end there, however. Shortly afterwards, based on an inaccurate report, Colles accused Gonne of continuing to receive a substantial army pension due to her father. In a confrontation that caught the imagination of the Dublin public, Colles was obliged to issue an apology, but not before Gonne was forced to face the rigours of a court cross-examination.[40]

After the relative success of the royal visit, and as the nationalist press found itself printing ever more numerous reports of British victories, many pro-Boers became despondent. James Connolly remained somewhat optimistic. In the *Workers' Republic*, he highlighted Britain's continued difficulties in South Africa, which had been compounded by the Boxer uprising in China. If only India rose in rebellion, he reasoned, 'then would come our Irish opportunity'. In contrast, the editor of the *Leader*, D.P. Moran, an important, mav-

---

35 *Freeman's Journal*, 28 March 1900.   36 McCracken, *The Irish pro-Boers*, 80–1.   37 *Limerick Leader*, 14 April 1900.   38 See James H. Murphy, *Abject loyalty: nationalism and monarchy in the reign of Queen Victoria* (Cork, 2001).   39 Alan O'Day, *Irish Home Rule, 1867–1921* (Manchester, 1998) 192.   40 See McCracken, *The Irish pro-Boers*, 85–6; Younger, *Arthur Griffith*, 15.

erick cultural nationalist, took a characteristically sceptical line by ridiculing pro-Boer rhetoric. 'Boers have no sentimentality in them', Moran wrote, 'We have little else ... The Transvaal is led by men, and not by ranters and exploded heroes.'[41] Later that summer, however, there was a renewed bout of 'Boer fever', with the return of Davitt from South Africa and the continuing guerrilla struggle in the Transvaal. Boer presidents and generals were again celebrated across the country, and the arrival of Kruger in Europe as an exile provided an occasion for the presentation of numerous Irish addresses of welcome. Irish nationalist newspapers continued to ridicule Britain's military performance and in March 1901, the *Weekly Freeman* printed a colour portrait of Kruger, wearing a green sash. Griffith was heartened by this revival, and sought to build on it by using the Irish Transvaal Committee to form the basis of Cumann na Gaedhal (which would later grow into the first Sinn Féin). News of the Boer surrender at Vereeniging on 31 May 1902 was met with dejection from many nationalists.[42]

Unionist responses to the war were quite different, given their continued loyalty to the imperial cause. They were however similarly varied. The Dublin-based *Irish Times* remained staunch in its support for the empire, and provincial unionist papers provided vivid pictures of local loyalism. The *Northern Whig*, traditionally a Liberal paper, but unionist by 1899, published detailed coverage of the war and its domestic impact. On 2 October 1899, its editor examined the nationalist pro-Boer protest meeting in Beresford Square, Dublin. He condemned the calls from the platform to Irish soldiers to cast off their British uniforms and join the Boers, and attacked those who had thanked Irishmen who, in the words of Patrick O'Brien MP, had 'upheld the honour of Ireland by joining the forces of the Boers'. The editor made it clear that the *Northern Whig* sympathized with genuine humanitarian opposition to the war but condemned those agitators who were taking advantage of the crisis. Irishmen, and Catholics especially, the editor pointed out, suffered under the laws of the Transvaal. The paper was 'ashamed to note ... the bad example' of Catholics members of one Ulster board of guardians, who, by passing a pro-Boer resolution, demonstrated their sympathy 'not with the oppressed, but with the oppressor'.[43] Two months later, against a background of British defeats by the Boers in 'Black Week', the editor analysed the strengths of pro- and anti-war factions in Liberal parliamentary constituencies in Britain, and related these factors and wider imperial issues to the position of Ireland within the empire. The editor hoped that in any future election voters would see what was really at issue in the struggle, not only in the empire but also in Ireland.

41 D.P. Moran, 'If the Boers were Irish', *Leader*, 15 September 1900. The author is grateful to Professor Roy Foster for this reference. 42 McCracken, *The Irish pro-Boers*, 88–92. 43 *Northern Whig*, 2 October 1899.

They will ask themselves whether they dare trust a party, a large section of which has suggested by its utterances that if it had unfortunately had the opportunity it would have trifled timorously or played fast and loose with British interests in South Africa and secondarily throughout our whole Colonial Empire. They will ask themselves whether those men are to be trusted even with domestic questions who have not disavowed a policy which would have conferred most mischievous powers upon Irish Nationalists, who have been breathing out seditious threatenings and praying for Boer victories. There is only one possible answer.[44]

The editor supported a suggestion that the city of Belfast send a Christmas gift to the Royal Irish Rifles (RIR), which would serve to 'emphasise in a very emphatic and striking manner that bond of sympathy which should, and we are glad does, exist between a loyal community and the military forces of the Crown'. Dismay at the reverse suffered by the RIR at Stormberg was 'somewhat lightened by the knowledge that, like the Royal Irish Fusiliers, the Rifles fought bravely and pluckily until borne down by overwhelming odds'.[45] The paper lamented the Dublin city council resolution supporting the Boers. Significantly, perhaps, the paper also noted that the votes of moderate nationalists, had they been used, might have combined with unionist votes to defeat it.[46] A week later, it praised Trinity for conferring an honorary doctorate on Chamberlain. Its report of the visit differed considerably from accounts in nationalist papers. According to the *Northern Whig*, Chamberlain was given a great welcome. Public hostility was 'muted, apart from the "residuum" of the population on whose support [the agitators] depend'.[47]

On the Easter weekend of 1900, the attention of the *Belfast Weekly Telegraph*, 'recognised organ of the Orange Society', was drawn to the reverses suffered by the Royal Irish Rifles at Reddersburg, and as with papers elsewhere in the empire, the focus of the reports was often on individual casualties. The paper noted for example the death in Cape Town from disease of 28-year-old Private William Ross, which had occurred only three days after his arrival in South Africa with the Canadian contingent. Coverage of Ross' brief life story demonstrated the colonial 'fresh start' that was available to Irishmen in a globalizing imperial world. At six-foot-two-inches, Ross, described in the press as physically 'one of the best specimens of Canadian manhood', was born in Belfast and taken as a child to Ottawa by his widowed mother, where he had served as a policeman for several years before joining the Canadian Mounted Rifles in South Africa.

Although unionism was developing a strong Ulster regional identity at

44 *Northern Whig*, 11 December 1899. 45 *Northern Whig*, 12 December 1899. 46 *Northern Whig*, 13 December 1899. 47 *Northern Whig*, 19 December 1899.

this time, the *Telegraph* claimed to speak for an 'Irish' as well as an Ulster identity. In the same issue, 'An Irishman's Diary' noted the prominence of Irishmen in the siege of Kimberley.

> The part which Irishmen have played in the present war is well known. They have come prominently to the front from the first with such bravery and dash that they have earned themselves the respect and admiration not alone of the British Empire but of the people of every civilized country in the world.

It was not surprising, the columnist concluded, to find 'men of the old sod', including Ulstermen, in the imperial front line in the northern Cape Colony.[48] The royal visit in April 1900 meanwhile provided an occasion for an out-pouring of monarchical sentiment. In 'The Queen – God bless her', Saul Cowan MA made up in sincerity for what he lacked in poetic ability.

> And naught shall stop or stay them when love and freedom
>   sway them,
> Till tyranny's home, Pretoria, shall surrender,
> Or Britain's guns shall claim it, and England's sons rename it
> Victoria, fair freedom's proud defender.[49]

Elsewhere in Ireland, in strongly nationalist and pro-Boer parts of the country, the concerns of numerically heavily outnumbered unionist commu-nities, mostly Protestant, were also conveyed by their local newspapers. The *Galway Express*, for example, reflected the strongly imperial allegiances of its readers at the outset of the war. The paper also demonstrated, however, greater sensitivity to Catholic feelings than did its northern counterparts. In an editorial headed 'A United People' the paper painted a stirring picture of a globe girdling empire 'from Malaya to Malta' that was as united as the Cabinet in dealing with a war that had been forced upon them. In particular it emphasized the support of the self-governing Dominions, claiming that, with their independent spirit, these communities would not have supported an overbearing policy. The paper acknowledged that '[n]aturally we have in Ireland treasonable utterances'. However, the paper claimed that 'The best men in the Nationalist Party [were] holding back', and rightly doubted whether the majority of Irish in South Africa were pro-Boer.[50] The paper's editorials regularly dealt with the war and its impact. In November 1899, an editorial entitled 'Liberal Imperialism' analysed the significance of the election of a 'Conservative Imperialist' in the Bow and Bromley by-election. Calling on 'Little Englanders' to adopt the Liberal imperialism of Lord Rosebery, the

48 'A Belfast Canadian', *Belfast Weekly Telegraph*, 14 April 1900. 49 *Belfast Weekly Telegraph*, 1 April 1900. 50 *Galway Express*, 7 October 1899.

paper went on to argue that 'The policy of the government is decisively vindicated; [by] the arms of our brave soldiers fighting in Africa the cause of our country are strengthened.' The paper went on to refer disdainfully to Galway urban district council's acceptance of a pro-Boer resolution referring to Joseph Chamberlain as 'Judas' and Rhodes as 'hypocritical'.[51] The sentiments of a patriotic article noting the departure of Galway reservists for the war in Black Week stood in contrast with a proposal then before the council which would result in the changing of 'imperialist' street names to nationalist ones: Eyre Square to Parnell Square; Eglinton Street to Wolfe Tone Street; Victoria Street to O'Neill Place, and William Street to Washington Street.[52] The paper meanwhile printed an account of a pre-Christmas Oratorio Service for soldiers, widows and orphans, held at St Nicholas' Church of Ireland, where a 'Special Prayer for Times of War' was said.[53]

Other southern unionist papers proved to be even more sensitive to the views of wider Irish society, and sought to distinguish moderate nationalists from the hardened pro-Boers. In May 1900, for example, the conservative *Kerry Evening Post*, carried a report of a recent speech by John Redmond in Glasgow, in which he highlighted the 'absurd' situation whereby the self-governing colonies were rallying to Britain in its hour of need, while Ireland was deprived of similar status. He confessed that although he was opposed to the British cause in this war, he was proud of the bravery of Irish troops. 'It was quite possible', he said, anticipating his Great War policy, 'their Irish brethren might, by their heroism, have done something to advance the National cause.'[54]

The complexity of Irish attitudes towards empire, as expressed by the press during the South African War, was further demonstrated by the *Irish Catholic*. While rejecting the necessity for war, the paper nevertheless concerned itself with the practical and spiritual needs of Irish soldiers and clergy, in reports that showed great pride in Irish Catholic devotion and martial prowess. The paper reported the thanks of an Irish nun in South Africa for medals, scapulars and rosary beads provided for poor wounded Catholic soldiers of the British army, while a missionary lamented the baneful effect of the conflict on Irish efforts, admittedly difficult, to convert the Boers to Catholicism.[55] The sense that, in spite of Irish popular attitudes to the conflict, South Africa lay within Ireland's spiritual sphere is conveyed by an account of the solemn profession as a Dominican in Pietermaritzburg of Sister Mary Columba Healy, sister of Tim Healy (the Irish nationalist MP, who was heavily involved in the promotion alongside Griffith of MacBride's election in South Mayo, and who later became governor-general of the Irish Free State). 'The ceremony', the paper noted, 'was exquisitely touching in its

51 *Galway Express*, 4 November 1899. **52** *Galway Express*, 16 December 1899. **53** *Galway Express*, 23 December 1899. **54** *Kerry Evening Post*, 12 May 1900. **55** 'The land of the Boers', *Irish Catholic*, 6 January 1900.

sacred beauty ... in striking contrast to the angry strife and turmoil that raged around' that had recently robbed the sisters of the convent of their home. But Sister Mary Columba was apparently safer in wartime Natal than she would have been in the Ardoyne district of Belfast, where the relief of Mafeking was greeted by loyalist crowds who attacked Catholic churches and presbyteries. In one case a Sister of Mercy was set upon and dragged about by a body of 'mafficking' drunks, until rescued by a few Catholic workmen.[56]

The *Irish Catholic* regularly published letters from Irish nursing sisters on the course of the war.[57] A message received by the mother-general of the Sisters of Nazareth from one of her nuns typified a widespread sense of pride in the Irish Catholic soldiers of the British army.

> The Leinsters landed here during the week – a splendid lot of men. One could not help saying God help the Boers they chanced to come across ... The Sisters met one poor fellow who took off his cap to show the shamrock he had brought from Ireland. Another poor fellow came up and said: 'Sister, I have a brother at the front severely wounded. There are five of us. I am proud to say that four of us are fighting for Queen Victoria' ... The Leinsters are all Catholics. They surround the Sisters asking for Rosaries, Scapulars, etc. I am afraid the Sisters will come back to me some day after having given away the minor parts of their Habit, namely their own Rosaries and Crucifixes, they are so anxious to supply the poor fellows leaving for the front ... The Sisters begged of the soldiers to go to Confession which, thank God, some of them did, although they had such a short time.

The same issue reported the return of Father Morgan, who had ministered to British prisoners in the Transvaal. The paper argued that he deserved a general's welcome.[58]

The *Irish Catholic* sounded a less pro-imperial note in an editorial on famine in India. The editor referred to a meeting in the Dublin Mansion House held the previous week, presided over by the lord mayor, to discuss the Indian famine and went on to draw analogies between India and Ireland. It was 'nothing short of shameful that, at the close of a century and a half of English dominion in one of the fairest, most fruitful, and wealthiest countries in the world, many millions should be menaced by the awful fear of death by hunger'. The English exchequer was replenished by 'enormous sums ... annually drawn from India – just as they are from Ireland'. Huge amounts were being paid to hordes of British civil servants on the backs of the 'toiling and starving millions', and these officials spent their money outside the country.

---

56 *Limerick Leader*, 21 May 1900.   57 See also for example *Limerick Leader*, 9 June 1900.   58 *Irish Catholic*, 16 June 1900.

Like the absentee gentry and aristocracy of Ireland, they regard India as a kind of milch cow created solely for the supplying of their necessities. One strong and real bond of sympathy, however, exists between Ireland and India. Both are equally the victims of a system of rule which is unjust and, consequently, injurious ... It would be strange indeed if in Ireland, which has suffered so much from the effects of alien government, no proof were forthcoming of appreciation of the needs of those who have been plundered, alike of their natural rights and revenues, precisely in the same way in which our own people of all creeds, parties, and ranks have been robbed by English Chancellors of the Exchequer.[59]

While the *Irish Catholic* was thus not unthinkingly supportive of empire, significantly, unlike Maud Gonne, it did not criticize the 'Famine Queen', and reported Victoria's visit to Dublin as a credit to her and to Dublin's citizens. The paper was anxious to point out that she was not responsible for her ministers' wrongs, or for the decay of Ireland.[60] Indeed, the visit provided an opportunity to express, conditionally but enthusiastically, Catholic loyalty to the crown. On St Patrick's Day, 1900, a carefully composed editorial entitled 'The Queen's Visit' admitted that there had been a varying response to the impending royal visit from 'different sections of our people'. However,

In saying so much as this we are far from suggesting that it will enter into the mind or thought of any Irishman to adopt towards her Majesty [any] other attitude than that which accords with her exalted rank as monarch, and with the respect due to an aged and gracious lady who will, for the time being, be the guest of this nation.

While the editor noted the widespread suffering that had prevailed in Ireland during Victoria's long reign, he did not doubt that she had always played the role of constitutional monarch and would sign a Home Rule bill as readily as George III had signed the act of Union. He also accepted the word of the viceroy, Lord Cadogan, that the visit was non-political. Any attempt to 'parade the Throne among the paraphernalia of faction ... [would be] regrettable', the editor warned. The queen might visit an Ireland in which equal laws prevailed, in which 'the Catholic enjoyed the same rights as the Protestant and in which the profession of national principles was not held forth by a narrow and insolent clique of self-seekers as synonymous with disloyalty and crime'. Once the royal visit was underway, the *Irish Catholic* was enthusiastic in its coverage. Victoria's visits to the Mater Hospital and Mount Anville Convent

59 *Irish Catholic*, 2 June 1900. **60** *Irish Catholic*, 14 April 1900.

of the Sacred Heart in Dublin were reported in detail. At Mount Anville there were long strips of red, white and blue bunting on both sides of the avenue leading to the school, where a Royal Standard and a large Union Jack were flying. 'Cead Mile Failte' was written in large gold letters over the gate, and the boarders sang 'God save the Queen' as the carriage drew up.[61]

The ambiguous reaction to the royal visit reminds us that Irish newspaper responses to the imperial connection were complex, particularly among nationalist organs. Criticism of British policy in South Africa was published in papers that also reported, without comment, the everyday reality of Ireland's imperial existence. The *Galway Observer*, for example, dispassionately printed details of the latest Royal Irish Constabulary transfers in Galway, on pages otherwise given over to pro-Boer rhetoric.[62] Moreover, in spite of its pro-Boer stance, it could still take pride in Irish valour in the ranks of the British army. One report of a Boer reverse from Mr Regan, their correspondent in London, noted that all the Boer guns had been captured by the Royal Dublin Fusiliers 'with great dash'.[63] Under the heading of 'The War in Galway', the paper reported the capture of Father Matthews, Chaplain to the Royal Irish Fusiliers, who assured his interviewer that 'The white flag was not hoisted by the Irish Fusiliers'. Doubtless, such ambiguity would have been less apparent in the columns of the *United Irishman* and other more relentlessly pro-Boer newspapers. Nevertheless, these, and other references point to a less than unified response to imperial issues both among nationalists and unionists. Significantly, perhaps, many press references to Ireland's relationship with the British empire in this period were comparatively prosaic. The *Waterford Mail* reported that 'the unexpected prolongation of the war has caused low-priced Australian shares to be sought after by speculative investors'.[64] Ward Brothers, a Waterford shipping agent, advertised passages to North America, Australia, Africa and India,[65] while the *Irish Catholic*, the *Belfast Weekly News*, the *Cork Examiner* and other provincial newspapers printed a report promoting land in Canada for prospective Irish immigrants of whatever political hue. Under the captivating heading of 'no rent, light taxes, free schools, good markets, splendid climate, sunny skies', interested persons were encouraged to apply to Mr Devlin, Canadian immigration commissioner for Ireland. For all the furore caused by the South African War, and despite its enduring significance for Irish nationalism and unionism, the practical advantages of Ireland's imperial connections remained an ever-present part of normal, everyday life.

61 *Irish Catholic*, 21 April 1900. 62 *Galway Observer*, 14 October 1899. 63 *Galway Observer*, 21 October 1899. 64 'Gold and the War', *Waterford Mail*, 16 April 1900 (listed in the *Newspaper press directory* as a national paper advocating 'progress and liberty and providing details of colonial intelligence'). 65 *Waterford Mail*, 17 April 1900.

10. An Irish perspective on empire: William Flavelle Monypenny

JACQUELINE BEAUMONT

The contribution made to the national press in the UK and to the imperial press in South Africa by the Irish-born journalist William Flavelle Monypenny was a controversial one, but one that is not fully understood. Monypenny played an important and distinctive role as editor of the Johannesburg *Star* and as Johannesburg correspondent of the London *Times* in the months leading up to the outbreak of war in South Africa in October 1899.[1] Otherwise, his name is primarily associated with a biography of Disraeli, of which he completed the first volume just before his death, known to generations of students as 'Monypenny and Buckle'. He was only 46 when he died of tuberculosis, after several years of poor health. Had it not been so, he may well have established a greater historical reputation for himself. George Buckle, the editor of *The Times*, thought highly of his talents from the first and, if Monypenny had been younger, and presumably fitter, Buckle would have preferred him as his successor.[2] This essay explores what it was about Monypenny that the establishment at *The Times* liked so much, and what this tells us about Monypenny, his newspaper, and their perspectives on the British empire.

William Flavelle Monypeny – he only adopted the familiar spelling after he joined *The Times* – was born on 7 August 1866 in the small town of Dungannon in County Tyrone. On his father's side the family was Protestant (Methodist by the nineteenth century), Scottish in origin and most probably descended from Thomas Moneypeny, laird of Kinkell, in Fife, who applied for and was granted 1,000 acres in County Fermanagh by King James I on the setting up of the Ulster Plantation.[3] The grandeur of the title 'laird' would

1 Monypenny was first brought to prominence in J.A. Hobson, *The war in South Africa: its causes and effects* (London, 1900), particularly 206–28. For further consideration of his role in South Africa see Alan Jeeves, 'The Rand capitalists and the coming of the South African War, 1896–1899', *Canadian Historical Association Papers* (1973) 61–83 and Andrew Porter, 'Sir Alfred Milner and the press, 1897–1899', *Historical Journal*, 16 (1973) 323–39. 2 News International Archive (henceforth NIA), London, WFA/3/1/27 G.E. Buckle to A.F. Walter, 12 July 1894; PPG/3/2/2/1 Sir Evelyn Wrench to George Walter Buckle, 5 March 1953, quoting a letter from G.E. Buckle to Geoffrey Robinson (Dawson), August 1912. 3 See the nascent Monypenny website at http://members.aol.com/chuckm7518/money3.html. According to this site Thomas sold his interests in 1625 and returned to Scotland. But his four nephews,

undoubtedly have appealed to Monypenny, who all his life remained conscious of his status as a gentleman. What his father, also William, did for a living is not known; he is described by J.B. Capper of *The Times* (who wrote the entry for the *Dictionary of national biography*, and had known Monypenny since he first joined *The Times*) as a small landowner of Ballyworkan (a rural district outside Portadown) in County Armagh. If so, he very likely rented the land and made his living by some other means in Dungannon. Those means were sufficient to provide for and educate a family of several children; Monypenny was his second son.

His mother, Mary Anne Flavelle, was born in Dungannon. The Flavelles, like the Monypennys, had already started to move out of Ireland before Monypenny was born. Several Flavelle brothers and sisters left for Canada and the United States in the 1840s and 50s. According to the Flavelle and Monypenny family websites there were, by the time Monypenny was born, members of both families in North America and Australia. One of Monypenny's brothers emigrated to Canada, where some members of his mother's family had prospered. His cousin, Sir Joseph Wesley Flavelle, son of his mother's older brother, became a highly successful businessman there. The Irish Flavelles kept in touch with their Canadian relatives; Monypenny's mother died in Canada in 1909.[4] Thus from childhood he must have been aware both of his family's association with the Protestant ascendancy, dating back to the seventeenth century, and of the existence and the practical necessity of the empire as a field in which families such as his own could prosper.

After an education at the Royal School in Dungannon, Monypenny went on to Trinity College, Dublin. Searches of the Trinity registers and year books reveal that he excelled in mathematics, in which he gained a first class degree, and in logic, for which he won several prizes.[5] He seems not to have participated in the flourishing debating society, where other near-contemporaries who subsequently launched into careers in politics and journalism practised the craft of public argument about the topics of the day. He was then for a short time in Oxford, at Balliol College. According to Capper, he had to leave due to the first of a succession of bouts of ill health that were to dog his short life.

We find him next working for the *Spectator*, a national weekly paper. The most influential member of staff (and the paper's proprietor from 1898) was

all brothers, followed their uncle to Ireland. They were James, Arthur, Henry and Andrew. It is believed that all Monypennys in Ireland, and thus all in the United States, descend from these four brothers.   4 Information about the Flavelles is to be found on the Flavelle family website at http://www.flavelle.com/Tree/irish/D1.html. See also NIA, CMB1 Monypenny to Bell, 24 November 1909, requesting that a notice be inserted in *The Times* after his mother's death in Canada from pneumonia.   5 *Trinity College, Dublin Calendar*, 1888 and 1889.

John St Loe Strachey, who had been an undergraduate at Balliol. It is quite possible that Monypenny owed his introduction to journalism to the good offices of Balliol's formidable Master, Benjamin Jowett, well known for his leadership of the party within the university that favoured the training of graduates for public service, including journalism. He was also, despite an intimidating manner which terrified many a young man, quietly very supportive of those in trouble, financially or otherwise, and quick to spot a winner and place him in the right niche.[6]

There is no evidence that Monypenny dabbled in student journalism, or had any publication record before joining the staff of the *Spectator*. But for two years, until the end of 1893, he had a relatively gentle, indeed gentlemanly, introduction to Fleet Street journalism. Being a weekly paper, there was not the daily, or rather nightly, hustle to put the paper to bed. In fact his subsequent application to join the editorial staff of *The Times* in November 1893 suggests that he only worked intermittently.[7] Monypenny seems to have gained the approval of the co-proprietors and co-editors of the *Spectator*, Townsend and Hutton, both of whom wrote in support of his subsequent application to *The Times*. What influence Strachey had on Monypenny, we do not know. But he seems to have maintained some contact with Monypenny after he left; Strachey was one of the select few who contributed to Monypenny's funerary plaque in 1912.[8] Strachey was a convinced 'imperialist' and also took a close interest in American politics, rightly believing that the affairs of the USA were of prime importance in the modern world. Monypenny was soon to evince his own faith in empire, together with an interest in matters American, perhaps influenced by his family connections and stimulated by Strachey.[9] Their enthusiasm for empire and for Anglo-American amity reflected a strong belief in the supremacy and ruling genius of the 'Anglo-Saxon race', a conviction shared by Cecil Rhodes among others.[10]

Monypenny started work for *The Times* on 1 January 1894.[11] Within a year he was sent to the United States to report on the political situation there. The result was a long analysis for the benefit of *The Times'* business manager, Moberly Bell, of the shortcomings of the paper's coverage of American affairs and the way in which Printing House Square might develop a virtual monopoly in supplying the American press with news from Europe.[12] Bell,

---

6 See Geoffrey Faber, *Jowett: a portrait* (London, 1957). Examples of Jowett pointing promising students in the appropriate direction are many. That of Arnold Toynbee is one of the best-known and remarkable examples. See A. Kadish, *Apostle Arnold: the life and death of Arnold Toynbee, 1852–1883* (Durham NC, 1986), especially 24–32. 7 NIA, Monypenny managerial file. 8 Bodleian Library, Oxford, Alfred Milner papers, Milner Dep. 44 ff. 7–8. 9 John St Loe Strachey, *The adventure of living: a subjective autobiography* (London, 1922). 10 See Cecil Rhodes, 'Confession of faith', 1877, printed as appendix to John Flint, *Cecil Rhodes* (Boston, Mass., 1974) 248–50. 11 NIA, Monypenny managerial file. 12 NIA, CMB/1 Monypenny to Bell, 10 Feb. 1895.

always looking for ways to improve the finances of the paper and increase the returns on the paper's investment in news services, seems to have listened to this suggestion. *The Times* never achieved the monopoly which Monypenny had hoped for, but when war broke out in South Africa, the Chicago *Tribune* paid £1040 a year for the sole US rights to publish *Times* telegrams from South Africa.[13]

Bell also listened when Monypenny urged him to appoint a better correspondent in the United States. At that time *The Times* used a correspondent based in Philadelphia, dependent for his news on telegrams from the American news agencies and with no access to the main sources of inside information to be found in Washington and New York. 'You might as well expect an adequate treatment of the affairs of the British Empire from a correspondent living in Birmingham and dependent on the Press Association for his information.'[14] Leading American politicians whom he had interviewed had commented on the poor coverage given to American affairs by *The Times*. Moreover, and this was an important point for Monypenny, the British ambassador in Washington, Sir Julian Pauncefote, 'seemed to think it a personal grievance and an abdication of its natural functions by The Times that we had not a man there whom he could take into his confidence and use as a medium for communicating with the public at home'.[15] Pauncefote cited as an example the leaking of a draft agreement about the Behring Sea which was published by an American journalist and then circulated around the world as the actual agreement, much to the embarrassment of all concerned. It would not have happened if there had been a *Times* man readily available to nip it in the bud.

> The interchange of ideas between the two nations, and the interest felt by each in the other, is increasing, and if we do not soon step in we are sure to be anticipated ... The Times has gained a clear ascendancy throughout the British Empire. But it cannot allow any other English paper to take the lead in our English speaking nation of sixty millions without a great loss of prestige.[16]

It was not long before the unsatisfactory Cook of Philadelphia was replaced by George Smalley, previously Washington correspondent for the *Morning Post*, who held the post for some ten years. His sharp, sometimes viciously acerbic reports on the activities of Bryanites and other pro-Boers in the US and on the (in his view) malign influence of the British Liberal James Bryce, were to enliven the pages of *The Times* during the South African War.

13 NIA, Moberly Bell Letter Books, Bell to A.L. Clarke (London correspondent of the *Chicago Tribune*), 1 Nov. 1899; Bell to F. Cook, 14 Dec. 1899.   14 NIA, CMB/1 Monypenny to Bell, 19 Feb. 1895.   15 Ibid.   16 Ibid.

Monypenny made his mark at *The Times* very quickly. By the end of 1898 he was second assistant editor. But this was to be the most senior post he ever held as an employee of the paper. For in November of that year, Alfred Milner, the British high commissioner in South Africa, came home on leave. Alongside his plans for briefing the British press on affairs in South Africa was a project to find a suitable new editor for the Johannesburg *Star*. This paper, owned by the South African Argus newspaper group, in turn controlled by the mining conglomerate Wernher Beit & Co, was until 1895 ably edited by Francis Dormer. His successor, Finlason, was no match for the editors of the other English and Dutch papers in the Transvaal. The English language *Standard and Diggers' News* was, after the failure of the Jameson Raid (an attempted coup that took place in 1895), particularly critical of the *uitlanders* (the foreign population living in the Transvaal and mainly working in positions related to the mining industry) and their leaders, and extremely hostile to the foreign mining capitalists in Johannesburg. It blamed them all for the Raid and advocated firm control by the Kruger regime. It was in response to these bitter attacks that those in the mining industry who wished to make reasonable terms with President Kruger's government concerning the financial and economic conditions in which the industry should operate, decided that the *Star* had to be placed in the hands of a more effective editor. Various efforts were made by the Argus company to find a suitable man to replace Finlason.[17]

Eventually that man was found, not by the company, but by Milner, who was eager to help the Rand capitalists in order to ensure that the *Star* had an editor he too could work with. He arrived in England bringing with him a list of those he wished and needed to see while he was home, among them Fleet Street journalists, most of whom were old friends. The list included several members of staff at *The Times* – Flora Shaw, the imperial editor, MacKenzie Wallace, then still the foreign editor, Moberly Bell, the business manager and Buckle, the editor.[18] Buckle and Milner discussed the problem of the editorship of the *Star* and by mid-January had agreed that the new editor would be Monypenny. He was appointed to combine the editorship of the Johannesburg *Star* with the post of correspondent for *The Times* in Johannesburg. For Milner this was part of a plan to keep the public in Britain informed of the situation in South Africa as he saw it and prepare public opinion for the conflict which he already regarded as being inevitable, an agenda which was not the same as that of the mine owners. For *The Times* it was a conveniently inexpensive way of ensuring that it had a hand picked correspondent in a place which was to be of paramount importance that year.

17 Jeeves, 'The Rand capitalists'; Porter, 'Sir Alfred Milner'.   18 Porter, 'Sir Alfred Milner', 332–4

The salary of £3000 paid by the proprietors of the *Star* apparently covered Monypenny's work both as editor of the *Star* and correspondent of *The Times*.

Monypenny was not Milner's first choice; he would have preferred an older and more experienced journalist, such as Henry Norman, then assistant editor of the *Daily Chronicle*, well known as a supporter of Milner. But by Christmas he knew that Norman would not accept the post. Characteristically, Milner subsequently wanted Monypenny to appoint a nominee to act as *Times* correspondent, while actually doing the work himself, so as to disguise the connection between the *Star* and *The Times*. Monypenny, while grateful to Milner for giving him the opportunity of an editorship at the age of 30, was not happy with this suggestion and, having discussed it further with Milner, Conynghame Greene (the British agent in Pretoria) and others after his arrival in South Africa, decided to act openly as *Times* correspondent.[19]

His reports on the significance of events in Johannesburg from the months before the war until early in September 1899 (when he fled to Natal, fearing arrest or worse) were among the most important to appear in Britain, because of the status enjoyed by *The Times*. From the start, Monypenny took an independent stance. That is, he followed his own political judgement without considering the aims of the mine owners, the proprietors of the *Star*. In practice this meant that he was Milner's man, doing for Milner the tasks which Pauncefote had expected of *The Times* representative in America. But Monypenny went much further than explaining mistakes arising from draft documents leaked by ill-informed journalists. He took charge of the Johannesburg *Star* on 15 March 1899 and his first full telegraphic report to *The Times* was sent ten days later. It was an account of the handing in to the British Agent in Pretoria of the second petition to the queen, signed by 21,000 British subjects. The petition requested the British government to intervene to force Kruger to legislate for civil and political liberties for the *uitlanders*.[20] Great care was taken to ensure that public opinion at home was sympathetic. The tone of Monypenny's account was neutral and dignified, as always. But in setting the scene he clearly sought to present a partial picture, arguing that a body of decent, respectable British citizens had been ground down by a despotic, unsympathetic regime. 'The Uitlanders possess most of the wealth and intelligence in the country, and they have no voice in its government. In spite of the promises of the Transvaal government and the petitions addressed to the President, there have been no practical reforms.'[21]

Monypenny arrived in South Africa at a critical moment. As he subsequently told Bell,

---

19 NIA, PPG/2/12 Milner to Buckle, 22 Jan. 1899; CMB1 Monypenny to Bell, 20 Mar. 1899. 20 A previous petition in 1898 had failed on technical grounds. 21 *The Times*, 27 Mar. 1899.

> I took over control ... in very difficult circumstances, knowing of strained relationships between the Governments and also of the negotiations between the capitalists and the Government – hampered by my knowledge of these things to neither of which I could refer and by want of knowledge of everything else.[22]

Readers would not have guessed from his confident reports and editorials, however, that he suffered from any 'want of knowledge'. Moreover, as Andrew Porter has pointed out, within a few days of arriving in South Africa he had come to the firm conclusion that 'the Boers are very Oriental, treacherous and cunning in a small way, but with no backbone and no real cleverness', a view most probably provided by Milner's secretary.[23]

How much he knew about the secret negotiations taking place between the Transvaal government and the mining interests, and to what extent he was kept informed about the quickly shifting story at this stage can only be guessed at. The probability is that he was soon fully briefed by Percy Fitzpatrick, 'the only man in Johannesburg with a head for politics', whom he met for the first time on 20 March.[24] It was Fitzpatrick who successfully sabotaged the negotiations by ensuring that *The Times* in London received leaked copies of crucial documents. It was Monypenny who forwarded these to London, thus ensuring that *The Times* had a scoop when on 3 April the paper published the response of the mining industry to the Transvaal government's proposals and printed a memorandum about the *uitlander* franchise delivered to the State Secretary F.W. Reitz by Fitzpatrick on 28 March. The effect of this disclosure was immediate and disastrous for those wanting compromise, and the negotiations broke down.[25]

In the months that followed, Monypenny mounted a crusade through the pages of the *Star* for the granting of full franchise rights to the *uitlanders*, and conducted a smear campaign against the Boers. What he wrote in Johannesburg was often sent back to London in his despatches for *The Times*. The latter were largely presented as news reports, not letters, and therefore appeared on the news page. The received wisdom of the time, subscribed to by editors, journalists and members of the public, was that the news page constituted 'facts', which were incontrovertible; debate and opinion was to be found in separate editorials and articles. What one read on the news page was believed to be inherently 'true'. What Monypenny wrote in his capacity as correspondent of *The Times* in Johannesburg was therefore printed by *The Times* as 'fact', even though the facts were sometimes quite selective and their presentation slanted.

22 NIA, CMB1 Monypenny to Bell, 20 Mar. 1899.   **23** Porter, 'Sir Alfred Milner', 335.   **24** Ibid.   **25** See Iain Smith, *The origins of the South African War, 1899–1902* (London, 1996) 229–62 for a detailed account of events leading up to the breakdown of negotiations.

Reading his accounts of events, one is struck for example by how the activities of a few hundred Johannesburghers become 'public opinion', by his emphasis on the very 'British' decency and respectability of these solid citizens and the reasonableness of their demands. As an example, we may look at his account of the mass meeting arranged by the South African League for Saturday 10 June, following the breakdown of negotiations between Milner and Kruger at Bloemfontein over the *uitlander* demands. The following Monday *The Times* published Monypenny's report of the reaction in Johannesburg to these events.

> JOHANNESBURG, JUNE 9
> Johannesburg is disappointed that the Bloemfontein Conference has led to no result, but the public are greatly gratified and encouraged by the firmness of Sir Alfred Milner, and are impressed by the ability, tact, and grasp of the position which he showed in the negotiations. The President's proposals are condemned as entirely unsatisfactory, and Sir A Milner's proposals are thought to err on the side of moderation, though the Uitlanders would accept the latter through their earnest desire of a peaceful solution ...

> JUNE 10
> The meeting called for tonight is evoking extraordinary enthusiasm. 600 signatures have been received to the requisition, and there has been great eagerness to sign even among those who were previously trimmers.
> The Government ... are taking precautions to protect the meeting, and, after another building had been secured, sanctioned the use of the Wanderers Hall. The State Secretary has issued an ungracious notice, warning all not to disturb the meeting, but especially urging those well disposed to the Government to remain away.

> LATER
> The meeting tonight was the greatest ever held at Johannesburg. 500 people passed through the turnstiles of the Wanderers Club. The proceedings were entirely orderly, but enthusiastic.

Given that this was all written in the dignified language required by *The Times*, it is nevertheless a pointedly biassed report. There is no doubt that Monypenny knew what he was doing and why. He had started to pile on the pressure as soon as the second petition was presented to the Kruger government, expecting that Kruger would 'wriggle' but eventually climb down.[26]

26 NIA, CMB/1 Monypenny to Bell, 7 May 1899.

He was part of a small committee, also including Fitzpatrick, that decided to set up the meeting of 10 June, specifically to unite public opinion in Johannesburg behind the paramount importance of the franchise question. Writing to Walrond, Milner's secretary, on 14 May he complained

> It made me swear the other day to find how ready everybody was to come forward and talk about a mere side issue like the liquor business while no one can be got to utter a word about the main question. It is like fiddling while Rome is burning. They do not even back me by writing anonymous letters to the papers.[27]

The meeting of 10 June, which he acknowledged was orderly because opponents who might have created trouble were prevented from coming by order of the government, enabled him to present a politically useful picture of the atmosphere in Johannesburg. The activists, numbering a few hundred, become 'Johannesburg'. This implied that there was total support for Milner's stance among a populace characterized by its mature approach to the democratic process, as shown by the reasonable and orderly conduct of the meeting. It could have been taking place in any industrial centre at home. This illusion of a solidly 'British', respectable, hard-working community was no doubt cultivated in order to ensure that 'opinion' at home among readers of *The Times* was sympathetic to the cause of the *uitlanders* and, more particularly, their ambition to be enfranchised

Monypenny continued in this mode for the rest of the summer, fully expecting the Boers to climb down. Other reports dwelt upon the brutality of the Boer response, the venality of the police and civil service and the sufferings of the *uitlanders*. The plight of the *uitlanders* was presented as comprising major breaches of civil liberties to which they were naturally and legally entitled. Monypenny had never heard the term spin doctor, but his interpretation of Johannesburg, its inhabitants and their preoccupations provides an excellent example of the technique. And Milner, who always appreciated the value of 'educating' public opinion, and on more than one occasion took a hand in the matter himself, was happy to harness his talents during these tense months.

Monypenny kept in touch with Milner, mainly through his secretary Walrond, and joyfully informed him that

> the Times people, after being a little reluctant at first to support us, have now gone a header and are wholly with us. They were afraid of getting left again in South Africa [as during the Jameson Raid] and

27 Milner papers, Milner Dep. 229 Monypenny to Walrond, 14 May 1899.

though I have not yet heard I fancy the change has been caused by their hearing from Chamberlain that he means business. Nothing has encouraged me so much.[28]

Two days after the meeting of 10 June he wrote to Moberly Bell that

It has had a most enormous effect here in rallying and consolidating the community, in strengthening the weak and bringing in the waverers. Throughout South Africa its effect will hardly be less and I hope it may be useful at home. In a way it is a personal triumph for me – three months ago it would have been impossible. I do not mean that I have done everything or even more than many others but the daily drip of discussion in the "Star" has undoubtedly done much to educate opinion. Milner is now the hero of Johannesburg and if this thing is peacefully settled he will be a bigger man in South Africa than Rhodes.[29]

Not everybody went along with Monypenny's interpretations however. In Johannesburg his delineation of the Boer character in the columns of the *Star* caused offence. On 24 April he was attacked in his office. An account of the incident appeared in *The Times* the following day, taken from the *Standard and Diggers' News*.

An inflammatory article in the *Star* referring to the ignorant and prejudiced Boers, led Mr Theron, a solicitor, to insist upon its withdrawal and apology for the insult.

An interview took place, and high words ensued between him and Mr Monypenny, the *Star* editor. In the result Mr Theron struck Mr Monypenny, smashing his eyeglass, and then left the office. Strong indignation is expressed at the unworthy attempt of Mr Monypenny, who is the *Times* correspondent, to precipitate another crisis. His telegram to the *Times* of Saturday last to the effect that Johannesburg is only awaiting a signal from England to rally all classes and nationalities in an anti-Pretorian demonstration is utterly false, and at variance with the facts.[30]

Leading Liberal 'pro-Boers' in Britain were also sceptical. The acknowledged expert on South African affairs James Bryce, who was in touch with many senior political figures in South Africa, told J.A. Spender, editor of the *Westminster Gazette*, that

28 Ibid.   29 NIA, CMB/1 Monypenny to Bell, 12 June 1899.   30 *Times*, 25 Apr. 1899.

> You must not believe the half you hear as to the "terrible position"
> of the Uitlanders as we are called. In no place in the world at the
> present time can a British working man do so well as in the
> Transvaal. It is the same party that made the trouble in 1896 when
> they came to grief over the Jameson Raid.[31]

Bryce was one of the few who had visited South Africa, and he was there at
the time of the Jameson Raid. In order to counter the increasingly alarmist
reports coming from Johannesburg, the radical press had to rely mainly on
reports from Cape Town, where Albert Cartwright did his best to inform
readers of the *Daily Chronicle* and the *Manchester Guardian* of the attitudes
of the Boers and the Cape Dutch. But it was not until J.A. Hobson was sent
out by the *Manchester Guardian* in July 1899 to take a closer look at what was
happening that any informed critique of the accounts written by Monypenny
and others became available. By the time they started to appear in radical
newspapers in September it was too late for them to affect the issue. What
happened during these months arguably knocked the stuffing out of any illu-
sions that Liberals might still have had about the role of the press as an educator of the newly enfranchised masses.

Hobson adopted Boer accusations against Monypenny, stating that he was
the mouthpiece of the 'capitalists', too young and headstrong for the job
entrusted to him.[32] Hobson was in some respects wrong and to some extent
disingenuous about Monypenny. He never made the connection between
Monypenny and Milner, or realized how their objectives differed from those
of the owners of the *Star*. His criticism of Monypenny's youth was also mis-
placed. Thirty was young, but it was not unusual for an editor to be appointed
at that age, sometimes even younger. Lord Glenesk had become owner and
editor of the *Morning Post* in 1852 when he succeeded his father at the age
of 22. Delane was 23 when he became editor of *The Times*, Buckle was 28.
Spender was 34 when he became editor of the *Westminster Gazette*. Moreover,
in South Africa it was always difficult to attract older, more experienced men
to editorial positions. Garrett of the *Cape Times* and his successor Saxon Mills,
and Basil Worsfold and Geoffrey Dawson who both succeeded Monypenny,
were all young men in their thirties when appointed. Monypenny's huge
salary of £3000 a year, on which many commented, was also a red herring.
The cost of living in Johannesburg was much higher than in London and
acted as a further deterrent in the recruitment of older men.[33]

31 British Library, London, J.A. Spender papers, Add. MSS 46391 J.A. Bryce to Spender, 28
May 1899.   32 Hobson, *The war in South Africa*, 206–8. Smith, *Origins of the South African
War*, 216–17.   33 Brotherton Library, Leeds, Glenesk-Bathurst Collection, Lord Glenesk to
Oliver Borthwick, 1 Dec. 1902.

Nevertheless Hobson had detected something in Monypenny which made him more dangerous as an opponent than obvious rabble rousers such as R.J. Pakeman, editor of the *Transvaal Leader*, whose editorials Hobson quoted so liberally.[34] Monypenny was as much a 'conviction journalist' as any of the other imperially-minded editors in South Africa at that time, but, unlike most of them, he spoke in the tones of 'civilized' Fleet Street, as had Edmund Garrett, editor of the *Cape Times* until ill health forced him back to Europe in July 1899. This was an asset much prized by Milner, who was very anxious that the tone of debate should be gentlemanly. He knew that, unless it was, opinion-formers and policy directors in Britain were less likely to accept what they read.

But even a Fleet Street tone could not disguise the objectives Monypenny was pursuing. Nor was his writing in the pages of the *Star* always restrained. Early in September a warrant for his arrest was issued. The news hit Fleet Street on 4 September, by which time Monypenny was safe in northern Natal. The radical *Morning Leader* rejoiced at his ignominious retreat, commenting that 'He who writes and runs away lives to write another day.' It expressed no surprise that this had happened and quoted from an article in the *Star* in which Monypenny had referred to the Transvaal government as a 'corrupt and scheming oligarchy', and another describing Boer actions with regard to the ongoing negotiations on the franchise question as

> not frank and praiseworthy efforts of men striving for peace and prepared to accept the responsibilities of their action, and come out into the open when their advice is rejected, but the work of schemers plotting how little they can give and still save the cause of injustice, misgovernment, and racial ascendancy from disaster.[35]

Such language, argued the *Morning Leader*, belied claims that the press in Johannesburg had been muzzled by the Transvaal government. Monypenny 'would have had a poor time if he had been an Indian journalist in India'. The paper's correspondent in Cape Town, very probably Albert Cartwright, bluntly stated that

> His writing during the last few weeks would not have been allowed in any other country, but friends and foes alike decline to believe that, having incited others to rebellious action against the Government, he has disgraced his Volunteer uniform and his Sovereign's commission by bolting at the first rumour of danger.

34 See Hobson, *The war in South Africa*, 211–14 for examples.   35 *Morning Leader*, 4 Sept. 1899.

The point being made was underlined by cartoons, one of a puny monocled Monypenny wearing the uniform of the London Irish Rifle Volunteers,[36] the second of Monypenny and Pakeman, heavily disguised in women's clothing, fleeing Johannesburg.[37]

But Monypenny was in fact prepared to demonstrate his loyalty to queen and country by taking up the sword in place of the pen. He joined the newly formed volunteer regiment, the Imperial Light Horse, among whose officers were many of the Johannesburg *uitlander* leaders, including several of the Jameson Raid 'Reformers'. Initially he was told that he could combine a commission with reporting for *The Times*. But Sir George White's censor refused to allow it and Monypenny chose to be a journalist, feeling himself to be under an obligation to *The Times*. In that capacity he made his way to Dundee, the coal mining area of northern Natal to which a portion of the British troops had been sent. As a journalist he covered all the events at Dundee, although not one of his telegrams got through to *The Times*. He witnessed the battle of Talana and the death of Penn Symons, the general commanding the garrison there, which he wrote up for *The Times*, and marched knee-deep in mud back to Ladysmith after Dundee was evacuated. Here he was told that only one man could represent *The Times*, so, with some relief, he returned to his regiment. He had not enjoyed being a war correspondent, objecting to 'the incivility and patronage of jacks in office' which 'almost convinced me that it was not the trade of a gentleman'.[38] By the end of the year he was, like many others in Ladysmith, suffering from a variety of ailments due to poor food and contaminated water and spent the last month of the siege in the military hospital suffering from typhoid. For the rest of that year, after he was allowed to leave Ladysmith, he recuperated.

It was not possible to return to Johannesburg until the end of 1900 and the *Star* remained closed until 1902, when Monypenny once again took up a journalist's pen after more than a year spent working for Milner in the administration of Johannesburg. But his new start was not to last long. Relations with Milner had become strained over the question of the location of the Transvaal's capital. Monypenny favoured Johannesburg, Milner preferred Pretoria. The two eventually parted company irrevocably over the question of Chinese 'coolie' labour. From May 1903 Monypenny expressed opposition to Milner's scheme to import Chinese labourers into the Transvaal to make good labour shortages. It was a scheme which Milner considered necessary for the economic future of the mines and which had the support of Monypenny's employers, the Rand mine owners. Monypenny favoured an 'exclusionist' policy. Back in London at *The Times*, Moberly Bell also dis-

36 *Morning Leader*, 5 Sept. 1899.   37 *Morning Leader*, 6 Sept. 1899.   38 NIA, CMB1 Monypenny to Bell, 7 Mar. 1900.

agreed with him. The correspondence between them illuminates their personal attitudes towards questions of race relations.

Having read Monypenny's analysis of the issue, Bell wrote to him in a long letter that

> I think you are wholly wrong because I think that if that much battered Anglo-Saxon race can't dominate a continent without resorting to exclusion we had better stop talking about our governing genius … I want to see the yellow and the black man put and kept in their proper place as the hewers of wood and drawers of water of the white races. For the present I am content to see inferior whites like Germans and Frenchmen used as servants but they will get civilised by and by and the black and yellow will either dominate us or we must dominate them. Exclusion is a Russian and childish way of shirking the difficulty and will no more succeed than Mrs Partington and her broom or Australia which is now trying to exclude even English labour. Of course they & you & the Tsar can all succeed for a time. But for how long?[39]

In his reply to Bell Monypenny wrote

> I am sorry you do not agree with me about the labour question … I am not [for] expelling Chinese from SA nor even excluding them. I am only objecting to the mine owners going to China, and bribing or cajoling its inhabitants to come here to the exclusion of Europeans. Not that I should shrink from the stronger methods if I had the power …
>
> But you say if we cannot dominate South Africa without excluding Chinese we had better stop talking about our 'governing genius'. Now in the first place their admission will have a very intimate bearing on the question of whether we or the Boers dominate South Africa which you will admit is of some importance and in the second place you are guilty of exactly the same fallacy as the extreme free traders. You win South Africa by your prowess. You maintain order and erect a shelter of government by your governing genius and then you invite an inferior race who could have done neither to come and compete with you in the narrow economic sphere in which by virtue of their very inferiority they can beat you, tying your hands behind your back in the meantime in the interests of 'free competition.' Give a hundred thousand of us who fought in the war rifles and land a

39 Ibid. Bell to Monypenny, 28 May 1903.

million Chinamen, with rifles if you like, and then let us try [*sic*] which will dominate South Africa. That will be something more like free competition.[40]

Monypenny may have been influenced in his views by his local knowledge of the poor and worsening relations between the white and Asian communities in Natal, and have feared that another influx of indentured labour would lead to more widespread problems in South Africa.[41] His view that South Africa should be primarily a white man's country was not unique, though his statement that he was prepared to go to war over the issue was admittedly extreme. Like Bell, he believed in the superiority of white Anglo-Saxons over all others; unlike Bell he did not apparently believe that in South Africa that superiority would necessarily prevail without a swingeing immigration policy.

At the end of 1903 Monypenny resigned his editorship of the *Star* over the Chinese Labour issue. Despite his disagreement with his proprietors and with Milner, despite views which suggested an autocratic and warlike streak at odds with Bell's concept of how Britain should run its empire, Moberly Bell still thought highly enough of Monypenny's journalistic abilities to offer him on his return to Britain the choice either of replacing Flora Shaw, now Lady Lugard, as imperial editor, or the elderly, cantankerous George Smalley as head of *The Times* service in North America.[42] Monypenny refused both posts. He decided that he had 'spent quite long enough dealing with the performances of other people in the political arena and should like to have a turn myself'.[43] Later, he suggested that he might spend some time as freelance roving correspondent for *The Times*, travelling to and writing about each of the Dominions in turn.[44]

In the event he neither became a politician nor did he travel in the empire. His health, never strong, and probably further undermined by the bout of typhoid during the siege of Ladysmith, gave way as he travelled home. For the rest of his life, another eight years, he was periodically under the doctor's care. It was not until the summer of 1905 that his health was good enough for him to consider taking on a new project. When he did, it was the biography of Disraeli, which Moberly Bell had been contemplating for some time. Monypenny was not his first choice; he would have liked a 'big name', but Lord Rosebery, Milner and others declined the honour, and Monypenny was free and willing.[45] He spent the rest of his life researching and writing

40 Ibid. Monypenny to Bell, 5 July 1903.   41 Joy Brain, 'Indentured and free Indians in the economy of colonial Natal' and Surendra Bhana, 'Indian trade and traders in colonial Natal', both in Bill Guest and John M. Sellers (eds), *Enterprise and exploitation in a Victorian colony: aspects of the economic and social history of colonial Natal* (Pietermaritzburg, 1985).   42 NIA, CMB1 Monypenny to Bell, 5 July 1903.   43 Ibid.   44 Ibid. Monypenny to Bell, 11 Jan. 1904.   45 Milner papers, Milner Dep. 216 Bell to Milner, 7 and 29 Jan. 1904; Milner to Bell, 31 Jan.

the first volume. He was also elected to a new board of directors at *The Times* after Northcliffe took control of the paper in 1909. During his last years he spent more and more time at the Nordrach Spa in Scotland, being treated for the TB of which he eventually died.

His last major effort was devoted to a discussion of the problems of his own country, Ireland. In the year of his death, 1912, after spending several months in Ireland as *Times* special correspondent, he wrote a series of articles for the paper, subsequently published as a book entitled *The two Irish nations: an essay on Home Rule*. This, his swansong, was also his most impressive piece of sustained argument. It enjoyed some vogue at the time.[46] The title recalled the 1886 Home Rule debates, when the phrase 'the two Irish nations' was used both by Chamberlain and Lord Salisbury, but it was not a concept taken up by unionists in Ireland at that time.[47] For Monypenny it became the fundamental premise upon which his whole argument rested. He examined the historical development of the two nations in Ireland, divided by religion and hating each other for a multiplicity of reasons, yet living side by side in many parts of the island. He analysed them from political, ethnographic, religious and geographical angles in order to explain the complexity of the problem posed by the two nations, a problem that he considered was often ignored or misunderstood by politicians at Westminster. He discussed whether Home Rule – the 'Home Rule menace' as he called it – would work, and whether the proposed Home Rule bill had any chance of success. He concluded that the complex problem of the two nations did not for the present permit the acceptance of Home Rule.

> Home Rule … cannot be applied to Ireland without at the same time violating those very principles to which its advocates appeal. In Ireland, as we have seen, there are two nations, not one, and self-government for either in the isolated Home Rule sense means subjection for the other. It was so when the Protestant ascendancy existed; it will be so when, to use the least invidious term, a Nationalist ascendancy is substituted in its place. I have shown how deep is the feud between the two nations, how it has contrived to draw its bitterness from all the various animosities of race and class and religion, and maintains itself on the memories of centuries of struggle. We may regret that there is such a cleavage in Irish soci-

1904.   **46** G.K. Peatling, *British opinion and Irish self-government, 1865–1925: from unionism to liberal Commonwealth* (Dublin, 2001) 125. My thanks to Simon Potter for this reference.   **47** James Anderson, 'Ideological variations in Ulster during Ireland's first Home Rule crisis: an analysis of local newspapers' in Colin H. Williams and Eleanore Kofman (eds), *Community, conflict, partition and nationalism* (London, 1989) 163. My thanks to Dr Mary Harris for this reference.

ety; we may look forward to the day when it will have ceased to exist;
but at present it is as much an ultimate fact of the situation as the
Irish Sea itself.[48]

According to Monypenny, only subordination to the Imperial Parliament at
Westminster guaranteed continued stability.

One chapter of the book was devoted to considering the idea of granting
Ireland the responsible self-government enjoyed by the settler colonies – essentially Dominion status – and another to the analogy often drawn between
Ireland and South Africa. 'Nothing,' Monypenny averred, 'has done more to
weaken the aversion with which Home Rule was at one time regarded by the
vast majority of thinking people in Great Britain than the striking success
that has attended the bold policy of granting self-government to the conquered colonies in South Africa.'[49] The argument ran that Dominion status
had worked in South Africa and therefore would work in Ireland, reconciling Ireland to Great Britain and the empire and putting an end to the 'secular feud' between the two Irish nations. Monypenny rejected both arguments. While Dominion status had improved the Transvaal's constitutional
position, facilitating reconciliation, in the case of Ireland it would mean a ret-
rograde step, since there would no longer be Irish MPs at Westminster.
Monypenny argued that in effect Ireland would become a dependency instead
of a part of the UK, since Britain would not tolerate any real signs of independence from an Irish Dominion. He claimed this dependency would be
resented by many in Ireland – that is, by Irishmen of his way of thinking.

Nor did Monypenny believe that Dominion status would heal the rift
between the two nations in Ireland, as had apparently occurred in South
Africa. The divide in Ireland was too deep and too ancient to be capable of
cure; that in South Africa was more recent and much less bitter.
Interestingly, Monypenny argued that a more accurate analogy could be
found in the case of Canada.

> Pitt's Constitutional Act of 1791 treated the French and English
> provinces of Lower and Upper Canada, now Quebec and Ontario, as
> two separate colonies. In the Act of 1840, which followed the Durham
> report, the blunder was committed of uniting them into one, but the
> experiment was so unsuccessful that in 1867 they were separated
> again, and at the same time merged in the larger unity of the
> Dominion [of Canada]. If we put Ulster in the place of Ontario,
> Nationalist Ireland of Quebec, and the United Kingdom of the
> Dominion of Canada, the analogy is complete. Irish animosities are

48 W.F. Monypenny, *The two Irish nations: an essay in Home Rule* (London, 1913) 65. 49
Ibid. 80.

at present lost or held in check in the larger unity of the United
Kingdom; the Government proposes to unchain them by going back
from the Canadian position of 1867 to that of 1840, segregating
Ireland and compelling her two nations to live alone together, precisely as French and English when they were united in a single colony
before the formation of the Dominion.[50]

The Canadian example, so often used to support the case for Irish Dominion
status, was thus reinterpreted for Monypenny's own, unionist purposes.

So what conclusions can one draw about Monypenny? Although an
Irishman, with strong views about the future of his country, he lived abroad
for most of his adult life, either in London or in South Africa. The needs of
empire were of greater concern to him than the fate of Ireland, unless the
latter impinged upon the affairs of the former. When there were differences
of opinion either about Ireland or about events in the empire, he used his
undoubted skills in the techniques of logic to construct political arguments
to defend and legitimate his often strong prejudices. A white supremacist,
Protestant, unionist conservative, he was able to express his views, typical of
his time, particularly effectively and persuasively. His journalistic and organizational skills were much admired by senior staff at *The Times*, some of
whom shared his passionate imperial faith. His compatriot, James Woulfe
Flanagan, as pugnacious and as much a conviction journalist as Monypenny,
wrote impassioned leaders on imperial topics during the 1890s. *The Times*
had become the voice of this racist brand of cultural imperialism and
Monypenny contributed significantly to its development.

50 Ibid. 87.

11. The South African War, empire and the *Irish World*, 1899–1902

ÚNA NÍ BHROIMÉIL

When the South African War broke out in 1899, the United States had just concluded the Spanish American War, and was engaged in the process of taking the Philippine islands from Spain and quelling Filipino resistance. The country appeared to be abandoning its previous inward looking strategy and was beginning to expand overseas. These developments became noteworthy topics in the pages of the *Irish World* during the years 1899–1902. Published weekly in New York and edited by Patrick Ford, the *Irish World* had a circulation of 125,000 in the 1890s. The paper was primarily read by the American Irish and had an Irish nationalist and a socialist agenda obvious from its full title – the *Irish World and Industrial Liberator*. Regarding England and its empire as the enemy of Ireland and the Irish, the *Irish World* could not countenance the notion that its beloved republic of America might take on an imperial mantle and come to resemble in any way the old enemy. Neither could it conceive of American support for England, either formally through an Anglo-American alliance or tacitly through lack of support for the Boers. The Boers, after all, were not merely fighting England but were 'sister republics'. The paper's response thus had to be more sophisticated than a simple anti-English tirade. It linked the war in South Africa with the cause of all nations struggling against the might of empire and urged the United States, which had once banished the English empire from its shores, to desist from joining the ranks of the imperial powers.

The main audience and readership of the *Irish World* was Irish American, and the general mood of the paper was anti-English and pro-Boer.[1] Irish Americans' natural inclination was to be anti-English. Irish American nationalism relied on a sense of ethnicity generated by English rule in Ireland, reinforced by bitter memories of the Famine and nourished by anti-Irish prejudice in America.[2] Irish American nationalism was resurgent in 1900 as Clan na Gael reunited under the leadership of John Devoy and Daniel Cohalan[3] – indeed, Francis M. Carroll suggests that Clan na Gael sought to fight the

1 See for example *Irish World* (hereafter *IW*), 7 Oct. 1899. 2 Thomas N. Brown, *Irish American nationalism, 1870–1890* (Westport, Conn., 1966). 3 Kerby Miller, *Emigrants and exiles: Ireland and the Irish exodus to North America* (New York, 1985); Alan J. Ward, *Ireland and Anglo-American relations, 1899–1921* (Toronto 1969).

British empire in America by opposing the South African War.[4] The *Irish World* for its part proclaimed that a good general rule for Irishmen was 'to take, in all wars, controversies and disputes the side that England is against, the moral certainty being that in every case it will be found to be the honest side'.[5] When respected Irish leaders such as Michael Davitt denounced England's treachery towards the Transvaal the attitudes of Irish Americans were unambiguous. The *Irish World* carried many reports from meetings around the country, a typical example of which was headed 'Chicago mass meeting in sympathy with heroic Boers'. According to this report, the meeting passed 'resolutions of sympathy with the Boers and of undying hatred for England'. The resolutions were followed by 'musical numbers . . . which were well received by the audience which filled the hall'.[6] St Patrick's Day resolutions were particularly trenchant and the *Irish World* printed pages of resolutions and promises of aid:

> The convention of Irish societies of San Francisco ... announced that [it] had been decided to donate the profits of the entertainment to the ... Boer fund for widows and orphans.

> Resolved that we Irish Americans of the city of Cleveland, O., in mass meeting assembled have not forgotten the trails of blood, ruin and desolation that cruel and pitiless England left upon sad and sorrowful Ireland ... that to the Boers we extend our best wishes in their contest for the preservation of country, home and fireside.[7]

> The mention of the Boers by Mr Langtry (Springfield) was the signal for long applause, the women joining heartily with the men.[8]

St Patrick's Day parades also gave Irish Americans an opportunity to display publicly their sympathy for the Boer cause and Boer flags were flown and carried, particularly in the New York parade.

> At an early hour Irish flags were flung to the breeze from window, balcony fire escape and housetop, side by side with the stars and stripes and the Transvaal republic flag the latter to show sympathy of the people for the struggling Boers.[9]

> Boer flags carried in streetparades – New York's friendly sons cheer the Boers and hiss England.

4 Francis M. Carroll, *American opinion and the Irish question, 1910–23: a study in opinion and policy* (Dublin and New York, 1978). 5 *IW*, 25 Nov. 1899. 6 *IW*, 9 Dec. 1899. 7 *IW*, 3 Mar. 1900. 8 *IW*, 30 Mar. 1901. 9 *IW*, 23 Mar. 1901.

> In Chicago ... Although the green field with the golden harp was in
> the ascendant, there were plenty of American flags and the four col-
> ored banner of the Boers. Many of the marchers wore Boer badges.[10]

Flags and badges were constant features of the *Irish World*'s coverage of
the support for the Boers. The paper carried a drawing of the Boer Irish
Brigade crossing VanBrands Square in Johannesburg carrying a flag with an
inscription 'Remember Mitchelstown' and the following week carried a bigger
version of the same drawing on the front page with the caption given to it
by the *London Illustrated Graphic* – 'Traitors!' The *Irish World* reminded its
readers that Mitchelstown recalled 'an atrocious affair in Land League days
when England's armed ruffians murdered defenceless men women and children' and that the volunteers represented in the drawing were in fact true
Irishmen as 'every Irish man the world over ... must be an enemy of the
British empire'.[11] This belief appeared to be borne out by a cable from
Michael Davitt in Dublin the same month headed '10,000 people in Dublin
cheer Boers and groan Chamberlain' on the occasion of Chamberlain's visit
to Dublin. Davitt reported that the crowd displayed the Transvaal flag opposite Dublin Castle until the police captured it. The editor of the *Irish World*
added insolently that it was 'the only Boer flag taken by the British so far'.
That December the paper printed a picture of Paul Kruger holding aloft the
Boer flag with the victories of the Boers against the British inscribed on a
pennant above it. The text below wished 'A happy new year to the Boers!
May they continue to win victories till their standard sheet floats in triumph
and England's blood stained colors are in the mire!'[12]

The paper was keen to display publicly its support for the Boers. In
January 1900, in response to a letter to the editor suggesting that the *Irish
World* should advocate the flying of the Boer flag from the homes of all sympathizers, the editor responded that 'The idea of displaying the flag is a good
one. From the windows of the *Irish World* office, the Boer flag, with the Stars
and Stripes and Ireland's standard of Green flies every day.'[13] Should a less
ostentatious symbol of support be required the paper carried advertisements
for Boer buttons containing a portrait of 'Oom Paul' Kruger and the slogan
'Success to the Boers'. Because the Canadian customs officials had confis-
cated several thousand buttons, declaring them seditious and treasonable, the
makers (who also made St Patrick's Day buttons, badges and novelties)
believed that they should be worn 'by every lover of liberty the world over'.
Alternatively, sheet music for the song 'The Gallant Boers' could be purchased and played in the privacy of one's own parlour.[14]

---

10 *IW*, 24 Mar. 1900. 11 *IW*, 2 and 9 Dec. 1899. 12 *IW*, 30 Dec. 1899. 13 *IW*, 13 Jan.
1900. 14 *IW*, 10 Mar. 1900.

4 Cartoon from the *Irish World*, 30 December 1899. Reproduced courtesy of the
National Library of Ireland

Probably the strongest demonstration of Irish American support for the Boer cause was the departure of an ambulance corps under the auspices of the Red Cross society for service with the Boer army in the Transvaal in February 1900. The United Irish societies of Chicago and the Irish societies of Massachusetts equipped the ambulance corps, many of whom had been volunteers during the Spanish American War.[15] Although travelling as an ambulance corps the *Irish World* admitted in September 1900 that the Irish American brigade had seen more fighting and military action than medical service:

> The casual visitor dropping in upon the boys will not realize that he is in the presence of an ambulance corps, for all the talk is reminiscent of service in the trenches and saddle, and he will have to search industriously for anything in the camp that looks like a litter. But he will see all sorts of rifles and revolvers.[16]

There were six physicians and a nurse in the company. The remainder of the fifty eight men who left were designated as litter bearers but 'the Boers having no place in their army for them in this capacity ... went into the field as part of the Boer fighting force as soon as they could get guns'.[17] On their return to Chicago, when 5,000 people welcomed them home at the Rock Island railroad station, M.V. Gannon defended the corps for having enlisted in the ranks of the Boer army as 'it was the inalienable right of every Irishman to take up arms against the soldiers of England wherever he found them engaged in war'.[18] As the war progressed the enthusiasm of the Irish Americans for the Boer cause did not waver and it was boosted by visits from such pro-Boer stalwarts as Maude Gonne and Major John MacBride, who arrived in the United States in February 1901 to lecture on the war and to stop recruitment for the British army.[19]

One Boer trait that might not initially have endeared them to Irish Americans was their Protestantism. The *Irish World* denied however that this meant that the Boers were anti-Catholic, and it printed reports from people who had been to South Africa and who had first hand experience of the Boers. One of these reports was from Father James O'Haire, a former missionary in South Africa who had been, according to his own account, in almost daily contact with the Boers. He reported that he had never been denied hospitality by Boer families, and that room was always given to him in Boer houses to celebrate mass for the few Catholics living in remote places. He added that grace was always said before meals in Boer homes and that he was on many occasions 'politely asked by the Boer if I would read the Bible

---

15 *IW*, 24 Feb. 1900. 16 *IW*, 15 Sept. 1900. 17 *IW*, 24 Nov. 1900. 18 *IW*, 1 Dec. 1900.
19 *IW*, 2 Feb. 1901.

and say some prayers for them which I always did'.[20] Another man, John O'Connor, 'a fine looking and sturdy Boer soldier, American by birth and citizen of the Transvaal by adoption' stated to the *Irish World* that 'The Boers are Christians and always treat the traveller kindly. They have more feeling for the poor than the British.'[21] Dr Leyds, the Boer's European agent, had written a letter to William Redmond denying that Catholics were forbidden to hold office in the Transvaal, and giving the names of four Catholic officials of the Boer government.[22] The Irish Americans were therefore reassured that they were supporting a pious people. Indeed, one editorial suggested that the Boers were lucky to be Protestant, as religion was one thing that the English wouldn't try to take from them as they had in Ireland.[23]

This empathy with the Boers was highlighted in other ways also. As early as November 1899 the *Irish World* remarked on Boer kindness to prisoners of war and contrasted Boer treatment with that of the English. In an article stating that 'British officers in hospital at Glencoe show their appreciation for the extreme kindness shown them by Boer officers and men' the paper contrasted this attitude with Kitchener 'who in carrying brutality to its utmost in Egypt gave orders to kill the wounded'.[24] This comparison continued throughout 1900 with headlines contrasting 'England's butchers and "pig-stickers"' with 'Boers kind to prisoners'.[25] The Irish brigade in the Transvaal had also testified to the 'tenderness of Boers for their wounded foes'.[26] The English, whose 'savagery is inbred', meanwhile not only treated their prisoners badly but extended their cruelty to the most vulnerable of all, Boer women and children.[27] This theme became more pronounced throughout 1901. British brutality was condemned as 'foul and cowardly murder', not only by Irish nationalists such as Bishop O'Dwyer of Limerick but also by others in the Transvaal. The Reverend Dr H.D. Von Brockhuizen, Mrs Botha's pastor, quoted an official report made by Dr Ronald P. McKenzie of the British army to the British government on conditions in the camps: 'the conditions are horrible, the death rate appalling and the food furnished wholly unfit to eat'.[28] More graphic were the reports by Emily Hobhouse, the delegate in South Africa to the Distress Fund for South African women and children, often reprinted by the *Irish World* from the London *Daily News*. These reports, according to the *Irish World*, should 'send a thrill of horror throughout the civilised world', describing as they did 'the sort of war England is making on women and children in South Africa'.[29] According to the editor, these women and children were submitted to torture because:

20 *IW*, 17 Mar. 1900. 21 *IW*, 5 Oct. 1901. 22 *IW*, 25 Nov. 1899. 23 *IW*, 7 Oct. 1899. 24 *IW*, 4 Nov. 1899. This is a reference to the British campaign in the Sudan – see chapter 2 above. 25 *IW*, 10 Feb. 1900. 26 *IW*, 21 Apr. 1900. 27 *IW*, 5 Jan. 1901. 28 *IW*, 22 June 1901. 29 *IW*, 29 June 1901.

BRITISH WARFARE UP TO DATE.

GENERAL LORD CHUMLEY-CHUMLEY – "Forward, me brave lads! Those Boers wont dare to shoot their own women and children, dontcherknow!"

—From N. Y. Journal

5 Cartoon from the *Irish World*, 26 April 1902. Reproduced courtesy of the National Library of Ireland

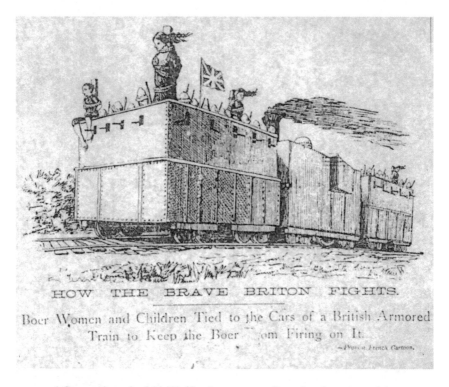

HOW THE BRAVE BRITON FIGHTS.

Boer Women and Children Tied to the Cars of a British Armored
Train to Keep the Boer from Firing on It.

~*From a French Cartoon.*

6 Cartoon from the *Irish World*, 4 January 1902. Reproduced courtesy of the
National Library of Ireland

their fathers, brothers, husbands and sons are perilising [*sic*] their
lives in defence of their native land. Not able to conquer these brave
fellows on the field of battle, England's representatives in South Africa
basely seek to conquer them by letting them know that if they do not
let down their arms their loved ones who are in the power of the
enemy will be slowly done to death.[30]

From 1901 on, a dual theme can be seen in the reports in the *Irish World*.
On the one hand, the horrors of the camps were described in great detail and
the headlines became unequivocal: 'Horrors of British "refuge camps"';
'Appalling conditions prevailing at the "concentration camps"'; 'England's
murder pens'; 'England's murder camps'; 'England's death traps'; 'England's
assassination camps'.[31] Conditions at the camp were detailed. 'No furniture,
no bedding, no decent food, burned by the sun and soaked by the rain,
women grow to living skeletons and children sicken and die by the scores.'[32]

30 Ibid. 31 *IW*, 13 July, 3 Aug., 28 Sept., 23 Nov. and 21 Dec. 1901; 8 and 15 Feb. 1902.
32 *IW*, 13 July 1901.

The *Irish World* reported that 'ten thousand Boer children [had been] murdered within eight months in Kitchener's refuge camps'.[33] The paper also
alleged that the camps were evidence of the cowardice of British soldiers.
Two cartoons depicted the use the British were making of the Boer women
and children. In one soldiers were portrayed fighting with women and children strapped to their bodies.[34] In January 1902 the *Irish World* also reproduced a French cartoon depicting a British armoured train with Boer women
and children strapped to the carriages and with a caption – 'How the brave
Briton fights'.[35] In April the paper carried a cartoon on its front page depicting the British shooting of the wounded Boer general, Commandant
Scheepers, who was unable to stand for his execution because of appendici-
tis. He was tied to a chair and 'riddled with bullets by a detail of coldstream
guards, firing at ten paces. He was buried where he fell, the chair broken up
and thrown into the shallow grave on top of him while the band played on.'[36]

Although the *Irish World's* criticism of England was trenchant and unre-
lenting, the paper sought at all times to stress the allegiance of the American
Irish to America and to the republican ideals of the founding fathers. While
the loyalty of hyphenated Americans to the United States was not addressed
as comprehensively as it would be during the period 1914–18, many of the
arguments deployed during the First World War were inadvertently rehearsed
during the conflict in South Africa.[37] The notion that the Boers were defending two small republics against the might of the British empire was reiterated
again and again in the *Irish World*. Chamberlain and Rhodes were determined
to 'destroy the little republic which blocks [the] British scheme of domination
in Africa' according to the editor in May 1899.[38] The description of the Boers
and their republics was consistent over the term of the war. The Boers were
constantly referred to as 'brave' or 'heroic', the republics as 'little' or 'small'
and England as rapacious and tyrannical.[39] In a cartoon taken from the
Pittsburgh Post and reprinted in the *Irish World*, republicanism was portrayed
as having sunk so deeply into the Boer republics that it was impossible for
anyone, even John Bull, to wipe it out.[40] According to the *Irish World*, a shared
republicanism should have led Americans to sympathize with the Boers, rather
than kow-tow to the subjects of a foreign monarch who had been banished
from the newly created American republic in the eighteenth century.

33 *IW*, 8 Feb. 1902.   34 *IW*, 26 Apr. 1902.   35 *IW*, 4 Jan. 1902.   36 *IW*, 12 Apr. 1902.   37
Edward Cuddy, 'Irish Americans and the 1916 election: an episode in immigrant adjustment',
American Quarterly, 2:21 (summer 1969) 228–43; William M. Leary Jr., 'Woodrow Wilson, Irish
Americans and the election of 1916', *Journal of American History*, 1:54 (June 1967) 57–72. For
a more general discussion on ethnicity and loyalty see Yossi Shain, 'Ethnic diasporas and US
foreign policy', *Political Science Quarterly*, 5:109 (winter 1994/5) 811–41.   38 *IW*, 20 May
1899.   39 See for example *IW*, 19 and 26 Aug. and 23 and 30 Sept. 1899.   40 *IW*, 27 July
1901.

J. BULL.—It's soaked clear through. I can't get at the gold whilst this blarsted republicanism is rooted in the soil. I must dig it out.   —FROM THE PITTSBURG POST

7 Cartoon from the *Irish World*, 27 July 1901. Reproduced courtesy of the National Library of Ireland

> Blood is thicker than water and these South African republicans are of the same blood with the New York and New Jersey immigrants of Holland and of Dutch Huguenot descent who fought England in the American revolution and again in 1812 when England still claimed a suzerainty right to search American vessels.[41]

This comparison between what the British were doing to the Boers and what they had done to the Americans was regularly made in the *Irish World*. In November 1899 for example a drawing appeared which represented visually the number of British soldiers in South Africa, and stressed that Britain has

41 *IW*, 16 Sept. 1899.

sent a force to crush the Transvaal three times larger than that which 'came to destroy the Americans'.[42]

American success in repulsing the British and resisting the empire in 1776 and again in 1812 should have made them forever wary not just of the British but also of overseas expansion in general, according to the *Irish World*. To remind the Americans of their history of clashes with the British the *Irish World* quoted from Herbert Paul, the London correspondent of the *New York Herald*.

> The language of the Marquis of Salisbury in the House of Lords which was almost textually reproduced by his son Lord Cranborne in the Commons, was very much the same as that used by Lord North and his colleagues at the time of the American war. Mr Balfour's was slightly milder and more sympathetic in tone but its substance was identical.[43]

Certainly this invocation of Lord North might have reminded Americans of the revolution but a starker depiction was outlined in a headline in the *Irish World* in March 1901, when the paper carried a quote from Judge Pennypacker of Philadelphia.

> As in 1814 he (the Englishman) burned the house of President Madison and the Capitol at Washington with its archives, books and papers, so today, with like gratification and futility he burns the home of de Wet.[44]

Again and again links between the American revolution and the war in Africa were reiterated. In September 1901 in an article entitled 'American revolutionists and the Boer patriots' the paper made connections between the 'fighting burghers' and George Washington's actions during the winter of 1777–8.

> The American revolution has had and is still having a powerful moral influence upon the South African war. The Boer generals are known to be closely acquainted with the history of General Washington and they derive great inspiration from the story of the hardships the colonists endured in the seven year struggle for liberty. In this dark hour de Wet, Botha and Steyn undoubtedly remember Valley Forge and are determined to continue the war, as the Americans did, at any cost to the bitter end.[45]

And as surely as the Americans won under Washington, the Boers would also beat the British.

42 *IW*, 18 Nov. 1899.   43 *IW*, 5 Jan. 1901.   44 *IW*, 2 Mar. 1901.   45 *IW*, 11 Sept. 1901.

Interestingly, in an article detailing Michael Davitt's proposal for 'A national address from Ireland to President Kruger', the *Irish World* stated that although Paul Kruger was the very antithesis of the Irishman, he could be favourably compared with Abraham Lincoln.

> Since Abraham Lincoln, there is no such figure as this great old man in modern history. His faith, his courage, his hopefulness, his coolness, his indifference to the sneers of his enemies, his belief in the righteousness of his cause, his splendid patriotism – they all went to make up a character worthy to be the head of a brave and gallant nation rightly struggling to be free, and especially worthy to be the head of the burghers of the Dutch republics, the bravest of the brave.[46]

If appeals to American republicanism and history were not enough to swing American support, then similarities between the Americans and Boers as people might convince the Americans, according to the paper. This likeness was brought out very clearly in a poem entitled the 'Song of the Farmer men' which was written for the *Irish World* by E. Tone. The concept of the Boers as farmers was one that appealed to the *Irish World*, reflecting the American image of itself as at heart a nation of yeoman farmers, despite industrialization and urbanization. The farmer metaphor also likened the Boers to the Irish peasants who were and had been fighting the empire for a long time, albeit without much success. These three themes came together in the poem.

> There was a day, a long time ago
> When the men on Concord common
> Left plough and spade to lend their aid
> To freedoms cause and honor.
> And when on Bunker hill they stood
> Like stone wall, firm and steady,
> The Saxon ranks could play no pranks
> For the farmer men were ready.
>
> In Wexford fields in 'ninety–eight'
> The farmer men were reaping
> When the 'boys' swept down from the hill tops brown
> Of gallant Wicklow greeting.
> And like brothers true, the green and blue,
> Stood with pike and gun together,
> Till the Saxon host paid well the cost
> With their blood on Irish heather.

46 *IW*, 10 Nov. 1900.

The British were described as 'Saxon redcoat dandys [*sic*]' with 'dancing plumes' on their heads whereas the Boers were described as having 'big brave hearts' in their breasts and 'rifles, quick and handy' in their hands as they 'marched forth to fight for freedom'.[47] As the war progressed the idea of the Boers as a nation of farmers was expressed more directly. In July 1900 a head-line in the *Irish World* declared that there stood '250,000 trained butchers against 30,000 farmers' although the article underneath expanded the farmer class to include 'clerks, attorneys, shopkeepers and schoolboys'.[48] In fact, towards the end of the war the image of the Boers as farmers was used to convey the differences between the British as imperialists and the sturdy Boers. In a front-page drawing captioned 'King Edward's imperialists yield to President Kruger's farmers', published in March 1902, the paper depicted the destruction by the Boers of a convoy of wagons at Vodonop in the Transvaal.[49] Again, in an article on the end of the war in June, the bravery of the Boer farmers was extolled by the *Irish World*.

> For two years and eight months a brave people numerically weak have withstood the might of a world wide empire. Thirty thousand farmers have held at bay for almost three years half a million of English soldiers. And now when the end comes they do not surren-der like cravens but on terms which would never have been granted them if they had not given England good cause to fear them.[50]

What annoyed the *Irish World* throughout the war more than anything else was the attitude of the American administration towards the Boers. Not only was President McKinley supportive of the English in 'her defense of her eastern empire', but he was abandoning the very concept of a republic, imitating the British and attempting to transform the United States into an empire by subjugating the people of the Philippines. In July 1899, the paper carried a statement by George S. Boutwell, governor of Massachusetts, headed 'William Mc Kinley denounced as a greater criminal than Jefferson Davies'. Quoting from the statement the *Irish World* highlighted the fundamental issue as it saw it. 'The founders of this government preferred republicanism and peace to imperialism and war. President McKinley and his supporters are engaged in an effort to revise their work and to reverse their opinion.'[51]

'Imperialism' and republicanism were wholly incompatible in the opin-ion of the *Irish World* and this was to be a consistent theme throughout the war. The links between the war in South Africa and the war in the Philippines were repeatedly highlighted, as was the charge that the United States was attempting to model itself on the old enemy, England. The 'cant

47 *IW*, 10 Feb. 1900. 48 *IW*, 14 July 1900. 49 *IW*, 8 Mar. 1902. 50 *IW*, 7 June 1902. 51 *IW*, 22 July 1899.

JOHN BULL—"Why, if h'I bid them Stand on their
Blooming 'Eads they'll do it for Me!"

8 Cartoon from the *Irish World*, 10 March 1900. Reproduced courtesy of the
National Library of Ireland

and humbug' that suggested that empire and civilization went hand in hand
was 'borrowed from England'.[52] Cartoons carried in the *Irish World* in March
and June 1900 demonstrated just how much in thrall to the British the paper
believed McKinley's administration to be. In March, John Bull had McKinley,
his secretary of state, John Hay and the entire Republican party (which was
symbolized by an elephant) standing on their heads.[53] In June, a cartoon
reprinted from the *New York World* depicted McKinley refusing to receive
or listen to the Boer delegation in America as John Bull stood behind
McKinley's door, clearly in charge.[54]

The Boers sent envoys to the United States twice during the war, to
appeal to the government and people of the United States for assistance.

52 *IW*, 25 Nov. 1899.   53 *IW*, 10 Mar. 1900.   54 *IW*, 2 June 1900.

9 Cartoon from the *Irish World*, 2 June 1900. Reproduced courtesy of the
National Library of Ireland

Although a warm welcome was extended to the delegates by the common
council in Boston and by the municipal assembly of New York, the White
House reception was low key. The delegates were received as casual visitors
and met only by the president and secretary of state. The *Irish World* was out-
raged that 'the official head of the greatest republic in the world who in virtue
of his official position, should be the foremost champion of Boer independence, has not lifted a finger to aid the cause of the Boers'.[55] When Colonel

<hr />

55 *IW*, 22 Sept. 1900.

Lynch, commander of the Second Irish Brigade in the Boer army visited the United States in October 1900 he spoke of the amazement of the Boers at the unfriendly attitude of the Americans and asked of the *Irish World*: 'What has become of the boasted banner of American liberty? Shall the generous and devoted enthusiasm of a Lafayette be scoffed at as out of date and ridiculous in this material age?'[56] The second Boer delegation in 1902 was more circumspect about what they wanted to achieve. The *Irish World* reported that the delegates did not want the United States to intervene in the South African war, but wished that the authorities in the United States might request that 'civilised warfare be insured in South Africa'.[57] This time President Roosevelt was not criticized about the envoys' reception, although the paper reported that General Anson Mills gave a dinner at home in Washington for the envoys to which senators, representatives in Congress, army officers and distinguished citizens were invited. According to the report General Mills was 'inspired to this act of courtesy by the desire to show the visitors that they have the good will and sympathy of Americans of high standing in public and private life in the gallant fight the republics are making for existence'.[58]

The paper also maintained that the United States had in fact abetted England by initially recognizing the annexation of the Boer republics and by providing a supply base for England throughout the war. Officers of the British army had travelled to America for the purpose of selecting and purchasing horses, established a camp depot for the collection and shipment of horses and mules and demanded protection for the facility lest it be attacked by Boer sympathizers. This led the *Irish World* to question if in fact the United States was still a colony of England.[59] According to the paper,

> the great republic to which all men struggling for liberty were wont to look for moral support has so far fallen behind its high estate as to aid and abet a pirate empire in the work of exterminating a brave people who are battling to perpetuate and transmit to their children the inestimable blessing of self government. Hide it as we may, the ugly fact protrudes itself that by such aid ... we are England's partners in her attempt to exterminate the Boers.[60]

The *Irish World*'s attitude towards President McKinley was encapsulated in its call for the election of William Jennings Bryan to the presidency in the autumn of 1900. In an editorial in August entitled 'Republic or imperialism' the reasons for supporting Bryan were outlined. 'A vote for him means a vote against imperialism and a British alliance. In other words, it means a vote for the perpetuation of the republic which is so seriously threatened by imperi-

56 *IW*, 20 Oct. 1900.   57 *IW*, 22 Mar. 1902.   58 Ibid.   59 *IW*, 12 Apr. 1902.   60 *IW*, 22 Feb. 1902.

alism.'[61] In articles entitled 'Vote for Americanism' and 'Stand by the republic' the *Irish World* exhorted Americans to choose Bryan and to guard against the beginning of the end of the republic.

> Shall the form of government born of the constitution of 1788 and defended in 1812 against England's rapacity by American valor, and for which thousands of lives were sacrificed from '61 to '65 – shall this form of government to use the phraseology of Lincoln 'perish from the face of the earth'? The answer to this question will be given by fifteen million voters when they cast their ballots at the November election for or against imperialism which is the issue of issues.[62]

The danger of McKinley's re-election according to the *Irish World* was not only that 'imperialism' would ride 'roughshod over the principles and traditions which the American people have hitherto regarded as sacred' but also related to where the trappings of empire such as a big standing army and foreign alliances would lead the United States. Thus the paper urged 'every *Irish World* man to do his duty' and to 'get one convert at least' to Bryan's cause.[63]

This campaign was, however, in vain. McKinley won the election and the *Irish World* castigated his victory as a triumph for 'England's candidates' and the 'Anglo-American alliance' and carried, under a cartoon depicting the merging of England and the United States, a report asserting that Lord Salisbury hailed McKinley's election as a victory for the British empire.[64] The paper subsequently continued to assert that, far from upholding the constitution with which he was entrusted, McKinley was seeking to subjugate the United States to the whim of England. A drawing on the front page of the *Irish World* in December showed the Union Jack unfurled from the Capitol building in honour of the centennial anniversary of the founding of the seat of government in Washington, and two inserts reminded the readers of Valley Forge and the 'burning by the British of the National Capitol'.[65]

The *Irish World* hoped that, with the accession to the presidency of Theodore Roosevelt following McKinley's assassination in 1901, government policy would change. While recognizing that Roosevelt was committed to overseas expansion, the paper noted that his speeches and writing always showed him to be 'animated by a spirit of distinct Americanism'. It claimed that 'there will be no yielding on the part of Theodore Roosevelt if there should be an attempt to sacrifice the national interest to gratify Anglomania'.[66] These hopes were perhaps inevitably disappointed. Roosevelt proved willing to continue McKinley's policies in the Philippines. To the *Irish World*, America seemed to be taking on all the worst characteristics of the British empire. While the

61 *IW*, 25 Aug. 1900. 62 *IW*, 6 Oct. 1900. 63 *IW*, 3 Nov. 1900. 64 *IW*, 10 Nov. 1900. 65 *IW*, 22 Dec. 1900. 66 *IW*, 21 Sept. 1901.

SALISBURY TO McKINLEY: "Let Us Shake!"

10 Cartoon from the *Irish World*, 17 November 1900. Reproduced courtesy of the
National Library of Ireland

FLAG DAY in the Dependencies.

Oh, say, does that star-spangled banner yet wave
O'er the land of the Free and the home of the brave!

11 Cartoon from the *Irish World*, 6 July 1901. Reproduced courtesy of the
National Library of Ireland

English were 'shooting down liberty in South Africa' the United States was
doing the same in the Philippines – 'both governments were operating along
parallel lines'.[67] Worst of all, the Americans were imitating the barbarity of
the Spanish in Cuba and the British under Kitchener in South Africa, setting
up concentration camps in the Philippines, torturing Filipinos and shooting
women and children.[68] In an effort to illustrate the hypocrisy of the administration's imperialist policies in July 1901 the *Irish World* reprinted a cartoon
from the *Detroit News* depicting Flag Day in the American dependencies. The
cartoon depicted Uncle Sam hoisting the Stars and Stripes, stating that it
stood for liberty, equality, independence, justice and fraternity 'if Congress
or the President so will'. Meanwhile the ragged natives of Puerto Rico, Cuba

67 *IW*, 13 Jan. 1900. 68 *IW*, 21 Dec. 1901; 3 May 1902.

(The Design on the Left is from the Crest of the Rochambeau Monument Recently Dedicated in Washington to the Memory of the Liberty-Loving Frenchmen Who, with Washington and the Patriots of '76, Won for Us Our War of Independence from England.)

THE BIRD OF FREEDOM vs. THE VULTURE.

France Establishing the American Republic in 1782.
America Crushing the Filipino Republic in 1902.

12 Cartoon from the *Irish World*, 5 July 1902. Reproduced courtesy of the
National Library of Ireland

and the Philippines stood by.[69] Most damning of all was a drawing printed
on the front page of the paper following the passing of the Philippine bill in
1902, depicting the establishment of the American republic, symbolized by an
eagle, with the aid of France in 1782. A smaller image portrayed the same
bird attacking the Philippines. The drawing was captioned 'the bird of freedom vs. the vulture – France establishing the American republic in 1782;
America crushing the Filipino republic in 1902'.[70]

The *Irish World* meanwhile reported denunciations of England by France,
Russia and Germany, claiming that hostility to Great Britain was 'almost uni-

69 *IW*, 6 July 1901. Interestingly the next issue of the *Irish World* was suppressed and its sale
prohibited in Massachusetts and Connecticut on foot of a complaint about the desecration of
the flag. See *IW*, 13 July 1901.   70 *IW*, 5 July 1902.

versal'[71], and noted that money was being raised in Holland to send a corps to aid the Boers.[72] The paper also reported that the Holland society of New York, in a letter to the editor, had specifically requested the support of 'the people of Irish and German origin' for the Boers, and hoped that 'everybody, except Anglomaniacs and fools' would lend a helping hand.[73] The *Irish World* carried reports of meetings of German Americans supporting the Boer cause and opposing 'imperialism', which 'it was asserted meant militarism, and militarism had been the cause of a great number of Germans leaving the Fatherland'.[74] At a packed Chicago pro-Boer meeting in December 1901, which was organized by the American Transvaal League and addressed by Bourke Cockran, nineteen German musical societies opened the proceedings with a song.[75]

Indeed, the *Irish World* insisted at all times that, in spite of the administration's support for the British, American sentiment more generally was in fact pro-Boer and against the English, as evidenced 'by the large and enthusiastic pro-Boer meetings that have been held in various cities of the Union. These manifestations of American sympathy are forcing the English press to acknowledge that the pro-British attitude of the McKinley administration does not represent the views of the American people.'[76] Certainly some of the meetings reported by the *Irish World* were well attended. One New York meeting, held under the auspices of the New York Committee to Aid the United Republics of South Africa, saw twelve thousand people assembled to denounce England and the Washington administration and cheer the Boers and Ireland.[77] The Metropolitan Temple in San Francisco was 'filled and the streets blocked with thousands of Boer supporters' at a meeting to 'extend moral and material aid to the struggling little republics of South Africa' in January 1900. According to the report, flags of every nation on the globe 'barring the banner of England and the dragon of China were used to decorate the interior of the hall'.[78] As the war progressed, meetings were held around the country to protest against the concentration camps in South Africa and to contribute money, medicine and clothing for the sick and needy in the camps. The paper reported that the Women's South African League of New York organized concerts, the proceeds of which were sent to the relief funds for the women and children in the concentration camps.[79] An organization was formed in Jersey City 'to raise funds for the suffering women and children', prompted by 'the almost daily reports in the public press of the deplorable conditions existing in the concentration camps in South Africa'.[80] Governor Yates of Illinois issued a proclamation announcing the formation of a committee to hold and distribute funds.[81] In Philadelphia, $5,000 was collected at a meeting to send 'an American relief ship laden with food, clothes and medicine for the unfortunate victims of war'.

71 *IW*, 21 Oct. 1899.   72 *IW*, 11 Nov. 1899.   73 *IW*, 7 Oct. 1899.   74 *IW*, 21 July 1900. 75 *IW*, 14 Dec. 1901.   76 *IW*, 13 Jan. 1900.   77 *IW*, 3 Feb. 1900.   78 *IW*, 20 Jan. 1900.   79 *IW*, 22 Feb. 1902.   80 *IW*, 12 Apr. 1902.   81 *IW*, 14 Dec. 1901.

The subscription list was headed by the German societies who subscribed $1,500 and the Ancient Order of Hibernians who subscribed $1,000.[82] The ship was to sail under an American flag and there was 'a general outburst of enthusiasm' when this was announced. Indeed a meeting in Cleveland of 2,500 people in March 1900 epitomized the fusion of loyalties present at the meetings:

> The armory was profusely decorated with the flags of the United States, Ireland and the Transvaal, while pictures of Kruger, Joubert, Robert Emmet and others were conspicuous. Miss Julia Ryan led the audience in singing "The Stars and Stripes Forever" and "God Save Ireland".[83]

The cause of the Boers and Ireland were viewed as one, as they were both fighting the might of the British empire. The cause of the Americans and the Boers were also believed to be as one, as they were both republics. The Irish Americans therefore, with Irish blood and American citizenship, were duty bound to aid the Boers.

Without doubt, the American Irish were galvanized by the South African War. With the reunification of the Irish Parliamentary Party under John Redmond, they were poised once again to support actively Irish political nationalism. Yet, throughout the war, the cause of Ireland, while important to the *Irish World*, had not been the primary issue. Certainly, there was an expectation that the American Irish were intrinsically anti-English because of their history and because of the manner of their emigration. But the *Irish World* drew on the experience of its American Irish readers of American republicanism at least as often as it drew on their Irish origins, and used their condition as citizens of a republic to exhort them to support the Boers. The paper also resisted the tendency of the US administration to turn to imperial ambitions of its own. The *Irish World* urged its readers to vote against McKinley because he was regarded as an imperialist. When an Irish American Union was formed in New York to fight militarism and 'imperialism' the paper was quick to support it, declaring that the Irish Americans 'would insist that this country should continue to be a republic and that the flag of America should wave over no man who was not a free man. We wanted no colonial policy and wanted no territory annexed to the United States out of which states could not be formed.'[84] Therefore, unlike much criticism of the British empire in Ireland itself, the American Irish attitude to the South African War was not designed purely with Ireland in mind, and extended to a more general critique of empire, including American overseas expansion. None of this was incompatible with the paper's continued condemnation of England. *The Irish World* regarded England as the proponent and epitome of empire. As long as America appeared to be aping the hated enemy, overseas expansion would be seen by the American Irish to be wrong.

82 Ibid.   83 *IW*, 3 Mar. 1900.   84 *IW*, 1 Sept. 1900.

12. John Bull's other empire: Roger Casement and the press, 1898–1916[1]

ANGUS MITCHELL

Analysis of Roger Casement's association with the press offers a unique insight into how print culture was harnessed during the late nineteenth and early twentieth centuries for different national and international ends. As an accomplished and relentless propagandist, Casement used the press for his own disclosed and undisclosed purposes, working outside British Foreign Office protocol to improve colonial government and scribbling anonymously as an Irishman involved in the movement for national independence. Both the generation and circulation of printed matter in the form of official reports, books, press articles, reviews, pamphlets, letters to the editor and subscription lists were central to his three interconnecting campaigns: in the Congo Free State (1898–1913), in the Putumayo region of the north-west Amazon (1910–16) and in the Connemara region of western Ireland (1913–14).

His published political writings on Ireland can be traced back to late 1905, soon after the founding of Sinn Féin by Arthur Griffith.[2] His press contributions appeared under various pseudonyms in various papers, notably the *United Irishman*. After 1912, with the deepening of the Home Rule crisis, Casement grew increasingly critical of press coverage of Irish politics, which he condemned as a weapon of division and conflict. On his public entry into the political arena for the cause of 'advanced nationalism' he was promptly dropped by almost all the editors and journalists who had supported his radical position on humanitarian reform. After the outbreak of war his outbursts continued in the pages of the *Continental Times*, where his ferocious attacks were aimed at the failure of political leadership, the manipulation of 'truth' and the encouragement of anti-German sentiment that he believed had pushed the world into the abyss. Press coverage of the opening of his trial for high

---

1 *John Bull's other empire* is the title of a short pamphlet written by Casement during 1914. This borrows from the play by George Bernard Shaw, *John Bull's other island*, with its controversial 'Preface for politicians.' 2 As he awaited trial for high treason, Casement wrote two important memos about his published writings. See the National Archive: Public Record Office (TNA: PRO), London, HO 144/1636/331643/32A 'Pamphlets, articles, letters etc. of mine on Ireland, against England, or pro-German that may be brought against me – directly or indirectly'; and National Library of Ireland (NLI), Dublin, George Gavan Duffy papers, MS 10764 'A private note for my solicitor', 14 June 1916.

treason might be assessed for what it reveals about censorship and the machinations of fledgling First World War propaganda agencies intent on controlling public information through a combination of secrecy and misinformation.

After his death, the continuing debate over Casement's place in history might be read as a metaphor for the unresolved destiny of the Irish independence movement. If his reputation has long been a painfully contested space for both popular and academic history, it is now significant for what it reveals about the lasting impact of propaganda, official secrecy and the political need to silence traumatic aspects of the past. Because so much of Casement's writing was pseudonymous it is hard to trace, and there is much material still to be uncovered.[3] However, by unearthing part of this buried body of work, it is possible to reconstruct an important strategy of hidden resistance, and a fierce critique of empire.

I

While there are references to articles published by Casement over the winter of 1889/90 during a tour of America,[4] his earliest identified contributions appeared in the weekly publication the *Outlook*, a journal launched in February 1898 and widely distributed throughout the empire. Contributors included the novelists Joseph Conrad and Robert Louis Stevenson, the socialist agitator and popular historian R.B. Cunninghame Graham and the antislaver and prominent Liberal politician, Sir Charles Dilke. The publication was strongest on African news with regular reports on the activities of Cecil Rhodes and most advertising space was supported by African mining companies. Much news, including the regular column 'A week of empire' was written by 'special correspondents' – Casement was possibly a contributor. His earliest signed piece of prose is 'Guti: a tale of Swazi life' – a prosaic short story about an African chief's desire for peace and reconciliation before he dies.[5] During the South African War the *Outlook* adopted an ambiguous editorial policy and, judging by its publication of the popular Fenian song, 'The wearing of the green', adopted an untypical position towards Ireland.

It was, however, the question of the Congo that would expose Casement to his first press and propaganda campaign. Manipulation of press reports,

---

3 James Carty, *Bibliography of Irish history, 1912–21* (Dublin, 1936) remains the most informed effort to identify the enormous amount of pseudonymous writings published in the build-up to the Rising, although much of Casement's work was penned before 1912. 4 Marcel Luwel, 'Roger Casement à Henry Morton Stanley: un rapport sur la situation au Congo en 1890' in *Africa – Tervuren*, 4:14 (1968). 5 *Outlook*, 23 Apr. 1898. This short story was republished in the Royal Irish Academy publication, *Roger Casement in Irish and world history* (Dublin, 2000). Casement's other contributions to the *Outlook* included 'England, England', 24 Sept. 1898; 'Nelson', 22 Oct. 1898; 'The peak of Cameroons', 25 Mar. 1899; and 'Love's horizon', 12 Aug. 1899.

destruction of significant parts of the archival record and the maintenance of
a policy of silence and secrecy has made the story of the Congo Free State
difficult to piece together.[6] The Congo was opened up rapidly by Leopold II
following diplomatic recognition of his enterprise under the Berlin Act (1885).[7]
His imperial project demanded careful management of the press to justify the
'civilizing process' and to satisfy a public curiosity for photographic representation of 'Darkest' Africa. To support and disseminate his imperial vision,
Leopold II produced lavishly illustrated magazines in the build up to his
'Exposition Coloniale' of 1897/98, held to inaugurate the Musée du Congo
at the royal palace of Tervuren on the outskirts of Brussels.[8]

In response to Leopold's self-promoting image of philanthropic endeavour, matrices of resistance emerged. Word spread out first of all through the
unrepresented channels of the Black Atlantic that all was not quite as 'civilized' as 'civilization' was being led to believe. The African American lawyer,
journalist and historian George Washington Williams was the first to take the
issue up at a political level.[9] In Europe, gossip and rumour filtered back
through the ports of Liverpool and Antwerp. Missionaries returning to their
headquarters in London and Boston had stories to tell. The grand narrative
of exploration and adventure shattered into fragmented tales of atrocities and
horror. From the mid-1890s, the secretary of the Aborigines Protection
Society, H.R. Fox Bourne, became increasingly vocal and both the press and
specialized humanitarian journals such as the *Anti-Slavery Reporter* and the
Aborigines' Friend began to play a significant part in bringing the matter to
public attention.

New centuries often inaugurate new discussions, and opposition in Britain
to the South African War helped stimulate a different kind of conversation
among those with an ethical conscience. The founding of the African Society
in memory of Mary Kingsley, by the historian Alice Stopford Green, was

6 The best account remains S.J.S. Cookey, *Britain and the Congo question, 1885–1913* (London,
1913). The most important recent histories of the Congo are by Jules Marchal, *E.D. Morel
contre Léopold II: l'histoire de Congo, 1900–10*, 2 vols (Paris, 1996) and the popular, polemical
work by Adam Hochschild, *King Leopold's ghost: a story of greed, terror and heroism in colonial
Africa* (London, 1998). See also Daniel Vangroenweghe, *Du sang sur les lianes* (Brussels, 1986).
7 The papers collected in S. Förster, W.J. Mommsen and R. Robinson, *Bismarck, Europe and
Africa – the Berlin Africa Conference, 1884–1885 and the onset of partition* (Oxford, 1988) demonstrate the great divisions between Western academic positions and African positions on the significance and consequences of the Berlin Act.   8 Belgian publications include: *Indépendence
Belge, Journal de Bruxelles, Mouvement Géographique* and *Le Patriote*. Between July 1903 and
the end of 1904 six fascicules appeared under the title *État Indépendent du Congo: documents sur
le pays et les habitants*. Richly illustrated with delicate art-nouveau typographical details, the
series gave a totally sanitized view of Leopold's colonial project, mirrored in the vast marbled
exhibition halls of Tervuren.   9 See John Hope Franklin, *George Washington Williams: a biography* (Chicago, 1985) reprinting Williams' open letter to Leopold II and his report to the US
President.

one organization prepared to challenge the aggressive tendencies of a world system that remained largely ignorant of and uncaring towards local customs. The African Society was constituted along the lines of the Royal Asiatic Society and around it congregated a concerned administrative and political elite rooted in the tradition of Gladstonian Liberalism. Its list of patrons is impressive: the future prime minister H.H. Asquith, the anthropologist J.G. Frazer, the historian and statesman John Morley, and the governor of the Gold Coast Sir Matthew Nathan (later Irish under-secretary in 1916) all figured on a highly distinguished general committee. In October 1901 it launched the *Journal of the African Society*, which sought new ways of representing Africa.[10]

Within eighteen months political pressure and popular agitation obliged the British government to take active steps to honour the promises made in the Berlin Act. As a consequence of debate in the Commons,[11] and increasing support for reform in the British press, Foreign Secretary Lord Lansdowne ordered the British consul in the Congo to gather 'authentic information'. Casement later recalled how 'the Foreign Office was forced by parliamentary action to support the demands of the small group of "reformers" who had secured both press and widespread public support'.[12] As Casement set out on his voyage up-river,[13] a new newspaper was established in London under the editorship of the reforming journalist, E.D. Morel. In its inaugural edition the *West African Mail* recorded its intention not only to supply 'existing commercial, mining and industrial' news, but also to address 'political and administrative questions relating to the development of Western Africa'. In succeeding issues, it became apparent that this was a polite way of saying that it was going to expose Leopold II and his administrative malpractices in West Africa. Good wishes for Morel's paper were forthcoming from prominent figures associated with both commerce and government: the Ugandan Commissioner and Africanist Sir H.H. Johnston, the Liverpool shipping magnates Sir Alfred Jones and John Holt, the governor of the Gambia Sir George Denton and the 1902 winner of the Nobel prize for his research into tropical diseases Dr Ronald Ross, all endorsed the publication with messages of support. The position of honour however was given to a letter illustrated with a quarter page photograph of Winston Churchill.[14] Over the following months

10 J.D. Fage, 'When the African Society was founded, who were the Africanists?' in *African Affairs*, 94 (1995) 369–81; in 1944 the title of the journal was changed to *African Affairs*, which continues to publish leading academic work on Africa.   11 See debate on 20 May 1903, published in *Parliamentary debates (official reports)*, fourth series, cxxii, 1289–1331.   12 NLI, MS 13082 (6) undated manuscript entitled 'Congo atrocities and the World War', possibly written in prison, explains the intent of the movement.   13 The bulk of correspondence relating to this voyage is held in TNA: PRO, FO 10/804–815.   14 *West African Mail*, 3 Apr. 1903. Ironically, in 1922 Morel and Churchill would bitterly contest the parliamentary seat for Dundee. Morel won.

the *West African Mail* kept the story alive in mainstream national newspapers. Beyond its own extensive coverage it also reported on African news in the French, Belgium, German and African newspapers and syndicated its own articles, spreading the campaign internationally.[15]

Casement's journey up the Congo remained secret, known only to the foreign-policy-making elite. Working through the network of English and American Baptist missionaries, he navigated the waters of the Upper Congo, collecting testimonies from victims of the rubber resource war and gathering photographs of mutilated bodies. His deep knowledge of the region allowed him to make stark comparisons between what he was witnessing and the world he had observed sixteen years earlier. During the next two and a half months he travelled almost 1600 miles, gathering evidence of the brutal excesses and injustices of the colonial administration. As he left the territories of the Anglo-Belgian Indian Rubber Company in early September he was satisfied that he had enough information to expose the Leopold regime for its cruelty and decided to intervene, whatever the cost to his own career.

It was the *West African Mail* that first broke the story of Casement's return[16] and its strategy over the next few weeks illustrated the resourceful manner in which it was able to maximize publicity through distributing copies to other national papers. The following week its scoop had been picked up and it reported that: '*The Morning Post, Daily News, Daily Chronicle, St James' Gazette, Nottingham Daily Express* and *Midland Herald*, amongst other papers, reproduced the information we were able to give last week with regard to the travels and the result of the enquiries of the British Consul in the Congo.'[17] When Casement arrived in London on 1 December, the national and international press was eagerly awaiting his story. By now the news had also begun to reverberate internationally. When the *West African Mail* announced Casement's return officially it listed the international publications on the Continent that were now running with the story.[18]

Casement delivered his report confidentially to the Foreign Office on 11 December 1903.[19] The precise, dispassionate prose describing a violated people and ravaged environment was clearly intended to shock, and it succeeded. Inevitably, there was a certain amount of internal conflict at the highest level within the Foreign Office as to how the report should be handled, whether

15 In its report on the 20 May debate in parliament the *West African Mail* (29 May 1903) contained reports from Reuters and excerpts from *La Metropole, Le Matin, Le Petit Bleu, Tribune Congolaise, Journal de Bruxelles* and *Independence Belge*.   16 *West African Mail*, 13 Nov. 1903.   17 *West African Mail*, 20 Nov. 1903.   18 The newspapers listed were *Temps, Patrie, Petit Bleu de Paris, La France, L'Autorité, Correspondence Havas* (all Paris), *Gironde* (Bordeaux), *Petit Troyen* (Troyes), *Patriote des Pyrénés* (Pau), *La Journée* (Marseilles), *Droit du Peuple* (Grenoble), *Tribune de Genéve* (Geneva), *La Tribuna* (Rome) and *Petit Bleu* (Brussels).   19 The report is published in Séamas Ó Síocháin and Michael O'Sullivan (eds), *The eyes of another race: Roger Casement's Congo report* (Dublin, 2003) 48–178.

222

Angus Mitchell

it should be published or used behind the scenes to force reform upon Leopold. A decision was eventually made to produce a censored version for public consumption – a decision that was indicative of the increasing layers of secrecy surrounding the issue. A carefully edited White Book was presented to parliament on 12 February 1904.[20] Names of all significant witnesses had been replaced with code letters. Casement was furious but the tactic ultimately proved sound. Widespread publicity was generated and headlines boomed: 'A policy of extermination' and 'Land of desolation and woe'.[21]

The *West African Mail* published in consecutive editions illustrated and condensed versions of the report, describing it as 'the most appalling document which has probably been issued at any time, by any government'. Elsewhere it gave due thanks to the mainstream press for publishing the facts for the 'enlightenment of public opinion'.[22] The use of photographs of the mutilated victims stimulated further public outrage. After meetings with Morel in London and Ireland, Casement set out the organizing principles and supplied the seed money for the founding of the Congo Reform Association (CRA).[23] When the CRA was launched in March it boasted a very impressive line up of peers, bishops, members of parliament and newspapermen – a support base that was deliberately inclusive and could not be defined either by religious persuasion, national interest, class or political predilection. Over the following years, popular interest was maintained with lecture tours and magic lantern slide shows. Thousands packed halls across Britain to campaign for Congo reform.[24]

The war of representation, waged in the pages of the British and Belgian press, now entered a bitter phase, inaugurated by accusations of forgery, levelled initially against Morel.[25] To the patriotic Belgian press, British humanitarianism was motivated by imperial interests. Leopold II, believing that he could in some way turn public opinion around in Britain, spent an increasing amount of money in buying the support of journalists. Every missionary, explorer, adventurer and administrator returning from the Congo was interviewed in an effort to establish 'the truth'. The most overtly outspoken paper to emerge in Britain against the CRA was the *Catholic Herald*. Throughout 1904 it lambasted Morel and fanned the flames of sectarianism with accusations of 'gross invention', 'falsehood and calumny' and 'flagrant deception':

---

20 *Correspondence and report from His Majesty's Consul at Boma respecting the administration of the Independent State of the Congo*, Parliamentary Paper [Cd. 1933] (1904). **21** *Daily News*, 15 Feb. 1904; *Daily Telegraph*, 18 Feb. 1904. **22** *West African Mail*, 19 and 26 Feb. 1903 and 19 Feb. 1904. **23** W.R. Louis and Jean Stengers (eds), *E.D. Morel's history of the Congo reform movement* (Oxford, 1968). **24** Kevin Grant, 'Christian critics of empire: missionaries, lantern lectures and the Congo reform campaign in Britain' in *Journal of Imperial and Commonwealth History*, 2:29 (May 2001) 27–58. **25** *La verité sur le Congo*, Oct./Nov. 1903.

Some of the lies set forth on the wings of the Press are hereby nailed to the counter, and it is to be hoped that yourself, or your Society, will at once disprove, by any means at your disposal, charges which, if not so disproved, clearly show that your evidence in connection with these matters is discredited and untrustworthy, and that no one will be justified in paying attention to any statement of yours, unless supported by evidence that has not been purchased or invented.[26]

Casement went off the Foreign Office active service list at the end of 1904 and devoted himself during the next twelve months to the question of Congo reform, and to rekindling his interest in cultural nationalism in Ireland. By 1905, the Congo Reform Association had meanwhile made inroads into Belgium and a different type of attitude was emerging in the Belgian press.[27] The publication in early 1906 of a study by a respected Belgian intellectual, Felicien Cattier, is cited as the moment when the tide turned.[28] Cattier accused Leopold not merely of profiting hugely from his enterprise but also spending 'considerable sums in influencing the press to support the Congo administration'.[29] Casement had himself made similar complaints at the end of 1905, as Lansdowne's administration entered its last months, where he condemned 'the Congolese press agency in England'.

I have been subjected to a lengthy course of personal attack carried on by private individuals or inspired and subsidised press agencies who have alike drawn their inspiration and financial sustenance from the same official quarter – the headquarters of the Congo State Government in Brussels.[30]

Casement learned several lessons after the publication of his report: that the press was a fickle instrument of power, as capable of dishonesty as it was of honesty, and that 'truth' and 'evidence' were not absolutes but rather tools of authority. Many of the hard-learned lessons of this campaign were subsequently deployed and refined in the context of Irish affairs. Benedict Anderson has traced the relationship between print culture and national identity, arguing persuasively that 'the convergence of capitalism and print technology on the fatal diversity of human language created the possibility of a new form of imagined community, which in its basic morphology set the stage for the modern nation'.[31] If the founding of the *Nation* in October 1842 can be rep-

---

26 A copy is held in TNA: PRO, FO 10/812 'The anti-Congo conspiracy', 8 Dec. 1904. 27 *Le Peuple* was the most active newspaper in Belgium to speak out against the authority of the Congo Free State. 28 Felicien Cattier, *Etude sur la situation de l'Etat Indépendant du Congo* (Brussels, 1906). 29 Cookey, *Britain and the Congo question*, 155. 30 TNA: PRO, FO 10/815 Casement to Lansdowne, 9 Oct. 1905. 31 Benedict Anderson, *Imagined Communities* (London, 1991) 46.

resented as the moment when the formation of Ireland's modern national identity began, then the centenary celebrations in 1898 of the 1798 Rising and the cultural nationalism associated with organizations such as the Gaelic League helped stimulate a significant growth in the number of nationalist publications.[32] Although Casement's flirtation with these cultural transformations dated back to 1898, it was the 'gathering of Gaels' at the *feis* in the Glens of Antrim in 1904 that reawakened his sympathies. During his extended period of leave from the Foreign Office, he published his first wave of political writings on Irish affairs.

From the start of 1905 he began to contribute regularly to the *United Irishman* using mainly the letter 'X' to identify himself, although signing a few poems under his own name and initials.[33] These contributions, ranging from the historical to the satirical to the scurrilous, spoke of his father's involvement in the struggle for Hungarian independence, the Act of Union, the Irish College at Lisbon, enlistment, imperial expansion and nationality and football.[34] On his own admission he was also writing for *Sinn Féin* and the *Freeman's Journal*, but these contributions have not been so easy to retrieve. His interest and work on behalf of the Irish language movement also put him in contact with *An Claidheamh Soluis*, edited by the public educator, Patrick Pearse.

Although Casement later claimed that he did not contribute to the advanced nationalist press after his return to active service, this seems not to have been the case. After Casement's posting to Santos in 1906, Bulmer Hobson's shortlived Belfast-based newspaper, the *Republic*, published 'Sinn Féin in India' signed MacA (MacAsmund).[35] Here Casement lashed out at *The Times* for its reporting of the Indian National Congress, dismissing it as 'that unchanging organ of English greed ... the true mouthpiece of "Imperial" England'.[36] Other contributions published during this period include his review of Alice Stopford Green's *The making of Ireland and its undoing*, and his involvement in the controversy over the teaching and learning of Irish in

32 Many of these papers are in the microfilm collection of *Irish political and radical newspapers of the 20th century*. The best general account of the period is Virginia Glandon, *Arthur Griffith and the advanced nationalist press: Ireland, 1900–1922* (New York, 1985); also useful is James E. Combs, 'The language of nationalist ideology: a content analysis of Irish nationalist publications, 1906–1914' unpublished PhD thesis, University of Houston, 1969.   33 'The Irish language', 28 Jan. 1905 – signed 'Glens of Antrim'; 'A dream of the Celt', 11 Mar. 1905 – signed 'R.C.' and 'Quo Vadis', 24 Feb. 1906 – signed 'Ruari' (in Irish lettering).   34 'Kossuth's Irish courier', 25 Feb. 1905; 'Redistribution', 11 Mar. 1905; 'A forgotten nationalist', 29 Apr. 1905; 'Fraudulent enlistment', 14 Oct. 1905; 'Imperial expansion' and 'Nationality and football', both 30 Dec. 1905.   35 7 Mar. 1907. Controversy about the 'scientific' authentication of documents has, once more, recently dominated aspects of the Casement debate. This must now extend from the 'diaries controversy' to examine the attribution of pseudonymous and anonymous material.   36 Referring to an article in the *Times*, 2 Jan. 1907.

the national university.[37] Casement was also central to the funding and covert encouragement of advanced nationalist publications. Hobson remembered how Casement gave 'a few pounds' to the *Republic* and 'raised money ... to keep our small and insolvent newspapers in existence'.[38] In November 1908 the first edition of *Bean na hEireann* (Woman of Ireland) appeared, edited by Helena Molony, also supported by Casement.[39] Casement was actively engaged with the intellectual formation of cultural nationalism in a way that his biographers have generally overlooked.

II

Casement also deployed his accumulated skills in what was, until recently, his least understood crusade, investigating the Putumayo atrocities in the north-west Amazon.[40] Once more it was specialized, low-circulation weeklies that were responsible for bringing the story from the tropical periphery into the metropolitan centre, forcing larger newspapers to take notice. In a muddy side street of Iquitos, far up-river in the depths of the forested frontiers of the Peruvian Amazon, a committed socialist, Benjamin Saldaña Rocca, published two small newspapers *La Felpa* and *La Sanción* during 1907 and 1908. Saldaña Rocca, wrote, printed and largely circulated these papers himself until he was eventually run out of town by the main target of his attacks, the rubber baron, Julio Cesar Arana. When testimonies and statements published in these papers were brought to London by a young railroad engineer, Walt Hardenburg, the story was taken up by *Truth*. Condemning the 'Devil's paradise' as 'A British-owned Congo,' *Truth* ran regular stories on the controversy until the summer of 1913.[41]

The Foreign Office once more deployed Casement, then serving as consul-general in Brazil, to investigate. During 1910 and 1911 Casement made two dangerous 'special missions' into the north-west Amazon and once more revealed disgusting crimes against humanity committed as a consequence of insatiable global demand for extractive rubber. In July 1912, having returned to Europe via Washington, in order to obtain US presidential sup-

37 See *Freeman's Journal*, 11 Dec. 1908, attacking the Royal Dublin Society for refusing to have the book on their shelves, and the review (unsigned) in *Freeman's Journal*, 19 Dec. 1908; see also *Freeman's Journal*, 4 Jan. 1909.   38 Bulmer Hobson, *Ireland yesterday and tomorrow* (Tralee, 1968) 80.   39 Margaret Ward, *Maud Gonne – Ireland's Joan of Arc* (London, 1993) 96.   40 Angus Mitchell (ed.), *The Amazon journal of Roger Casement* (Dublin, 1997) and *Sir Roger Casement's heart of darkness: the 1911 documents* (Dublin, 2003) contain journals, fragmentary diary entries, correspondence and press reports relating to the first two years of this investigation.   41 The reporter who worked on the story, G. Sydney Paternoster, eventually published a book about the incident, *The lords of the Devil's paradise* (London, 1913).

port for his campaign, his reports were published as a Blue Book, prompting international outcry.[42]

Throughout the campaign that followed, Casement was aware of the need to maintain pressure on the Peruvian administration in Iquitos and Peru with the threat of adverse publicity. He returned from his first voyage with two Amazindians and introduced them into humanitarian circles in London to draw attention to the plight of their people. Through the co-operation of the editor of the *Daily News*, A.G. Gardiner, a front-page story described 'inferno in a paradise'.[43] During the course of this campaign, he sent at least three anonymous letters to the newspapers, stirring up debate at the national level. Signing himself as 'A Catholic Reader,' he attacked the Monroe doctrine for preventing direct action from Europe and demanded the publication of 'the Consul's report'.[44] More inflammatory comments appeared under the name 'D. MacCammond' condemning the fact that most rubber from the Amazon was conveyed to England in British steam ships, implicating British business in the crime.[45] A week after the publication of the Blue Book, he wrote to *The Times*, this time under the pseudonym 'O', quoting extensively from his own report.[46] This strategy of writing pseudonymously to draw attention to his own humanitarian campaigns was one that he would adopt with increasing frequency over the following years in the cause of Ireland, and was a crafty means of steering controversies. Nevertheless it clearly transgressed the protocol of his official position and he seems to have come perilously close to being revealed when the Foreign Office started to make inquiries as to who had made such damaging and well-informed criticisms.

Beyond the delay in the issuing of the report, much else went wrong in the campaign. Casement was unhappy that the Blue Book would be presented to parliament during the summer holidays when the public were less charitable, and when the story was leaked in advance in the US further impact was lost. He was also angry about the appearance of his image in the newspapers, which he had expressly wished to avoid.[47] The type of game Casement was playing, as he tried to negotiate his official position with his increasing commitment to both international and Irish causes, can be understood from an incident involving Lord Northcliffe. Northcliffe had agreed to open the columns of his newspapers to the Putumayo Mission Fund, on the condition

42 *Correspondence respecting the treatment of British colonial subjects and native Indians employed in the collection of rubber in the Putumayo district* [Cd. 6266] (1912). 43 *Daily News*, 1 Aug. 1911 44 London *Nation*, 29 July 1911. 45 *Daily News*, 1 Mar. 1912. 46 *Times*, 21 July 1912. 47 Casement's caution over the publication of his image in the newspapers was indicative of his concerns about his Irish involvement. When his 'treason' was eventually identified by the intelligence services after the outbreak of war in 1914, it was discovered that there was no photograph of him on the police file. An image of him on the Putumayo was published in the *Sketch*, 2 Dec. 1914 – see TNA: PRO, CO 904/195.

that Casement wrote a supporting article. Casement, however, refused, regretting that his position as 'a public servant' prevented him from such action.[48] A few weeks later, when the *Contemporary Review* ran Casement's article on the Putumayo,[49] Northcliffe was 'very much annoyed'.[50]

The public presentation of the Morel Testimonial on 29 May 1911 illustrated the press support Casement was able to draw on during this period, as well as the sophisticated methods of publicity that he had mastered. 1911 was a key year for the empire: besides the Coronation of George V there was the Crystal Palace Exhibition and the Universal Races Congress,[51] each of which contributed towards a new conversation on international relations. By then, the Congo Reform Association had largely achieved what it had set out to do. Leopold II had reluctantly handed over the Congo to an equally reluctant Belgian government in 1908. He died the following year. Morel was thus looking for a new crusade, and both Alice Green and Casement hoped that the occasion would breath new life into the slightly flagging campaign. Even if the financial response from the public was not as great as the organizing committee hoped, many influential figures attended. Two celebrities, the Earl of Cromer and Sir Arthur Conan Doyle, presided over the occasion, and many powerful newspaper editors were present.[52] In the following days a flood of publicity praised Morel for his 'sustained battle against embattled powers of evil more formidable than can easily be realised'.[53] 'No testimonial,' the *Spectator* claimed, had been 'more richly deserved'.[54]

III

After returning from South Africa in the spring of 1913, a few weeks before tendering his resignation to the Foreign Office, and with his reputation riding the crest of a wave of popularity, Casement involved himself in a relief campaign in the typhus-stricken districts of Connemara in the west of Ireland.[55]

---

48 NLI, MS 13087 (21/ii) Percy Browne to Casement, 8 Oct. 1913. **49** Roger Casement, 'The Putumayo Indians', *Contemporary Review*, Sept. 1912. **50** NLI, MS 13087 (21/ii) Browne to Casement, 8 Oct. 1913. **51** G. Spiller (ed.), *Papers on inter-racial problems communicated to the First Universal Races Congress held at the University of London, July 26–29, 1911* (London, 1911). **52** Including Sir Percy Bunting, editor of the *Contemporary Review*; Bertram Christian, editor of the *Morning Leader*; Robert Donald, editor of the *Daily Chronicle*; Robert Emmett of Reuters; A.G. Gardiner, editor of the *Daily News*; E.W.M. Grigg of *The Times*; R.H. Gretton, London editor of the *Manchester Guardian*; F.W. Hirst, editor of the *Economist*; Reverend T.A. Lacey of the *Church Times*; H.W. Massingham, editor of the London *Nation*; J.S.R. Phillips, editor of the *Yorkshire Post*; W.T. Stead, editor of the *Review of Reviews*; J. St. Loe Strachey, editor of the *Spectator*; and Fabian Ware, editor of the *Morning Post*, who gave a speech on behalf of the assembled press. **53** *Morning Post*, 30 May 1911. **54** *Spectator*, 3 June 1911. **55** Angus Mitchell, 'An Irish Putumayo: Roger Casement's humanitarian relief campaign among the

Through the letters page of the *Irish Independent* he deliberately connected his work in Africa and the Amazon to his increasing commitment to Irish separatism, using the campaign to convey a number of his own views on questions of social reform, preservation of the Irish language and the relocation of impoverished workers. His attack on the London press for failing to say 'a single word'[56] resulted in a full-page article in the *Financial Times* and their unprecedented use of Irish script.[57] Later that year he opened a campaign stressing the need for Ireland to establish autonomous economic connections with Europe and America, using the controversy over the decision by Cunard to abandon the use of Queenstown (Cobh) as a stopover on its route between England and North America to stir up popular sentiment.[58]

Although the Irish Volunteers were founded on 25 November 1913, the event was publicly announced in London five days before that date in an interview given by Casement to the *Daily Chronicle*.[59] In this interview Casement set out why it was necessary for the national movement to militarize, and over the next six months he was more prominent than any other leader in the drive for recruits. Beyond the letters pages of the *Irish Independent* and *Irish Times* articles written by Casement appeared regularly in the *Irish Review*,[60] the *Irish Volunteer*[61] and most vociferously in *Irish Freedom*.[62]

On the 28 June 1914, the day the Archduke Ferdinand was assassinated in Sarajevo, Casement delivered his last public address in Ireland in the Glens of Antrim, beside the cairn dedicated to Sean O'Neill. Afterwards he left for America, travelling via Glasgow and Montreal. In New York he made contact with John Devoy and his movements and views were fully recorded by the *Gaelic American*.[63] Casement had been quietly supplying Devoy with 'items of news' for publication from as early as 1910.[64] During a speech in Philadelphia on 2 August 1914, Casement launched a blistering attack on the British press:

Connemara islanders, 1913–14', *Irish Economic and Social History*, 31 (2004, forthcoming). **56** *Irish Independent*, 20 May 1913. **57** *Financial Times*, 30 May 1913. **58** See *Irish Times*, 10 Dec. 1913; *Irish Independent*, 16 Feb. 1914. **59** *Daily Chronicle*, 20 Nov. 1913. **60** Casement's identifiable political contributions to the *Irish Review* include: 'Ireland and the German menace' (Sept. 1912) signed 'Batha MacCrainn' and 'From "Coffin Ship" to "Atlantic Greyhound"' (Feb/Mar/Apr. 1914) signed 'An Irish American'. **61** 'From Clontarf to Berlin: national status in sport', *Irish Volunteer*, 7 Feb. 1914. **62** Casement's contributions to *Irish Freedom* include: 'The English hypocrite' (Dec. 1912) signed 'Irishman'; 'Ireland, Germany and the next war' (Aug. 1913) signed 'Shan Van Vocht'; 'Ireland a slave depot' (Feb. 1914) signed 'X.X.X.'; 'The elsewhere empire' (Mar. 1914), 'Victor Hugo, Victoria, & Ireland' (Apr. 1914) and 'The Volunteers' (June 1914) all signed 'The Poor Old Woman'; 'The British Army in Ireland' (May 1914) signed 'Mars Ultor'; 'Garibaldi and the Fenians' (May 1914) – unsigned. **63** Although John Devoy would turn against Casement shortly before his execution, the *Gaelic American* (henceforth *GA*) contained a steady stream of news about Casement throughout the war, as well as a number of Casement's articles, many of them reprinted from other journals. See for example 'Germany to win must cripple or destroy England', *GA*, 19 Sept. 1914. **64** John Devoy, *Recollections of an Irish rebel* (Shannon, 1969 [*c*.1929]) 408.

The truth is that all this turmoil comes from England, and largely from the British Press. There would be peace in Ireland to-morrow, amity and good will in Ulster between Catholic and Protestant, were it not for the English press and their agents in Ireland. I'd like to see all the editors given six months in jail, and then we should have peace to discuss our own affairs together. All these diatribes about 'Ulster on the brink,' 'The grim, determined men scarcely able to hold on any longer,' 'The powder magazine with the spark,' etc. etc. are merely designs to send up the circulation of vapid English journals and in order to achieve that end, they would gladly upset the circulation of our blood and spill it, too. But we are not going to play their game. The 'war correspondents' may go back across the Irish Sea. Ireland will send a horrid message to England and the London papers. Our answer to their full-blooded screams is this: 'We can mind our own affairs. Ulster will not fight and Ulster will be right. We, Ulster men are all Irishmen, and at bottom we know and understand each other and need no interference from British political parties, or from the English press.[65]

This was hardly the attitude that was likely to win Casement friends. The outbreak of war brought most other radical voices into line – Casement and Morel being the most obvious exceptions. In pamphlets and letters to the newspapers, Casement took up a very contrary position on questions of international foreign policy, and argued that Irishmen had no place in the escalating war.[66] But his position was publicly dismissed as 'extreme', 'cranky' or 'mad'. In the autumn he left New York with orders from the leadership of the Clan na Gael to put in place German guarantees for Irish independence. With the passing of the Defence of the Realm Act and Regulations in Britain in August 1914, Casement's isolation deepened. Several individuals involved in supporting Casement in Africa and South America were now recruited into intelligence and propaganda agencies. Press editors, in particular, were brought firmly into line behind the imperial war effort and there was irony in the appointment of Casement's eventual prosecutor, F.E. Smith, as first director of the Press Bureau.[67]

IV

Atrocity propaganda became one of the most malignant weapons in the wartime battle for hearts and minds.[68] Casement's name and work were both

---

65 'Philadelphia honors the martyred dead', *GA*, 8 Aug. 1914. The speech was delivered at the Forrest Theatre on 2 Aug. 1914 and was extensively covered in the Philadelphia *Record* the following day, as war was declared in Europe. **66** *Irish Independent*, 5 Oct. 1914. **67** John Campbell, *F.E. Smith, first earl of Birkenhead* (London, 1983) 372–94. **68** James Morgan Read,

used and abused on all sides. Belgium's own recent history in the Congo could be used for example to question the legitimacy of Britain's attempt to protect 'plucky little Belgium'. James Connolly dedicated a whole front page of the *Irish Worker* to 'Belgium rubber and Belgium neutrality'.[69] After arriving in Germany in late 1914, Casement was increasingly frustrated and isolated by his position. He produced his most pungent political writing for the *Continental Times*.[70] This broadsheet, published three times a week in Berlin, was aimed predominantly at demonstrating to an American readership that their neutrality had been 'contaminated' by 'slander and calumny'.[71] Casement argued that 'truth' had been the first casualty of the war. In an article entitled 'England's care for the truth', written 'By One Who Knows Both',[72] Casement, adopting a deeply satirical style, attacked what would later be identified as British intelligence strategies: interception of messages and the production of propaganda. His direct knowledge of Foreign Office practices gave him a privileged understanding of such techniques. His most disturbing revelations of state secrets were made in letters written under the name of J. Quincy Emerson.[73]

Other pseudonyms that can be identified as Casement's include Will E. Wagtail,[74] An American Scholar,[75] Henry Bower[76] and Diplomaticus.[77] By October 1915 Casement was prepared to put his name openly to a poem, 'In memoriam', commemorating the life and death of Charles Stewart Parnell[78] as

---

Atrocity propaganda, 1914–1919 (New Haven, 1941) remains a useful work. More recent examinations include Ben Novick, *Conceiving revolution – Irish nationalist propaganda during the First World War* (Dublin, 2001) and John Horne and Alan Kramer, *German atrocities, 1914: a history of denial* (Yale, 2001), although both studies suffer from insufficient or partial analysis of Casement's significance. **69** *Irish Worker*, 14 Nov. 1914. **70** An incomplete run of the *Continental Times* (henceforth *CT*) is held in the British Library (Colindale), including some issues from 31 Oct. 1909 to 31 Dec. 1917. Among Casement's prison papers is a note on his writings published in Germany stating that 'There are other articles and letters by me in *Continental Times* from Dec. 1914 to March or April 1916 – some signed – most unsigned.' See TNA: PRO, HO 144/1636/331643/32A. **71** *The Continental Times war book* (Berlin, 1915) contained a selection of articles published after the outbreak of the war. **72** *CT*, 30 July 1915. A positive identification of this article can be assumed due to its survival in manuscript form in NLI, MS 29064. Other contributions from 'By One Who Knows' include 'The calibre of Roosevelt', *CT*, 6 Oct. 1915 and 'Letter to Roosevelt', *CT*, 31 Dec. 1915. **73** Four letters in Casement's hand signed J. Quincy Emerson have survived in manuscript form in NLI, MS 29064 and are dated 14 Aug., 1 Sept., 14 Sept. (published *CT*, 24 Sept.) and 6 Oct. 1915. **74** *CT*, 16 Aug. 1915 includes a poem entitled 'A tale of tails'. **75** *CT*, 8/11/13 Oct. 1915 serialized 'British versus German imperialism'. The full text, in pamphlet form, has survived in the National Library of Ireland with Casement's pencilled marginalia. **76** NLI, MS 29064 letter to *CT*, 22 Sept. 1915. **77** *CT*, 13 Dec. 1915 published 'War depression: a pacific blockade' under the name 'Diplomaticus'. A typescript version of this article has survived in Clare County Archives, Ennis, signed in red crayon 'Sir Roger Casement' and dated '27/11/1915'. See also a further article, 'Free trade and neutrality: the Christmas dolls', *CT*, 29 Dec. 1915. **78** *CT*, 6 Oct. 1915.

well as his blistering attacks on the diplomacy of Sir Edward Grey,[79] and the historical reputation of James Bryce.[80] For four articles, including those on Grey and Bryce, Casement was paid 200 guineas by Count Blücher.[81] He passed the money on immediately to Father Crotty to help in his work for the Irish prisoners. Recently discovered correspondence between Casement and Blücher reveals something of his own publishing strategy:

> Here is another article towards the good cause. I hope you will be able to use. Please read it and if it suits your purposes have it translated and sent out to your clientele abroad. Also will you please, in all cases, have a typed copy of it sent to the *Continental Times*. Don't put my name to it or say it's from me – simply ask them to publish it at an early date ... If you could also send me back a typed copy I'd be very glad & I'd get it inserted in one of the Munich papers.[82]

Casement remembered that during his interrogation by the intelligence service chiefs at Scotland Yard over Easter weekend 1916, following his landing in Ireland and subsequent arrest, 'Thomson read the "Kitchener" articles (taken from an Argentine paper!)'.[83] The recent release of KV-2 military intelligence files and Special Branch files on Casement have been disappointing in terms of revealing anything new about Casement's propaganda work.[84] While clearly demonstrating the intelligence priority Casement became as soon as war was declared, the official archives are silent on his pseudonymous writings. Given the international distribution of the *Continental Times*, it is hard to believe that the British intelligence services were unaware of the masks Casement was wearing in order to publicize his position. Perhaps the last remaining SIS files, still withheld under the Official Secrets Act, will prove more revealing.

From the moment his capture was announced, Casement was vilified in public and private. Many of the distortions and myths implanted then have remained central to subsequent representations. The *Graphic* for example car-

---

79 *CT*, 18 Oct. 1915 has survived in manuscript form in NLI, MS 29064. It also appeared in *GA*, 20/27 Nov. 1915. 80 *CT*, 3 Nov. 1915, republished in *GA*, 4 Dec. 1915. 81 Beside the articles on Grey and Bryce the other two that appeared under his name were: 'The Emerald Isle and its giant parasite', *CT*, 15 Nov. 1915 and 'Ireland and the world war, 1815–1915: a parallel and a contrast', *CT*, 22 Nov. 1915. Copies of both are held in NLI, MS 13082 (6). 82 Clare County Archive, Casement papers, Casement to Count Gebhard Blücher, 26 Jan. 1916. 83 TNA: PRO, HO 144/1636/331643/32A 'Pamphlets, articles, letters etc.' The article on Lord Kitchener was first published in the *Münchener Zeitung*, 18 Nov. 1915. It was subsequently republished in Sir Roger Casement, *Irland, Deutschland & die freiheit der meere & andere Aufsatze* (Munich, 1916) 182–7. A typecript copy is held in NLI MS 13,082 (6) under the title 'Lord Kitchener's mission'. 84 TNA: PRO, KV 2/6–10 released on 25 and 26 Jan. 1999 and MEPO 2/10659–10674 released on 21 June 2001.

ried a very unflattering photograph beside the misleading caption 'Sir Roger Casement the ridiculous traitor, was born in Ireland in 1864, and entered consular service. He did much to stir up the Belgian atrocities agitation and ran the Putumayo business.'[85] Two weeks later, the same publication ran an illustrated double page.[86] Casement ordered his solicitor George Gavan Duffy to take a libel suit out against the editor. The *Graphic* was one of many publications whose reporting helped inspire a tradition that would gradually confuse Casement's revolutionary role, minimize his work in Africa and South America and cast aspersions over his significance for Ireland. Here the press helped shape popular imagination. With the leaders of the Easter Rising already unceremoniously executed, and Britain and the Allies about to launch the Somme offensive, the press turned on Casement with a vengeance. If the full weight of the legal system was aimed at this disgraced imperial knight, so too was the official and unofficial propaganda machine. Most of Casement's supporters fell away, especially after the whispering campaign concerning the 'black diaries', alleged evidence of 'sodomitical practices', had begun.[87] Just as Casement had once deployed text and images in his own crusades, that same combination was now used to bring about his public downfall. Only William Randolph Hearst's newspapers in the US, and a few informed and more impartial British journalists such as H.W. Nevinson, stood by their man.

The question of his diaries, papers and correspondence preoccupied Casement well before his capture, and throughout his time as a political prisoner. He wrote to Gavan Duffy requesting that his 'Irish writings [be] collected, edited and published'.[88] Alice Stopford Green tried to gather his widely dispersed papers, but much had already fallen into the hands of Basil Thomson and others. In the wake of the Easter Rising, the houses of suspected revolutionaries and their collaborators were raided for subversive material, and incriminating letters and much valuable material was destroyed. In 1956, an amateur historian, Herbert Mackey, published some of Casement's political essays but most of his writings and speeches are still buried in the seditious press.[89]

---

85 *Graphic*, 6 May 1916.   86 *Graphic*, 20 May 1916.   87 The earliest direct mention of the diaries appeared in the *Daily Express,* 30 June 1916 under the headline 'Paltry traitor meets his just deserts, death for Sir Roger Casement. The diaries of a Degenerate' and stated that 'It is common knowledge that Sir Roger Casement is a man with no sense of honour or decency. His written diaries are the monuments of a foul private life. He is a moral degenerate.' The *Daily Express* was under the guidance of Lord Beaverbrook, who in early 1918 was appointed Minister of Information by Lloyd George. The so-called 'black diaries' were discussed in a series of memoranda laid before the Cabinet on 17 July 1916. See TNA: PRO, HO 144/1636/311643/53.   88 NLI, MS 10764 'A private note for my solicitor'.   89 H.O. Mackey (ed.), *The crime against Europe: writings and poems of Roger Casement* (Dublin, 1958).

V

Edward Thomson, in his attack on British rule in India, hinted at the oppression of the printed word: 'when one side has succeeded in imposing its version of events on the whole world, when one side controls history or the press, then underground bitterness becomes something too poisoned and ferocious for expression'.[90] Recent academic histories of Africa, South America and Ireland have preferred to forget or ignore Casement's contribution to the evolution of the idea of ethical foreign policy and his exceptional position within Anglo-Irish relations. His propaganda writings remained a live issue long after his execution. A parliamentary paper published in 1921 traced the origins of Sinn Féin and the Irish-German alliance to Casement's writings 'in seditious Irish newspapers', circulated in pamphlet form as *Germany and the next war* and *The crime against Europe*.[91] Casement has been characterized as 'emotional', not an 'obviously systematic thinker', who 'wrote no book of lasting value'.[92] This fails to take into account the significant corpus of pseudonymous political writing buried in the advanced nationalist press. Other anti-colonial discourses are now being excavated from similar sources, revealing 'contact zones' of exchange between different sites of colonization.[93] It is in such a zone that Casement's writings in the press are best situated.

90 Edward Thompson, *The other side of the medal* (London, 1925), 26. **91** *Documents relative to the Sinn Féin movement* [Cd 1108] xxix (1921) 2. **92** Andrew Porter, 'Sir Roger Casement and the international humanitarian movement', *Journal of Imperial and Commonwealth History*, 2:29 (May 2001) 59–74. **93** On the concept of 'contact zones' see Mary Louise Pratt, *Imperial eyes: travel-writing and transculturation* (London, 1992). See also Elleke Boehmer, *Empire, the national and the postcolonial, 1890–1920: resistance in interaction* (Oxford, 2002) 2. Robert J.C. Young, *Postcolonialism: an historical introduction* (Oxford, 2001) locates Casement 'at the centre of a campaign for the human rights of "free" postcolonial indigenous Brazilians'. Another recent postcolonial reading, if somewhat distorted through neglect of the primary sources, is Richard Kirkland, 'Frantz Fanon, Roger Casement and colonial commitment' in Glenn Hooper and Colin Graham (eds), *Irish and postcolonial writing: history, theory, practice* (London, 2002) 49–65.

Index